Mini Cooper
The Real Thing!

JOHN TIPLER

VELOCE PUBLISHING PLC
PUBLISHERS OF FINE AUTOMOTIVE BOOKS

Other books of interest to enthusiasts available from Veloce -

Alfa Romeo Owner's Bible
by Pat Braden
Alfa Romeo Tipo 6C, 1500, 1750 & 1900
by Angela Cherrett
Alfa Romeo Modello 8C 2300
by Angela Cherrett
Alfa Romeo Giulia Coupé GT & GTA
by John Tipler
Biggles!
by Peter Berresford Ellis & Jennifer Schofield
British Car Factories from 1896 - A Complete Survey
by Paul Collins & Michael Stratton
Bugatti 57 - The Last French Bugatti
by Barrie Price
Car Bodywork & Interior: Care & Repair
by David Pollard
Car Security Manual
by David Pollard
Citroën 2CV Family Album
by Andrea & David Sparrow
Citroën DS Family Album
by Andrea & David Sparrow
Fiat & Abarth 124 Spider & Coupé
by John Tipler
Fiat & Abarth 500 & 600
by Malcolm Bobbitt
Lola T70
by John Starkey
Mazda MX5/Miata Enthusiast's Workshop Manual
by Rod Grainger & Pete Shoemark
Nuvolari: When Nuvolari Raced
by Valerio Moretti
Pass the MoT
by David Pollard
The Prince & I - My Life with the Motor Racing Prince of Siam (biography of racing driver 'B.Bira')
by Princess Ceril Birabongse
Standard & Standard-Triumph - The Illustrated History
by Brian Long
Total Tuning for the Classic MG Midget/A-H Sprite
by Daniel Stapleton

First published in 1994 by Veloce Publishing Plc., Godmanstone, Dorset DT2 7AE, England.
Fax 0300 341065

ISBN 1 874105 22 7

Readers with ideas for automotive books, or books on other transport or related hobby subjects, are invited to write to the editorial director of Veloce Publishing at the above address.

British Library Cataloguing in Publication Data -
A catalogue record for this book is available from the British Library.

Typesetting (Bookman, 10pt), design and page make-up all by Veloce on Apple Mac.

Printed and bound in England.

MORRIS · MORRIS S COOPER · COOPER · AUSTIN COOPER · Austin

(1961)
COOPER
997cc · CLOSE RATIO GEARS
FRONT DISCS · TWO TONE
UPHOLSTERY · OIL & WATER
GAUGES · BUMPER END BARS

(1964)
998cc
SEPT: HYDROLASTIC SUSPENSION

(1967)
MK II
AS 'S' · DISCONTINUED 1969

(1990)
LIMITED (1000) EDITION · 1275cc
TWO TONE PAINT · SIGNED COOPER
BONNET STRIPES · ALLOY WHEELS
DRIVING LAMPS · SUNROOF
TINTED GLASS · RED CARPETS

(1959)
MORRIS MINOR · AUSTIN SEVEN

(1964)
970cc
DISCONTINUED JANUARY 1965

(1969)
MK III
LARGER DOORS · CONCEALED
HINGES · WIND-UP WINDOWS ·
RUBBER SUSPENSION ·
DISCONTINUED 1971

(1990)
PRODUCTION MODEL
STRIPES · SUNROOF · LAMPS ARE
EXTRAS · 1991 FUEL
INJECTION & CATALYST
1992 'S' VERSION FROM
JOHN COOPER

(1963)
COOPER 'S'
1071cc · AS COOPER · 70BHP
(1964)
1275cc
JAN 1966 TWIN FUEL TANKS

(1967)
MK II
LARGER REAR WINDOW &
REAR LIGHTS · NEW GRILLE
BLACK UPHOLSTERY

(1991)
CABRIOLET
LIMITED (75) EDITION BASED
ON COOPER · BODY KIT · CHERRY
METALLIC PAINT · ALLOYS
1993 PRODUCTION MODEL

James Ruppert

©1992 ACTION AUTOMOTIVE PRODUCTS

ACKNOWLEDGEMENTS

I had to rely on many Mini Cooper afficionados for help with background and photographs. I particularly want to thank Philip Splett, Chairman and PRO of the Mini Cooper Register for his initial guidance and loan of pictures, brochures and personal memorabilia. I am also grateful for having been able to compare one of Philip's classic Coopers with a modern hatchback. I should mention John Parnell, also of the Mini Cooper Register, whose buyers' guide I referred to.

Many thanks indeed to Rover Group's PR lady Pam Wearing who organised my fascinating tour of the production line at Longbridge, introduced me to Alan Jones, Chief Engineer, Body-in-White, Geoff Powell, Principal Engineer, Conformance, John Speed, Development Engineer, Conformance, and Nigel Ravenhall, Production Manager, who gave the guided tour. Also for arranging the loan of the Rover Cooper test car which I thoroughly enjoyed. Thanks to Alastair Vines, Rover's Development Engineer, for the quick whizz round in his original rally S and useful background information. Paddy Hopkirk and David Vizard are quoted from interviews I have done with them,

and John Cooper very kindly wrote the Foreword. John Rhodes and Warwick Banks came up with some magnificent photos of themselves in action, as well as providing invaluable anecdotes from their racing pasts.

Other photos are courtesy of *Carweek* magazine, LAT, British Motor Industry Heritage archives at Gaydon, The Rover Group and Jem Marsh of Marcos,

And, finally, I have to acknowledge the enthusiastic and efficient input of my old chum and ex-Motor Industry Research Unit colleague Jeremy Boyce, without whom there would have been no book, given the constraints of my day job as a subeditor on *Carweek* magazine. The book should therefore really be regarded as a joint venture between Boyce and Tipler.

To be more precise, there really would be no book without Rod and Judith at Veloce, so thanks to them for making it happen.

I'd like to dedicate the book to Zoe Christabel, who became an ardent Mini Cooper fan during its compilation, and will undoubtedly drive one herself one day.

John Tipler

CONTENTS

FOREWORD
BY
JOHN COOPER

Let's get my sporting backgound in perspective to start with. At the time the Mini came out in 1959, I was already busy changing the face of Grand Prix racing, putting the engine where it's been ever since, behind the driver. My 500cc motorcycle-engined Formula Three cars of the immediate post-war period laid the foundations, and meanwhile such stars as Mike Hawthorn, and even Fangio, drove my Formula Two Cooper-Bristols. Stirling Moss and Maurice Trintigant had shown the way forward by winning Grands Prix at Argentina and Monaco with rear-engined Cooper-Climaxes, and Jack Brabham and I also intoduced the Indianapolis establishment to the rear-engined concept in 1961.

So I suppose I was already something of an old hand when Roy Salvadori and I took the prototype Mini for testing at Monza. Its potential was not lost on the Italian cognoscenti; Ferrari's chief engineer, Snr Aurelio Lampredi, remarked: 'If it wasn't so ugly, I'd shoot myself if that isn't the car of the future!'

During our World Championship winning years - 1959-1960 - 'the Boys', Jack Brabham and Bruce McLaren, were already using Minis as road cars and, naturally, starting to play around with them. We were well versed in tuning the 1100cc Formula Junior engine, which was essentially the BMC A-series unit built by Eddy Maher at the Morris Engines plant at Coventry. I de-

cided to try fitting one in the Mini. This motor had all the regular racing goodies, like nitrided crank, nemonic valves, a bigger oil pump and twin one-and-a-half inch SUs and adapted so that the gearbox was in the sump: it was a real flyer. A number of factors came together at the right time to make the Mini-Cooper work, and one of these was Lockheed's development of a suitable disc brake system. We also produced a remote gearshift.

I was rubbing shoulders pretty much on a day-to-day basis with the likes of Sir Alec Issigonis and Donald Healey, which perhaps isn't too surprising when you're World Champion Constructor, and one day in Spring 1961 I went to (Sir) George Harriman, BMC's Chairman and Managing Director, and said to

John Cooper outside his Ferring Honda dealership. Quite naturally he also specialises in the cars which bear his own name.

him 'Let's do one for the boys!' The depth of my rapport with BMC management was evident when George Harriman responded enthusiastically 'Yes! Go away and do it!'

Very soon the notion of capturing the European Touring Car title had taken hold. I told an incredulous Harriman: 'You'll have to make a thousand for Group II homologation by September. You only have to say you've made a thousand.' Harriman laughed. By the January of 1964, Paddy Hopkirk had won the Monte Carlo Rally in a Mini-Cooper S and we never looked back.

Astonishingly enough, there was never an official agreement between BMC and me with regard to developing the cars. We just received a nominal £2 a car for the R & D. Granted, this had been carried out to a great extent on Formula Junior engines, but perhaps £2 a car does seem rather minimal today. We were also provided with the wherewithal to go racing with the cars, which was of course something we excelled at. My drivers included John Rhodes, John Handley, Gordon Spice, Sir John Whitmore, John Love (who won the British Championship in 1962), John Fitzpatrick (who won the 1300 Class in 1964), Paddy Hopkirk, Steve Neal and Warwick Banks (who won the European Touring Car series for Tyrrell in a 1.0-litre car in 1964, by virtue of most class wins). Rhodes won the 1300 class in 1968. Also at this time a certain Ron

Dennis was an apprentice. He's done quite well for himself, too.

The arrangement we had with BMC was that Ken Tyrrell handled the European races, and this at a time when Jackie Stewart was racing F3s for him, while my team, managed by Ginger Devlin, took care of the British events. There was a certain amount of rivalry, during the 1960s, between us and the Broadspeed team for BMC funding, and driver poaching was not unknown ... Other challengers running Mini-Coopers with some success included Don Moore, Equipe Arden and British Vita. Rallying was handled by Stuart Turner, and later Peter Browning, at the BMC Competitions Department at Abingdon. The two disciplines, rallying and racing, produced different driving techniques. I remember being at Zandvoort for a demonstration and being driven round by Timo Mäkinen. He was dancing on the pedals, saying alternately 'Now we make Mini understeer, and now we make Mini oversteer,' just playing with it. I was quite relieved when we paused in the pits, only for him to say 'and now we do proper lap!' That was something else!

By now, I expect you have this sea of half-remembered famous faces swimming before you, easing in and out of Mini-Coopers and single-seaters of one sort or another. These were heady days, when almost anything seemed possible and we decided that now was the time to make a big one! The first

Cooper S had been the l070cc car, and a thousand 970cc cars had been homologated to go for the European title. Now I wanted to take the engine out to 1300cc but George Harriman was pessimistic. He thought the bore wouldn't go that far; it was, after all, still a production engine. 'Never mind that', I said, 'We'll bloody well do it!' And of course we did, but clearly it seemed outrageous at the time.

The works cars were fitted with rose-jointed suspension set-ups, anti-roll bars, the traditional Cooper racing wheels, copied, incidentally, by Minilite. When suspension went hydrolastic, I thought 'Great!', initially, especially in the wet. But the cars were down on their bump-stops anyway so it didn't matter a lot! I tested the ZF diff with Issigonis at Silverstone and it was a full two seconds a lap quicker so we got it homologated. You get the idea that nothing was particularly onerous to organise? It's not like that today. Alec wanted to keep the sliding windows in order to retain the door pockets: somewhere to keep the gin bottles from rolling around. You know, 30 years ago it must have been the cheapest car that ever won those big-time rallies. Since then everyone's copied the east-west engine configuration. Actually, Jack Daniels, who built the prototype, first had it the other way round with the carbs at the front.

I expect you know how the Mini got started. In 1955 when we were in the midst of the Suez crisis,

Leonard Lord said to Alec Issigonis: 'You'd better make a bubble car.' Alec, of course, went his own way and simply made a small car - under ten feet - with a big interior. On a minimal budget, too! They wouldn't give him money for jigs so he made his own, which is why the Mini's got seams down its roof pillars. These are jigging ribs, spot welded together, to save money. Sergio (Pinin) Farina once joked with Alec: 'Why don't you style the Mini a bit?', and Alec replied 'It'll still be fashionable when I'm dead and gone!'

It can't have been that undesirable to the Italians, of course, because Enzo Ferrari had at least three Mini Coopers. He used to take them up into the hills for fun. I had lunch with Enzo in 1958 and he said to me: 'Ferrari will never build a rear-engined Grand Prix car. The engine in a Grand Prix car belongs at the front.' After Clark's Lotus was impounded in 1961 after the Von Trips crash, they must have had a really good look at it! It wasn't long before they followed suit, anyway.

Our involvement with BMC ended in 1970 when Donald Stokes took over the helm at British Leyland. In contrast to people like Harriman and Issigonis he wasn't an enthusiast, and not at all interested in competition or, indeed, the promotional value of competition successes. Until Stokes came along, everyone got on well together. He asked me to define my involvement and I explained I was a consultant who won races and rallies. This wasn't enough for Stokes and the Cooper name and badge were dropped.

The sporting Mini became the rather lacklustre 1275 GT, followed by the 1300 GT which was only moderately better. And this was at a time when we were leagues ahead, developing not only an 1800cc Mini, but the legendary 'Twinny Mini', a double-fronted device with two engines. This creation very nearly cost me my life, for a rear suspension failure tipped the car over and I fractured my skull in the ensuing accident. I asked Harriman to make a thousand for rallying but after the accident he wouldn't hear of it. The twin-engined moke was a bloody good army vehicle, though.

By 1970, British Leyland was beginning to lose money and the Mini was over ten years old. I'd certainly had ten of the happiest years of my life, accident or not. After the shunt I got involved with Jonathan Seiff of Marks and Spencer and we toyed with the idea of a St Michael Racing Team! We ran Cooper-Maseratis for a while and Surtees and Rodriguez won in Mexico and Argentina.

I'm currently President of the BRSCC. I was on the BRDC Committee as well, but you can't do everything. I find the current saloon car racing scene very exciting. But as with the Mini Coopers, you tend to get one make which is dominant at one time, at least in its class. Now it's the Alfa 155; a couple of years ago it was the Sierra Cosworth. The budgets are very different, of course, particularly in Formula One, where something like £30 million, with free engines, is McLaren's stake, compared with the £50,000 it cost us to run the Grand Prix cars in 1959.

Funnily enough, my wife's nickname at school was 'Minie', and this was long before the car came out! But I feel people generally remember me more for the Mini Coopers than the Grand Prix cars because, of course, they are something the public comes into contact with. Although they probably haven't a clue who this bloke Cooper is, and don't necessarily make the connection with the racing cars. After all, it's a couple of decades since we were active in single seaters.

I'm proud of my influence on saloon car development. The Cooper

John Cooper keeps in touch with racing in the '90s.

S made the Mini the first family saloon to be a GT car. Then Colin Chapman, who was a great friend, made the Lotus Cortina. Other tuners helped things along, too. We dealt with Jan Odor of Janspeed, who was, of course, with Daniel Richmond at Downton Enginering, as was Richard Longman. We ran Downton engines from 1966, they did all the fuel injection engines and now Janspeed do all our head machining for our conversion kits. I feel the Mini's logical development was manifested in what Innocenti did with it; a facelift for the body and upgrading of instrumentation and interior brought it into the 1970s. I'm surprised how long it's lasted, though. Look at Japan! it's a cult there; Rover sold 10,000 Minis into Japan last year and over 50 per cent were Coopers.

I opened my garage at Ferring, England, in the early '70s. Until eight years ago it was a regular British Leyland dealership, but they were over-represented in the area at the time. Then I happened to be at Brands for the Grand Prix and I met old Nakamura. We'd supplied Honda with the basis for their 1962 Grand Prix car so we knew each other quite well and I said 'What

about taking a Honda franchise?' And he said 'Delighted!' So that's what we've been doing since 1985. We've a spacious, modern workshop and alongside the Hondas in the showroom are a 1969 Cooper S, a 5oocc Cooper-Norton F3 car and a bicycle marketed in Japan as a 'John Cooper'. Quite flattering, really.

As I've said, the Cooper is a cult car in Japan and in the mid-1980s the Japanese approached me to supply a performance kit for the 1.0-litre engine; the twin carbs and cross-flow head gave an extra 20bhp. We supplied these in a wooden box which fitted on the back seat of the Mini so there was no problem with type approval and it was a great success in Japan. We supplied over 1000 kits. *Autocar* magazine asked us to put a kit on a regular UK car for evaluation and we had over 70 orders straight away

At the 30th birthday party for the Mini at Silverstone I spoke to about 150 foreign journalists, along

with Paddy, announcing Rover's intention to market the Mini Cooper. The decision was made to drop the 1.0-litre unit and use a 1275 engine. The Metro 1275 engine was type approved in July 1990 and by September was in full production. Rover made 1000 Mini Coopers, all of which were pre-sold. Then the enthusiasts at Rover elected to go with the fuel injected system, which is still in production today.

I'm delighted to say that Coopers make up half of the current Mini production. In addition, my son Michael and I supply aftermarket performance and handling kits and all sorts of accessories to make Mini Cooper motoring even more enjoyable.

INTRODUCTION

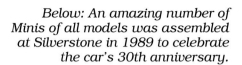

Below: An amazing number of Minis of all models was assembled at Silverstone in 1989 to celebrate the car's 30th anniversary.

It's not so much the car that needs introducing as the author, I'll confess now that I never used to be a great Mini fan; in the halcyon days of the mid-'60s I was an Anglia fan, delighting in taunting Cooper Ss with my lowered 1340cc Classic-engined Anglia. I can feel Cooper addicts' hackles rise! What! 'Why then is someone with no particular commitment to the model writing a book about it?' You have Rover's Longbridge PR department - who lent me a new, fresh-out-of-the-box Cooper S to try - to thank for that. I also compared Philip Splett's Cooper S with a colleague's new Citroën AX GT, the idea being that the Citroën could be the '90s successor to the Cooper. After hustling both cars around rural Essex, I concluded there was no comparison. If you wanted an easy time of it, you'd take the AX; but if you wanted something wlth soul, with fire in its belly, there was no contest. It had to be the Cooper S.

Discussions with Rod Grainger of Veloce sowed the seeds for the book. Everyone knows someone who had or has a Mini, so I was not unacquainted with the car; never having owned one, or had one on test before, I'd not got to know it intimately. The main reason for this is due to the cars' interior ergonomics: a little over 6ft tall, I never felt comfortable in Minis, despite in-

triguing accounts of in-car encounters and the physical contortions necessary to perform them!

Having excused myself, I'll get on with the story. The Mini Cooper's compact cheekiness encouraged familiarity and a mid-'60s Mini owner off to the pub or Brands might be asked 'Are you going in the "Box"?' Often the cars were referred to as Min-Bins or just Bins. There is a certain amount of grudging respect implicit here, recognition that the Mini was quite capable of looking after itself; other cars of the day like Anglias, A40s and the like never attracted such epithets. Only if it was modified did an Anglia become a 'fatty Anglia', for instance. When a car gains an identity, it must be special, and the Cooper's was quickly established.

Conceived as an economy measure for the late '50s, the Mini's running gear layout put it on a higher plane. Unlike other small cars which preceded it, such as the A30 and A35, the Mini was unique; no big-sisters to steal its thunder. Unlike the Hillman Imp which failed to materialise according to Rootes' schedule, the Mini had a smiling 'face'. The slab-sided rear-drive A40 was staid by comparison and, anyway, like the Anglia, it wore a larger shell. The Mini was a car of its time, innovative and born into a new, optimistic era.

Free from post-war austerity, the '60s were obsessed with the new and trendy with the accent, Liverpudlian or otherwise, on youth, sensation, frivolity and freedom. If something caused outrage in the older generation, so much the better, be it long haired blokes or convoys of parka-clad scooterists jamming the roads to seaside towns like Clacton, 'Skeggy', Margate or Brighton. Psychedelia was just too incomprehensible for parents! The hem of the mini skirt rose until hardly anything was left to the imagination. Anything traditional and smacking of the past was debunked, kitched-up or scoffed at, and cars such as the Mini, E-Type, Elan and, so help us, Beach Buggy, were flash and fashionable. Like the latter, the Moke was a rejected military project which was sufficiently 'off the wall' to attract its own cult following.

But then we know all that now. I am demonstrating how regular enthusiasts perceived the cars in their early days. There was the spate of banal Mini jokes, often pumped out over the PA during the pre-race lull at Brands Hatch; ones that went 'how many elephants can you get in a Mini? Answer: two in the back and two in the front', or something awful like that. There were rag-day competitions to see how many students could be crammed into a Mini, and so on. It's not true

to say there had never been anything like it, because the A30 is almost as diminutive. The Fiat Topolino of the '30s and the Fiat 500 and 600 were well in advance of the Mini, sizewise. The Mini's attraction lay just as much in what it was capable of, and what could be done with it when it was on the move, exemplified, in the public's imagination, in the classic film *The Italian Job*, starring Michael Caine and three Mini Coopers that leapt across Turin rooftops and led the Italian cops in their Alfa Romeo Giulia Supers a merry dance through the sewers; fabulous stunt driving by L'Equipe Remy Julienne immortalised the Cooper in a different way to its competition successes.

I have dealt largely with the introduction of the Cooper and its early competition years, which, I believe were the cars' finest hours: tyre-smoking John Rhodes, yumping Paddy Hopkirk. Many emulated their feats, making the Cooper the most consistently successful competition car of the decade and beyond. Considerations of space have led me to gloss over the interim period, but I have brought things up to date with the Rover Cooper because I am intrigued by its renaissance. Avoiding any cynicism about Rover's motives in relaunching the car, it demonstrates just how versatile was the original concept. What BMW, Rover Group's new owners, will do with the Cooper remains to be seen ...

I

IN THE
BEGINNING:
SIR ALEC ISSIGONIS

Mini history has its origins in the aftermath of the 1956 Suez crisis but, before explaining how this came to be, we should look at the fascinating life and works of the man who fathered the Mini. How did Alec, later Sir Alec, Issigonis come to drop this bombshell in a world of family motoring populated by miniaturised clones of American designs, Fiat 500s and VW Beetles? The answer is that he was a natural genius, a man who lived in times of great events to which, in his own way, he contributed.

Issigonis grew up with things mechanical, his family having been involved with marine engineering. He was born Alexander Arnold Constantine in 1906 in Izmir, Smyrna (which was part of the Ottoman empire and is now Turkey) to a Greek marine engineer with British nationality. When the family business was confiscated during the political machinations which

Father of the Mini, Sir Alec Issigonis had a good eye for a curve in the bodywork, and recorded his ideas in Leonardo da Vinci-like sketches.

followed the First World War, the family was evacuated by the Royal Navy and Alec travelled to Britain to study engineering at Battersea Polytechnic where he gained a diploma. He travelled extensively and, following a tour of Europe with his Bavarian mother, took a job, aged 22, as chief draughtsman at Edward Gillett's workshop in London.

Under development at the time was an automatic clutch, intended to work in conjunction with the opening and closing of the throttle. As a means of automatic transmission this was inferior to General Motors' evolving synchromesh gearbox, but in the course of the development Issigonis was introduced to a number of British manufacturers who were interested in the concept, including Humber and Rover. In 1934 he was offered a job by Humber and it wasn't long before Cowley beckoned: two years later; at the age of 30 he found himself in charge of rear axle design in one of the cells in Morris Motors' newly centralised engineering division.

Before long Alec was designing suspension systems, too. As a hobby he took to sprinting and hill-climbing an aluminium-bodied 750cc single seater known as the Lightweight Special, based on his Austin 7 Ulster, and with his friend George Dowson learned much about suspension and body stiffness, as well as exploring the limits of drivability and handling. This racer had independent suspension all round, using rubber rings for both spring and damper units. Camber changes to front and rear wheels could be executed swiftly, as a means of getting the power down efficiently. By 1939 he had designed an independent coil spring and wishbone set-up and rack-and-pinion steering for the Morris M10 series, but with the Second World War intervening, these components were first tried on the 1250cc MG Y-type saloon of 1947.

The arrangement endured in the MGB. During the war years he spent some time preparing designs for the Morris Minor under Chief Engineer Vic Oak, assisted by draughtsmen Jack Daniels on chassis suspension and steering, and Reg Job on the body. The original scheme was to use torsion bar front suspension, virtually unheard of at the time, 14in wheels and a VW-style flat four engine. The prototype

was overly tall and dumpy, which Issigonis cured by inserting a 10in wide fillet down the centre of the body. The Morris Minor was launched to much acclaim at Earls Court in 1948, despite the remarks of Lord Nuffield at the trade launch who described it as a 'poached egg'. Over 1.6 million Minors were built between 1948 and 1971 and, in terms of space and efficiency of handling and performance, it was a trendsetter which also gave excellent value for money.

Before long Alec was fiddling with his creation, experimenting with front wheel drive in 1951, which would have its place later in the decade, but was stalled by corporate marketing tactics following the merger that occurred in 1952. The Nuffield Organisation which owned Morris merged with Austin to form the British Motor Corporation, and Issigonis left to work for Alvis at Coventry, seeing his designs for Morris shelved, temporarily at least. Things didn't work out at Alvis either, as too much had already been spent developing Alec's first project, which included a new 3.5-litre, 90-degree, V8 engine and Alex Moulton's brand new Hydrolastic suspension system. There was to have been a two-speed automatic gearbox allied to a conventional overdrive, effectively giving four forward speeds, but it was shelved.

By 1956, Issigonis was back at BMC, now located at Longbridge, Birmingham, along with several designers from Alvis and Cowley,

An original Austin Cooper about to try a hill start on the Test Slopes before dispatch.

all under the Chairmanship of Sir Leonard Lord. Which brings us to the Suez crisis. Egypt's President Nasser had the canal blocked and the oil pipeline through Syria was cut. At a stroke, Europe was forced to reconsider its view of the motor car and the immediate upshot was the sudden abundance of bubble cars. These diminutive Heinkels, BMWs and Messerschmits were new and trendy and, although they provided very economical motoring for the impecunious driver, in the same way as home-grown three-wheelers, they were total anathema to Lord, who encouraged Issigonis to produce something appropriate to combat the invasion of Teutonic and Italian products. The idea was to utilise as many items from the

BMC parts bin as possible and, just as he had done with the Morris Minor, Issigonis worked with a series of carefully annotated freehand sketches to draw up his design for the new small car.

Between March and July 1957 his team of specialists built the wooden mock-ups. Alec, of course, went his own way and produced a small car - under ten feet long - with most of the space devoted to the interior. It was achieved on a minimal budget, too. BMC wouldn't give him money for jigs so he made his own which is why the Mini has seams down its roof pillars These are jigging ribs, spot welded together as a means of saving money. Assembly was to be a simple matter. According to Alan Jones, cur-

rently Principal Engineer Body-in-White at Longbridge and an apprentice there in the late '50s, one of Sir Alec's favourite saying was that the Mini 'could be built by a Bournemouth waiter!' Compared with today's robotisation, there was clearly some truth in the jest. The simplicity of assembly was of less significance to other contemporaries, like Pininfarina, who once joked with Alec: 'Why don't you style the Mini a bit?' Alec had the foresight to reply: 'It'll still be fashionable when I'm dead and gone!' John Cooper pointed out that the Mini can't have been that undesirable to the Italians, because Enzo Ferrari had at least three Coopers.

What became recognised as the key engineering innovations incor-

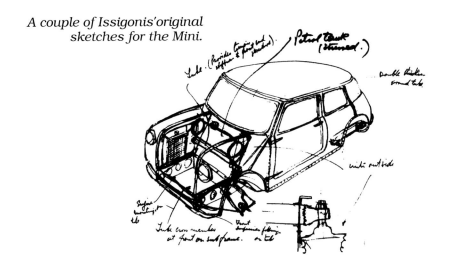

A couple of Issigonis' original sketches for the Mini.

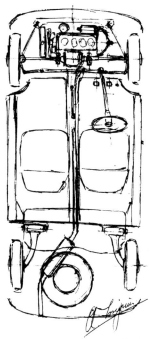

porated into the Mini's design were the placement of the gearbox under the engine in the sump as a means of saving space (something which had never been tried before) and mounting the power unit transversely in a frontal subframe. The engine used was the Morris Minor's 948cc A-series unit, with the radiator at the left-hand side of the car and air blown through it rather than sucked in. The original idea had been to create a new engine using half the Alvis' V8, giving a 1500cc slant four, and another abandoned project was a two cylinder engine composed of half a BMC 1100cc unit. The tiny ensemble ran on diminutive 10 inch Dunlop wheels. It took a year to iron out most of the bugs, including driveshaft/steering problems, and by mid-1959 the Mini was in production. It had cost £100,000 to develop.

Issigonis' second complete design, the Mini was followed by a line of similarly conceived family cars for BMC, increasing progressively in size and produced as badge-engineered models within the BMC family includlng MG, Riley, and Wolseley, as well as Austin and Morris. There were the four-door 1100 and 1300, the 1800 'land crabs' and Maxi derivatives. None achieved as much as the Mini, which revolutionised the world's motor industry and remains in production over thirty years later.

Issigonis received numerous accolades throughout his life, including a CBE in 1964 and a knighthood in 1969. A man of impish charm and good manners, who was throroughly enthusiastic about all he undertook, he was given to producing Leonardo da Vinci-style sketches of his ideas at the drop of a hat. A fan of model steam railways, he experimented with a steam-powered Mini in his Longbridge design shop. Alec Issigonis also enjoyed the finer side of life, including gourmet food and wine and holidays in Monte Carlo. A life packed with creativity and achievement ended in 1989.

II

THE COOPER STORY

Very, very few road cars are designed primarily with the intention of going racing and the Mini is no exception, despite being endowed, even in its most utilitarian form, with extraordinary handling. If, over thirty years after the Mini's introduction, you consider for a moment that a road test in 1993 (*Carweek*, 24 November 1993) rated the Mini Cooper's handling and roadholding better than that of the Fiat Cinquecento and Daihatsu Mira, and when others have preferred it to the most up-to-date, souped-up microcar from the Japanese, then you begin to get some idea of how genuinely sensational was this agility and grip when compared to its historical contemporaries. It was, after all, introduced in the late 1950s ...

It has been claimed that Issigonis was 'strongly against' using the Mini in competition. This may be an exaggeration, although it should be remembered that he considered the first 948cc Mini prototype too fast, whereupon it shed 100cc. In an interview, when asked how the Mini got into competition, he said that he 'never gave this one single thought', adding that it 'never occurred to me that this thing would turn out to be such a fantastic rally car'. This is slightly surprising if one remembers his own, not unsuccessful, forays into competition. The truth seems to be that he was unwilling to be distracted by the extra effort needed for competition work whilst the basic car - his peo-

ple's car - was still being developed. It must also be remembered that development work was not over on the day of the Mini's launch in August 1959, for Issigonis would still have had plenty to occupy him with various design faults which had come to light, such as wheels breaking off in competition (the Six Hour Relay at Silverstone in 1960 was where this came to a head), slipping clutches, electrics which were too vulnerable to wet weather and water entering the car creating that once-familiar 'Early Mini Odour'.

The existence of these last two problems on the production Mini can at least be partly explained by the very hot and dry summer of 1959, during which much of the car's testing was done. The relative dearth of rainfall thus failed to show up what was, in the case of the wet carpets, a great headache for Issigonis and his team. Only a re-design of the floor pressing and the way it went around a stiffening cross-brace cured the problem. The difficulty in finding the cause of the problem which, in the end, took three months, seems to have been exacerbated by the fact that only a certain combination of rainfall and speed would see the water entering the car, as it was apparently being sucked into an area of low pressure. Although such behaviour on a mass-produced model would be scandalous today, this sort of thing was really about par for the course for more than one car maker at that

Hopkirk and Crellin go for the Monte again in 1994.

time; it seems that in those days the customers for early models were used to carrying out the testing themselves!

Sparring partners

It was not long after the Mini's introduction that various firms started to offer engine conversions to provide more power. Improved brakes were also available, thanks to harder brake linings sometimes backed up with a servo. However, the person who eventually succeeded in getting the idea of a go-faster version of the Mini into official production was a person whom Issigonis had known for some time and who had occasionally been an adversary of his in competitions such as hillclimbs and speed trials.

John Cooper had taken his prototype 500 Special to compete in the 500 and 750cc classes at the Brighton Speed Trials in the autumn of 1946 and found himself matched against Issigonis, racing for the Dowson team in his Lightweight Special, a pre-war machine with a modified Austin Seven sidevalve engine and, significantly as it turned out, rubber suspension. His Cooper beat the older car and the two men became friends. Given the subsequent chain of events, it is interesting to conjecture whether the Mini Cooper would have happened at all, had Cooper's little racing car found itself alongside some other competitor at the start of the Madeira drive kilometre. Such is the way that whole

chunks of history can come about from what was at the time a most trivial detail.

Since Cooper was the first Grand Prix car maker of the postwar era to successfully demonstrate that placing the engine behind the driver in a Grand Prix car was better than in front, making such a layout universal, it is also interesting to note the comparison with Issigonis, whose transverse engine layout in the Mini is just about universal for all today's inexpensive family saloons. However, Issigonis, like Cooper with his rear-engined GP cars, was not the first person to adopt the transverse engine layout - DKW had a transverse engine before the war - but, like Cooper, Issigonis was the first to make an adventurous idea work properly. Little could these two men have realized the enormous and lasting influence they were to have on motoring and motor racing ...

In view of his achievements, an interesting and surprising point to remember about Issigonis is that he was a very poor mathematician. He has been quoted as suggesting that truly creative people cannot manage higher mathematics. He took his exam in this subject sev-

eral times and reckoned that his college eventually decided to allow him a pass so that he could continue with his course. If this is so, we must be more than grateful to Battersea Tech for its foresight.

As a result of this friendship with Issigonis, Cooper became a frequent buyer of BMC's A-series engine which, when modified, was used very successfully in his Formula Junior racing cars, competing in a formula that required the use of production engines. Successfully enough, in fact, that one John Young Stewart won the Formula Three World Championship in 1964, his car powered by the BMC A-series unit: clearly the Mini Cooper's engine was to have a good pedigree. John Cooper was therefore not ignorant of the Mini's development and he and Issigonis took a pre-production car to Monza for the Italian Grand Prix in September 1959, just after the Mini's launch and it's often repeated how they beat Reg Parnell, in his Aston Martin DB4GT, there. With the considerable straight-line speed differential between the two cars, this part of the story should be taken with a sizeable pinch of salt; after all, in testing at Silverstone in 1960,

What is interesting about this BMC publicity shot from Goodwood pits in 1962 is that the Mini's badge has been faked up on the photo to read 'Austin Cooper'. Bruce McLaren and friend appear to have spotted the 'fix'.

the Healey 3000s lapped in around 1m 18s and the Minis in 1m 32s ... What actually seems to have happened was that when they arrived at the twisty bits in the Alps, they let Roy Salvadori (down to drive an Aston Martin in the Grand Prix) take the helm and he proved faster over this section than Reg Parnell, once an F1 driver himself. This ability to embarrass the big cars on the corners was, of course, to become a Mini trademark.

More horsepower

Unsurprisingly, the Mini made such an impression on Cooper that he enthused to Issigonis how fantastic was the little car. 'Why?', asked its designer. Cooper, in reply, asked him if he had ever taken it around a racing circuit. 'No; should I have done?' was the answer. Undeterred by the Issigonis diffidence, Cooper made it something of a new goal to endow the Mini with the horsepower deserved by its remarkable chassis. It was not long before Cooper's two contracted F1 drivers, Jack Brabham and Bruce McLaren (featured in early advertisements for the car) were charging about in Minis of their own and, not unnaturally, were also requesting more power. Apparently this was answered by the installation of Formula Junior engine parts.

Around this time Cooper had been expending not a not insignificant amount of time and effort trying to change a Renault Dauphine into a racing car: no doubt attracted by the light weight of the basic car. It was to prove a hopeless project: even with the substitution of an exotic powertrain. Cooper has said that a recent drive in a DeLorean reminded him of it! Since a Dauphine would have proven a strong contender in the Flimsiest Car Awards, perhaps the bodyshell wasn't rigid enough for decent handling? That said, the Gordini version was the mainstay of French domestic saloon car racing. However, the aborted Dauphine project made Cooper look at the Mini as a racing car with an even stronger eye.

Issigonis' reluctance to commit himself to a 'hot' Mini was an obstacle to be overcome, but eventually Cooper seemed to have persuaded him to consider it. 'Let's go and see the headmaster', Issigonis said to Cooper, referring to George Harriman who was then boss of BMC. Since Cooper was the world champion car constructor in both 1959 and 1960, one wonders how he had time for all the wheeling and dealing to get the Mini Cooper into production? Encouraged, no doubt, by the modified cars of his two

drivers, he told Harriman they should make a proper factory version with disc brakes and a remote gearchange. 'Let's make some for the boys', was Cooper's oft-quoted remark to Harriman. 'Take one away and do it', was Harriman's pragmatic reply. Cooper designed the new gearchange himself and talks were held with Lockheed who were very interested in putting disc brakes on a Mini, since if they could be seen to work on a car with such small wheels, they would work anywhere. Also, the high profile thereby given to this new type of brake by being on a car as ubiquitous as a Mini, would be invaluable to them.

Just two weeks after George Harriman's encouragement, Cooper took this prototype Mini Cooper along for Harriman to try and he set off around the grounds at the Longbridge factory in it. Since this car apparently now had what was virtually a complete Formula Junior engine under the bonnet - as much as three times the original car's output! - Harriman presumably was kept entertained. On returning, he readily agreed to make more. Cooper explained that they'd need to make 1000, in order to homologate the car for rallying. Harriman didn't think they could sell that many, but gave the go-ahead anyway.

Factory commitment

And so the Mini was to enter competition with the official backing of the factory. Rallying was the only

form of competition overtly supported by Abingdon, although - as is so often the case - unofficial help was given to enter the Mini Cooper in track races. To find the reason for this one has to look back to the horrendous 1955 Le Mans disaster in which more than eighty people died. The car which triggered this much debated and worst-ever motor racing accident was an Austin Healey. In 1961 this was all a very recent and vivid memory, which explains why BMC were reluctant to give public support to their products being used for 'pure' motor racing. Joe Public thus saw that it was left to privateers to race the Mini on the circuits. This lack of official factory backing does not seem to have prevented the Mini from being staggeringly successful, winning more circuit races than any other full four-seater saloon ever made.

Limited by the homologation quest to 1000cc, it was decided that the production version of the new performance Mini should have a top speed of 85mph - some 15mph up on the standard car - and that 55bhp would be needed for this goal (one wonders what speeds were attainable with the car that Harriman tried?) This represented an increase in power of more than 50 per cent over the standard unit's rather meagre 34 bhp. This horsepower requirement was realised with various modifications, the most obvious being an increase in capacity. The stroke was lengthened by

almost 20 per cent and a reduction in bore size of but one half a millimetre kept the swept volume below one litre. Twin carburetters were used, along with various internal mods such as larger valves and a stronger cylinder block. All these parts were pretty well standard production items, however, the engine being similar to that found in the contemporary Austin Healey Frogeye Sprite.

Apart from the extra performance, the remote gearchange was also praised, giving a great improvement in change quality over the example found on the original Minis - sometimes described as 'like a spoon in a Christmas pudding'. However, the actual speed of the change was hampered by rather parlous synchromesh. That the new disc brakes were much praised will surprise no-one who has attempted 'frisky' driving in the standard car and remembered the unsettling moments caused by the heat induced brake fade when, in dire circumstances, one merely rolled gently to a stop even while heaving mightily on the middle pedal! Despite the improvement over drums it was not long before the brakes on this first Mini Cooper were considered too fade-prone. In retrospect, part of the problem was due to a poor choice of pad material; we must not forget that such a tiny disc brake was all very new technlogy in 1961. Both the remote gearshift and front discs would, in time, find themselves fitted as

standard on the basic Mini.

Various cosmetic enhancements and refinements found their way onto the Cooper version of the Mini, the most salient being the two-tone paint jobs with contrasting roof colours. This readily-distinguishing feature of the Coopers was soon applied by the factory to the Mini Super, presumably to make the buyers of this more prosaic model feel they had bought something with Cooper panache, although it certainly did not perform like one. This undoubtedly diluted the exclusivity of the Cooper to some degree. Three decades later, the same piece of marketing saw the mundane VW Golf Driver dressed up to resemble the GTi.

Extra sound-proofing was fitted to the Cooper Minis, partly because they were, after all, made to be up-market versions of the Mini, and partly as the increase in engine speed obviously made more noise. A ride today in an original Cooper is a noisy experience. In 1961 one magazine called the soundproofing measures 'a triumph of applied accoustics'. However, the modern car buyer can feel comforted by the real progress made in the refinement of small cars in the last 30 years. Unsurprisingly, the press of 1961 went pretty wild about the Cooper, declaring it even more fun than the original Mini. No changes to the suspension were made. This is a tremendous compliment to the original design and once again serves to remind us just how amaz-

MORRIS MINI-COOPER *'S'* TYPE

The S type was produced between 1963 and 1971. A highly successful sporting saloon, it achieved numer-ous rally victories. This is an original, postcard-type brochure.

ingly high were the original Mini's levels of handling and roadholding. Thus, equipped with more 'urge', the new 997cc Cooper soon found itself in competition.

Turner's urge

Despite the great success of the first Mini Cooper, Issigonis was still not convinced of the car's potential as a competition winner. Some time around the early international rally wins he relaxed his coolness to the hot Mini syndrome and brought his enthusiasm to bear on the design of the first S-Model Cooper, a car which owes its conception to the urgings of Stuart Turner. It was also a case of Issigonis being able to afford the time, now that the basic car had

entered its fourth year in production and many of its faults had been ironed out. Later on he admitted being very much indebted to John Cooper for all the competition success and publicity that the Mini Cooper was earning. The result, with a more co-operative Alec Issigonis, was to be the 1071cc Cooper S, the larger engine size being achieved by taking the bore out to its practical limit, some 8mm more than the 997cc car. The stroke had to remain the same as the original Mini's, because of a crankshaft-machining problem, thus explaining the rather odd capacity. Apart from this enforced piece of make-do, the 1071 engine was far less mundane than the 997

engine, which was made up, more or less, from stock parts.

This first over-square Cooper engine produced a 27 per cent power increase over the previous unit and internal modifications to the new engine were many, if not radical. Larger valves, oil pump and oilways, together with stronger crankshaft and connecting rods, all found their way into the new engine, which owed a lot to the BMC A-series competition motors, as fitted to the Formula Junior racing cars. The gearbox was also strengthened with improved bearings. These modifications found their way into the cars because of weaknesses which had showed up under racing condi-tions, thus giving pretty strong sup-

20

port to the adage 'Racing improves the breed' and good reason to continue with competition work, publicity benefits aside.

Almost as significant as the power boost was the improvement to the brakes, which were now half-an-inch greater in diameter and one-eighth-of-an-inch thicker. These apparently meagre increases in size resulted in an increase in swept volume of almost 80 per cent with a corresponding improvement in heat-sink and, therefore, resistance to the dreaded brake-fade. A servo was now added, as one of the criticisms of the first Cooper was that the pedal pressures were too high, especially in relation to the other controls in such a small car. The servo's fitment also permitted harder pads to be used, further delaying the onset of fade. It would be true to say that the improvement to the 'stopping' over the previous car was every bit as great as the improvement to the 'going'.

New model introduced

The British Motor Corporation was certainly busy with its Coopers at this time, for a few months later it brought out the 998cc version to replace the 997 car. Although there was merely a single cubic centimetre increase in engine capacity, many owners would never realise how different the engine was internally, being much 'squarer' than the outgoing car, with a larger bore and a shorter stroke. This unit was developed from the engine in the Mk 2 version of the Wolseley Hornet and Riley Elf (lovely motors, squire!). With maximum power unaltered, the torque was increased slightly, but at its peak was some 600rpm lower - a very worthwhile difference. This accounted for the useful improvements in low speed pulling power and, consequently, overtaking performance.

Hydrolastic suspension arrives

Just over one year after the introduction of the 998cc Cooper, Hydrolastic suspension, borrowed from the Austin/Morris 1100 range, appeared on all models in September 1964. For the most part the new suspension did a far better job at providing a comfortable ride than the rubber cones and shock absorbers could ever manage. No conventional shock absorbers were fitted, the Hydrolastic units themselves housing valves which acted as dampers. The difference in roadholding between the new suspension and the old was absolutely minimal - in road use. It is true that those who raced them sometimes converted the Hydrolastic cars back to dry suspension, but the difference between motor racing and even the fastest road use - however much the road driver likes to think otherwise - is a yawning chasm. Perhaps those who state their preference for dry suspension too loudly are just being a wee bit macho, a bit like those who think manual transmission is oh-so sporty: after all, Formula One drivers don't wrestle with gearsticks any more. Besides, several rallies were won with Hydrolastic cars and John Cooper actually put Hydrolastic suspension on a Formula Junior single-seater. It performed quite well in the dry and was actually a bit better in the wet!

Nevertheless, one inconvenience of this fluid suspension system was the attitude of the car if heavily laden. Just like the contemporary 1100s and 1800s, to fill the car with adults plus luggage would cause the headlamps to light up the tops of trees on main beam and antagonise one's fellow motorists on dip. Testers at the time commented that new suspension allowed the Mini to squat, dive and roll slightly more during eager driving but that the car's actual grip was largely unaffected. Perhaps you could say that the car had become slightly softer in order to widen its appeal - rather the same thing that happened to the Volkswagen Golf GTi, a car which is a spiritual descendant of the Mini Cooper. The 998cc Cooper remained in production for almost six years, easily longer than all other Coopers except the 1275S. It does not seem to have found its way into competition, certainly not as a works entry. The main reason for this would be the introduction of the fastest standard Cooper of all, the 1275 Cooper S.

But it wasn't all plain sailing. John Cooper had more trouble get-

ting the idea of the 1275 car past Harriman than the original 997 Cooper. It seems Harriman would not believe that the engine could take it, complaining that 'It is supposed to be an 850cc engine!' Much muttering went on during the meeting concerned and Cooper decided to leave. When he got to the door, Harriman stopped him and said 'We're bloody well going to do it!' Such a choice of words sums up very well what sort of a bloke Harriman was. He is talked of with great affection by everyone.

Introduced in the spring of 1964, this car all but managed the magic 100mph and reached 60mph in not far off half the time of the first 997 Coopers, whose performance was considered pretty impressive at their introduction. Since this had occurred less than two and a half years earlier, BMC had clearly made plenty of progress. To give an idea of how rapid the 1275 Cooper S's acceleration was in 1964, it was faster to 60mph than, for example, the Austin Healey 3000 MkII and Triumph TR4A, both of which were two-seater sports models with much larger engines (and price tags!) The 4.3-litre Ford V8-engined Chrysler Sunbeam Tiger only bettered the new 1275 S Cooper in the dash to 60mph by a second and a half. Although the Cooper's well-known lack of aerodynamic prowess, which usually saw its Cd compared unfavouraby with that of a house brick, meant the more powerful cars drew ahead after about 70mph, on the corners the small car would leave them all floundering.

Apart from the tremendous acceleration, the press was quick to praise the top gear performance. Having the same 71mm bore as all the S models, the 1275cc Cooper now had the longest stroke, some half a millimetre more than that found in the 997cc car. This combination delivered enough torque to enable this largest-engined Cooper, using top gear only, to out-accelerate the average smallish car at the time, being driven flat out through the gears. Since the fifth gear of recent cars is usually an overdrive ratio, any comparisons with modern machinery should be with their 4th gear acceleration - and this 1964 Mini Cooper would still leave most behind. For example, the latest Renault Clio RSi, with an 1800cc fuel-injected engine, recorded the same 30-50mph time in 4th as the Cooper did in top some 29 years previously. Since cars have become much faster in that time, one can get some idea how impressive the Cooper's flexibility would have been in 1964. In traffic, as any press-on driver will know, this top gear flexibility is much more relevant to rapid progress than mere off-the-line performance and some academically high top speed. Indeed, this latest Cooper even recorded a very respectable 10-30mph time in top gear, and one which was quicker than the 997cc Cooper car could manage in third! Around town this flexibility, allied to the car's tiny size and wonderful agility, helped to make it almost uncatchable.

Inside information

All this performance was not arrived at easily, however. Although the S-type Cooper engine may seem simple and even crude to us today, this notion reveals some ignorance of what was going on inside. By the time it was fitted in the 1964 1275 S-model, this engine was delivering nearly three times the power of the original A-series unit's 28bhp and more than doubling the output of the standard Mini's 34bhp as it appeared only some four and a half years before. BMC could not be accused of idleness; to win rallies and races one had to keep up the pressure of development; which was all good stuff for the customer, of course.

The cylinder block on all the S-type Coopers - the 1071, 970 and 1275cc models - had to have its middle two bores moved inwards and its outer two outwards in order to accommodate them. The EN40B steel crankshaft was nitrided, which means that the nitrogen content of the surface layer was increased, thereby improving its hardness and, in turn, resistance to wear. This was done by Rolls-Royce and the crank now with 2in diameter big ends. The specially-made pistons and connecting rods were joined by gudgeon pins of extra thickness. The valves, which ran in cupronickel guides, were of Nimonic 80 steel and had Stellite tips to resist wear where they met the rockers, which were forged and not pressed. As mentioned before, the oil pump and oilways were enlarged. Clearly, these engines had come a very long way from the originals. Nevertheless, the 1275 unit was far from being highly-stressed, since its output was several bhp lower than the smaller one-litre Formula Junior version of the A-series unit - and this engine's output was kept down by having only a single carburetter and an intake restrictor. That maximum output of the engine in road form, at 76bhp, was so much less than ungoverned race-tuned outputs of around 130bhp, shows how lightly-stressed it was. Indeed, the 1275cc engine produces only 8bhp more than the 1071 version, equal to a specific output some 10 per cent lower than the smaller engine. One complaint by the Abingdon competition department was that they were handicapped in rallies - where they had to stick to standard, albeit homologated, production parts - because the 1275S Cooper was supplied with such a 'soft' camshaft in order that 'a District Nurse could drive it in traffic', as Stuart Turner ruefully put it. This helps to explain the lusty and much-enjoyed torque of the car at low engine speeds. The 970S has a specific output higher still than the 1275 unit's, although this car was only in production for ten months - the shortest-lived of all the Cooper variants.

The 970cc car has been erroneously described as a sales flop. It was never intended to make more than 1000 examples to homologate the car for the Group 2 European Saloon Car Championship and it seems around 980 were completed, available only to special order. The engine was by far the most oversquare, with the usual Cooper S bore dimension of around 71mm mated to a stroke of 62mm - shorter than the basic Mini's. It should surprise nobody to know that it was the most high-revving and smoothest of all the Cooper engines. The 970S Cooper was introduced at the same time as the 1275S in March 1964, both cars getting Hydrolastic suspension six months later.

When the desired quota of 970cc cars had been reached, this model was discontinued, leaving the 1275 to soldier on as the only S-model Cooper representative. It graduated to become the Mk 2 model in late 1967, gaining uprated Hydrolastic units, twin tanks and an oil cooler as standard on the way. The new car also had better trim and a larger rear window. More significantly, an all-synchro gearbox was introduced at this time, although this was not found on all cars until one year later. The 998cc Cooper was discontinued in November 1969, at which point the 1275 GT appeared. I can't bring myself to say that the 1275 GT was a replacement for even this ordinary non-S Cooper. The Mk 3 version of the 1275S came out in spring

1970 and sported wind-up windows and concealed door hinges. The Cooper was gradually becoming more civilized without losing its basic appeal. Then along came Lord Stokes.

A Longbridge too far

We know that BMC was in deep fiscal ordure at the time it merged with Leyland to form the British Leyland Motor Corporation - BLMC. Donald Stokes was the man who found himself with the task of trying to put right a company with some 200,000 employees spread across 72 factories, a company that was really in a terrible mess and for many different reasons, not least of all appalling trade union problems. An unenviable task, to be sure, and it is so easy with hindsight - 20/20 vision - to lay all the blame on Stokes. They really were up the creek without a paddle.

No future in competition

However, Stokes and his team apparently could not see the benefits in a rallying or racing programme, thus making an interesting contrast to BMC under Sir George Harriman. They were soon to shut down the competitions department at Abingdon, thereby preventing any more track and rally successes for BMC, so considerably lowering the company's international profile. The consultancy agreement with Cooper was up for review in August 1971 and it was decided not to renew it. Apparently, Stokes approached

Cooper and actually said, 'And what do you do?' Possibly slightly insulted by such a question, Cooper replied that he came to the factory once a fortnight 'to wind Issigonis up'. The excuse given for axing the Cooper name was that the high insurance premiums for the Cooper models was depressing sales. This would be a nonsense even today, at a time when most of us seem to be far from happy with our car insurance. Probably the desire to save the £2 per car which was paid to Cooper was the real reason. Although a seemingly piffling amount now, this sum may equate to several times that figure in today's money, but the prestige generated by the Cooper name both at home and particulary abroad would have easily outweighed this levy. This bean-counting serves as a grim example of the narrow-minded thinking of those who - to quote Wilde - knew the price of everything and the value of nothing.

The association with Healey was also terminated, despite - once again - all the rally victories earned by BMC products wearing that badge. The Triumph competitions department vanished, too. Also under Stokes, Jaguar's Browns Lane factory was to be named 'Leyland Large Car Plant Number Three', thus

working wonders for the morale of the Jaguar workforce. It is now known that Cooper was working on an 1800cc version of the Cooper Mini and this, of course, never went into production. The name of Lord Stokes will be a long time in the forgetting.

And so the last 1275S Mini Cooper left the works in July 1971. The only car that now remained for anyone who wanted a faster Mini with the benefit of full factory back-up was the 1275GT, which had already been in production for some 20 months. Seldom have the initials which once stood for Gran Turismo, and which once graced such fine machines as the Aston Martin DB4 and the Ferrari 330, been so severely diluted as the day they appeared on the 1275 GT Mini. Never claiming grand touring was its forte, being too small and no tourer, the Mini Cooper was horribly emasculated after the removal of the Cooper badge. Not content with reducing the power of the engine, the car was offered with that sad attempt at modernising the Mini's appearance: the square front of the Clubman - a pretty daft name. The result of this misguided disfigurement is that the 1275 GT now looks dated and a Cooper does not (ditto basic Clubman compared to a

basic Mini). Just to add to this sorry tale, the GT suffix given to the new car caused it to be put in the same insurance category as the outgoing 1275 Cooper S, despite its considerably inferior performance, being both heavier as well as less powerful. Cooper urged them to call it a 1275E - for Executive, but he was ignored. Why don't the planners in car companies pay at least some attention to the enthusiastic driver who would often have a better idea than they what sort of machine their company should be offering to the public? The 1275 GT was not only less lively, it was also rather ungainly: it would not be long before it began to look outdated. It was no substitute at all for the real thing.

What began nearly ten years earlier as a perhaps optimistic run of 1000 homologation specials with the 997cc car, had now ended after five different Cooper models and over 145,000 units. What this suggests is that, fuel injection excepted, the Mini Cooper was really the original GTi. The car that BL deemed fit to stop making at the beginning of the 1970s, Volkswagen introduced just a few years later, thus taking the credit for the creation of a whole new genre.

III

PRODUCTION HISTORY AND EVOLUTION

We'll look at the way the cars were, and still are, actually made in another chapter in our walk round the Longbridge lines. First, here is the chronology and detail changes.

The Mark 1 Cooper

The Mark 1 Cooper was in production from July 1961 to November 1963, when it used the 997cc engine, and from November '63 to September 1967 with the 998. Austin chassis numbers were

specifications as the Cooper from 1961 until 1966.

There was a choice of nine variations of the two-tone paintwork theme, the roof colour being the second 'tone'. However, a few Mark 1s left the factory as single colour finishes, usually special orders. Also, the tartan red with white roof combination was reserved for the Works cars and was never a factory option. The door window surrounds were in chrome and the bumper

Mk 1 Morris Cooper in a parkland setting - D-plate indicates 1966 registration.

prefixed C-A2S7 and Morris with K-A2S4. Visually, the Coopers had a number of distinguishing features, although the Mini Super DeLuxe shared the same body and trim

overriders had chromed corner bars. The Morris Cooper grille had seven slats, the Austin had ten. Any car built before June 1964 would have had a plain front valance and, sub-

This Mk 1 Austin Cooper 1275 S looks completely original: Austin grille is perhaps neater than Morris version.

sequently, there were ventilation slits below the bumper at each end. Headlights became sealed-beam units in January 1966.

Without exception, all production Coopers used twin one-and-a-quarter inch SU HS2 carburettors with GJ needles, (GY in 998), topped with a black twin-filter air cleaner. The first 997cc cars used individual pancake filters. The 997 cars had a metalastic crankshaft damper and 998s had double valve springs. Some cars had domed high compression pistons; this may be checked against the engine number prefix: for 997 it would be 9F-Sa-H for high, or 9F-Sa-L indicating low compression concave-top pistons, and similarly for 998cc cars, 9FA-Sa-H and 9FD-Sa-H, or 9FA-Sa-L or 9FD-Sa-L. To extend the numerology, head casting numbers for 997s are 12G185 and 12G195 for 998s. Heads had nine studs. The metal plate with the engine number stamping is to be found riveted to the block above the dynamo, and the chassis number plate on the cowl between radiator and inner wing. Curiously for a car of unit-constuction, there is also a plate for the body number which is spot

welded to the bonnet catch mounting point. The final drive ratio was normally 3.765:1, giving 14.7mph per 1000rpm in top gear, but the optional 3.44:1 provided 16.05mph at 1000rpm in top.

Hydrolastic suspension came in in late September 1964, before

which date it had been the dry rubber cone variety. Mark 1s ran on the standard 10in diameter x 3inJ pressed steel wheels, painted old English white and sporting 'deluxe' wheel trims. There were 7in disc brakes at the front and drums at the rear, but no servo assistance. 998 cars had a smaller bore master cylinder plus a larger fluid reservoir. The 997 had a single silencer in its one-and-five-eighths inch exhaust system; the 998S had two.

Whatever one may think of the austerity and tackiness of '60s car interiors compared to today's plush, cosseted driving environment, it

Mk 1 Morris Cooper S in the paddock at Silverstone during the '87 Norwich Union rally. The right-hand filler cap indicates second fuel tank.

must be remembered that we were then entering a brash new decade, when new synthetic materials offering scope for design innovation were tried which, if proved hard-wearing as well as cheap, were pressed into service. The Cooper's interior was characterised by its contemporary jauntiness, for it was actually a lot more spirited than the remarkably dull interiors of Fords of the time, and actually a model of good taste compared with what I saw them trimming the Metros with recently at Longbridge! The Mk 1 Cooper seats were in two-tone vinyl, lined in grey and sometimes with silver (in early 997s) or gold brocade. Seats upholstered in almond green, tweed and smoke grey had plain grey liners and seat inserts and no brocade. There were five horizontal flutings in the front seats - three in very early cars - and carpets matched seat trim accordingly. They were woven in wool untll November 1965 and in a sort of velvety flock material from then onwards. The dash rail and screen pillars were clad in black vinyl and the headlining was as for regular Minis.

Small detail changes help to establish the authenticity or history of the cars, and are fascinating, if not almost addictive as one discovers more. For instance, cars built before September 1964 were equipped with interior rear-view mirrors in crackle-black cast metal, changing over to cream plastic housings after that. Similarly, the sun visors only became padded at this point, and fitted on single mountings at the corners of the windscreen, whereas previously they were simply vinyl-covered boards fixed to a central chromed swivelling mounting with a pair of chrome crosshead screws. The steering wheel was the distinctly unsporting standard Mini issue.

Unlike the regular Mini, the Coopers all had a remote shift, a blessing compared with the early cars' long, porridge-stirring device which seemed to have a life of its own and could easily interfere with one's clothing! There was no syncromesh on first gear, however. Up to September 1964 the Cooper's gearshift was painted black, then subsequently chromed, as were the interior door handles and the steering column support bracket. The dash-rail ashtray had a solid chrome lid and the push-button window catches were chrome until May 1963. It follows that these touches of glitz were subtle ways of making the Cooper a higher status vehicle than its bog-standard sister. In Minis the driver always looked to the left for the instrumentation, housed in the familiar simple binnacle in the middle of the dashboard and containing the Smiths Industries speedo, calibrated to 100mph with five digit mileometer, plus the electrically operated oil pressure and water temperature gauges, with the control switches mounted on a grey painted panel below. You could opt for extras such as the fresh-air heater and a radio. Round the back, certain Mark 1 Coopers were given double-skin boot lids, otherwise there was simply a black blockboard lining to the lid. Five brackets simply pop-riveted to the boot floor, rear firewall and lower boot edge held the bootboard deck in place, although from 1966 those on the firewall were spot welded. The factory had taken the trouble to match the boot carpet to that of the interior with the early cars, but it was soon standardised to ubiquitous grey. A contentious point is the presence of a second right-hand petrol tank; while all Mark 2 and 3 Cooper Ss had one as standard, hardly any Mark 1 Ss built before 1966 were so equipped.

Mark 1 Cooper S

Between April 1963 and August 1964, the Mark 1 Cooper S was powered by the 1071cc engine; the 1275 unit came in from April 1964 to September 1967 and between June 1964 and April 1965 the 970 engine was fitted. Engine number prefixes were 9F-SA-H and 9FD-SA-H for the 1071, 9F-SA-Y, 9FD-SA-Y and 9FE-SA-Y for the 1275, and 9F-SA-X, 9FD-SA-X and 9FE-SA-X for the flat-top piston 970 variant. The heads now had ten studs and one bolt, necessitating the insertion of a notch at either end of the rocker cover to clear the extra stud and bolt. There were also two rectangular tappet chest covers on the rear of the block, and one-piece forged rockers and double

Here's a good comparison between two Morris Coopers only a year apart in age; the 998 Mk 1 Cooper, right, and the Mk 2 1275 S.

valve springs were in use. Head casting numbers were 12A-185 on early cars and AEG-163 thereafter. On S models the engine mounting bracket was cut away to accommodate a one-piece crankshaft damper pulley.

Other idiosyncrasies include the placement of the voltage regulator, fitted on the off-side inner wing above the bulkhead on later cars, having previously been on the bulkhead itself. Cooper S models have no vacuum advance on their distributors. Mark 1 'S' Austin models bore chassis numbers starting C-A2S7, and Morris were prefixed K-A2S4. The identification plates were located at the same points as the standard Cooper's.

Bodily there was no difference between the Mark 1 S and the ordinary Cooper, but the former appear to have been more frequently painted in green or red with white roofs. Twin fuel tanks and oil cooler were options, with the second five gallon right-hand tank becoming standard in January 1966. Clips for the tank breather pipe were spot welded onto the rear firewall and there was now a rectangular bracket to support the tank.

A horizontally mounted oil cooler also became standard, at first braced with a diagonal strut mounted against the grille support panel, and then two vertical brackets to the base of the front panel. The oil pipes were covered in rubber hose with threaded brass unions. Apart from the instrumenta-

tion (which now included a 120mph speedo and fresh-air heater), interiors were identical to the Cooper, although, curiously, coppers' Coopers, cars used by Police forces, had plain red seats (like the Redcoats, so you couldn't see the blood?) and zips in the roof headlining!

Reclining seats were optional from late November 1965. The 1071 cars had the Moulton rubber cone-type suspension, and the 970 cars had hydrolastic systems. The long-stroke 1275-engined cars started off with the rubber cone set-up, switching after five months to the hydrolastic. All models ran on either 3inJ or 4inJ steel wheels which were pierced by nine cooling holes, the drive coming through solid Hardy-Spicer drive couplings from April 1966. There was a Lockheed type 5 servo, 7in discs at the front and built-in spacers in the rear drums, and the brake master cylinder was larger than the clutch's.

Mark 2 Cooper

Cars bearing the Mark 2 designation were built between October 1967 and November 1969, to works commission number 2-50S. There was an amalgamation of grille design and a compromise on eight grille slats for both Austin and Morris, with two slight angles breaking up the curved shoulders of the grille surround. Rear light clusters were now larger and squared off, and the rear window aperture size was increased slightly. The same colour choice was available as for the Mark

1 cars, although there was a tendency for later Coopers to be painted a single body colour like the Mark 3 cars: the chrome door window trim remained in place, but the chrome overrider bars on the bumper ends disappeared. Chassis numbers went from C-A2SB for Austins and K-A2S6 for Morris, and the body number was 250S. Location of chassis and engine number plates was the same as for the Mark 1 cars, but the chassis plate for later Mark 2 Coopers was on the bonnet catch mounting. The bootlid was now double skinned, and the bootboard, sitting on spot welded brackets, was finished in grey or black on later cars. Hydrolastic suspension was the norm and, until May '68, rear radius arms had grease nipple shrouds. The Cooper continued to use the standard 10in wheels and still had 7in disc brakes at the front with drums at the rear, but no servo assistance. Engine numbers varied according to whether there was synchromesh on all four gears; it was 9FD-SA-H for three synchro and 9FD-XE-H for full synchro gearboxes. In addition, engine number prefixes varied according to whether the car had a dynamo or an alternator; with a dyno it was 99H 377CH and with alternator, 99H 970CH. The early metal fan was swapped for a plastic example, and the specification also included double valve springs and D-top pistons. The head casting number was 12G 295.

28

Mk 2 1275 S of 1967 has angular corners to its grille, looks good with optional Minilites.

A Mk 1 998 Cooper poses with the very last Mk 3 1275 S.

Mark 2 Cooper S

Many aspects of the Mark 2 S were the same as the Mark 1 1275cc car; the twin tanks were standard, whilst suspension and brakes were unchanged. Wheels were most often 4inJ rims without chrome trims to the hubcaps. There was a trend towards single body colour and, as with the Mark 2 Cooper, the grille and rear light clusters were changed. A 130mph speedo graced the instrument binnacle, now with rounded bezels instead of pointed ones, and seats, liners and carpets were very nearly always upholstered in black. Recliners were optional. The Mark 2 S was in production from October 1967 to March 1970, outlasting the standard Cooper by four months. Chassis numbers began C-A2SB for Austins and K-A2S6 for Morris. Again, engine number prefixes depended on the synchromesh situation; with three, it was 9F-SA-Y and with four it was 9F-XE-Y.

Mark 3 Cooper S

As standardisation crept in so the extrovert identity of the Cooper S was suppressed. Colours were the same as for the standard 850 and 1000 Minis, as were interiors, apart from the 130mph speedo. The car's badging had become identical to any Mark 3 Mini, except for the austere rectangular boot badge stating MINI COOPER S. The bonnet bore the blue British Leyland Mini shield emblem and the BL logo appeared on the front wings behind the wheelarches. Only export models were identified as being an Austin or a Morris by a second badge on the bootlid. Otherwise, the owner had to consult his log book to see whether he had the right model or not. The most obvious difference in the outward appearance of the Mark 3 car was the absence of the door hinges, which had been tucked away internally. The new bootlid had a smaller handle and the rear number plate was fixed to it, instead of being hinged in order for it to hang down and be visible if travelling with the boot open, as had previously been the case.

The specification was unchanged from the earlier S, including twin tanks, centrally-mounted oil cooler, hydrolastic suspension and 3inJ or 4inJ wheels. The Lockheed type 6 servo differed in that it was rather deeper than the predecessors'. There was synchromesh on all four gears, and late Mark 3s used a 3.65:1 final drive ratio. Production lasted from March 1970 to June 1971, with chassis numbers running from XAD-1 45441A to XAD-1 458987A. Commission number prefix was N20-D,

They usually only look this good when they leave the factory: the inner wheelarch of this immaculate Mk 3 1275 S is so clean it suggests a very recent restoration job.

Sunday afternoon by the village green, from left, a Mk 2 Morris Cooper S, Mk1 998 Morris Cooper, and Mk 3 1275 S.

body prefix was B-20-D, and engine numbers began 12H 397F if the car had a dynamo, or 12H 398F for alternator models. There was an electric fuel pump. The power units themselves which, like earlier Cooper Ss ran with forged rockers were painted BMC green. They were later replaced with pressed steel rockers and the engines painted black.

Innocenti Coopers: the Italian jobs

The arrangement between BMC and Innocenti involved supplying components PKD (part knock down) for assembly at the Lambrate plant in the suburbs of Milan. At this point in time, Innocenti was busy supplying Britain's swinging '60s mod culture with scooters, for which I have to admit to being a regular and eager customer. (Lambrettas

tended to be more robust and reliable than Vespas, the panels and running gear less easily damaged when you fell off!)

Innocenti was originally a successful manufacturer of steel tubes and scaffolding, based in Rome in the '20s before moving back to Lombardy in 1931. After the second World War when its factory was devastated, the firm got going again by responding to the demand for economical transport, making scooters and those absurd three-wheeler delivery vans. Under the guidance of its founder, Ferdinand Innocenti, the company started producing cars under licence in 1961, building the A40 and Ghia-bodied

Austin Healey Sprite and, from 1963, the Morris 1100. Just after the company began building the Cooper in March 1966, Ferdinand died and his son Luigi took control. In May 1972, British Leyland bought out the car manufacturing side of Innocenti and the company was split up. The scooter concern was moved to Spain and the machine tool producing arm, which, in 1966, had entirely equipped Lada's Togliatti plant in Russia, passed into government control. By mid-1975, Innocenti was in deep financial trouble, some £10m in the red, with models like the Allegro and Bertone-styled Mini on stream, and additionally burdened with marketing the whole gamut of BL products in Italy.

So BL sold up to the Italian government's GEPI rescue agency, which promptly did a deal with Maserati owner Alejandro de Tomaso. The company continued to produce Innocenti Minis with such models as the Mini Mille in 1980 and the Mini 90SL in 1982, but when British Leyland engine supplies were threatened in 1981, the shrewd de Tomaso came to an arrangement with Daihatsu for provision of their three-cylinder motor. *Innocenti had improved interior, different wheels, wind up windows.*

The box-nosed 1275GT was ushered in with the British Leyland regime, and was not really an adequate replacement for the Cooper; it looks very dated today.

In turbocharged and naturally aspirated form, this unit powered the boxy but stylish Innocenti Tre from 1983.

The Innocenti Mini Cooper Mark 1 used the 998cc engine, and was built from March 1966 to September 1968. Chassis number prefix was B39/1 and the Mark 2 followed on until February 1970. The Mark 3, chassis numbered from B39/2, retained the 998 engine until January 1971, when the Innocenti Mini Cooper 1300 was introduced. In its final incarnation, it bore the nomenclature of the new regime and was called the Leyland Innocenti Mini Cooper Export: chassis prefix was B39/7 and it was made from February '73 to January '75.

In the main, Innocenti Coopers gave the impression of being more sophisticated cars than their British-made companions. All were left-hand-drive, and there were wind-down windows and opening quarterlight windows in the doors, although these didn't actually open on cars destined for Germany. Other differences included the two-tone colour scheme and different bootlid pressings which featured a square, as opposed to rectangular, location for the rear numberplate. Immediately above this was a chrome number-plate light, and there were additional indicator flasher units on the side of the front wings. The Innocenti cars had stainless steel bumpers with no overriders and the radiator grille was slatted in black with its own personal logo on a central horizontal chrome strip. The IPRA-made oil cooler was mounted on two brackets, there were two-speed wipers and other neat touches included a plastic battery box cover, heated rear window, interior bonnet release and a grown-up, full-width, six-dial instrument panel made of moulded plastic; the special needs of the typical Italian motorist were catered for by the fitting of twin horns!

The instruments were made by Veglia Borletti or Jaeger and, as well as the usual speedo, (calibrated in kmph), oil, water and fuel gauges, also included rev-counter and ammeter. Cars for Germany had orange front indicators and what were known as 'Mini-special' wheelarch spats. Virtually all trim and ancilliary components were sourced in Italy. There were two colour schemes for the upholstery: seats trimmed in black vinyl with grey cloth centres, or beige vinyl with beige cloth, and carpets either black, beige or grey. Recliners were a later option. The later 1300 export models used the 1300 GT engine, which was painted black and badged as a Morris unit. These had alternators, carbs were one-and-a-quarter-inch SUs, and they employed the Cooper S three-branch exhaust manifold. Unlike the Mark 3 Cooper S, which had a remote gearshift, the Innocenti 1300 had a rod change gear linkage, although it used the 1275 ratios and pot-joint driveshafts. The Cooper S type braking system was split front and back, equipped with an Italian servo on the front and a dual circuit master cylinder. And finally, the Innocenti Coopers never had the right-hand fuel tank.

End of the line
The end came for Cooper's involvement with BMC in 1970 when Donald Stokes took over the helm at British Leyland. He was not an enthusiast and not at all interested in competition or, indeed, the promotional value of competition successes, in contrast to people like Harriman and Issigonis. 'Up until Stokes came along, everyone got on well together,' said John Cooper. 'He asked me to define my involvement, and I explained I was a consultant who won races and rallies. This wasn't enough for Stokes and the Cooper name and badge were dropped. The sporting Mini became the lacklustre 1275 GT, followed by the 1300 GT which was only moderately better. And this was at a time when John

The factory brought out special models to mark the Mini's 25th and 30th birthdays, and these cars from Philip Splett's collection bear the year of manufacture in their number plates.

Cooper was leagues ahead, developing not only an 1800 Mini, but the legendary 'Twinny Mini', a double-fronted device with two engines. This creation very nearly cost Cooper his life, for a rear suspension failure tipped the car over and he fractured his skull in the accident.

IV

BUILDING
THE
COOPER

'They don't make 'em like that anymore', is an assertion usually reserved for vintage-type cars, never cars still being mass-produced in their thousands. However, in the case of the Mini such a remark, unlikely as it may seem, would prove to be absolutely untrue, since modern robotic methods, with their great strides in efficiency, are not available to the little car from Longbridge. For this reason, the Mini could claim to be hand-built; a description which, when applied to cars, brings to mind the Morgan, maybe, or some lovingly-created bespoke carriage of a long-gone age. 'Hand-built' in this case is a bit misleading, even if true, for modern robotised assembly systems give us mass-produced cars with better standards of panel fit than any vintage Rolls-Royce could display.

At the time of writing the Mini has entered its 35th year of continuous production in its country

Mini front sub assemblies trundle along the line at Longbridge West Works on their way to meet the sides, rear and roof; rough edges are sanded off even at this stage.

Right: Seams are first tack welded to unite the body panels.

Bottom right: Not a robot in sight; these cumbersome welding tools with their myriad umbilical cords are state-of-the-art 1959, and are run up and down the Mini's body panels to effect a seam weld.

of origin. Talking in terms of mass-produced cars, only the Citroën 2CV has beaten this. The Volkswagen Beetle was also produced for a long period and sold in far larger numbers than the Mini, but the manufacturer from Wolfsburg held on to the car as its staple trade for so long that the company was in danger of going bust. (Precisely the same thing happened with the Ford Model T). However, unlike the Mini, the Beetle was an inherently illogical design - the pendulum handling factor - and was only kept going by one of the cleverest car advertising campaigns of all time. Production may yet be transferred back to Europe from South America in a bid by Wolfsburg to emulate Longbridge. The Mini itself has long since ceased to be one of its maker's best-sellers: because it now sells only 10 percent of the numbers it did 20 years ago, it is simply not economically viable to update its production process.

Each Mini takes about 50 man hours to make, compared to an average of around 20-30 hours for a small recent design. A modern GTi equivalent to the Mini Cooper is rather more complex, with electric windows and mirrors (several small cars are now thus equipped), rear wash/wipe, sophisticated engine management, split and folding rear seats and so on. Despite this greater complexity, the modern vehicle is still easier and quicker to build than a Mini. It was Issigonis' intention to make the car easy to assem-

ble and, compared to its real contemporaries, it was. However, relentless cost pressures on car makers, particularly in the last ten years or so, have meant that greater effi-

ciency on the production line has become a *sine qua non*. Robots have been one of the main ways to achieve this, but the Mini was simply not designed to be built by robots -

Left: The line moves at an almost imperceptibly slow pace, as two men work on each car. Jigs hold certain components like the front valance in place during the welding process, and bins of components, such as the rear shelves, stand ready for fitting.

Bottom left: Two completed shells - minus doors - wait beside a line of long-nosed 'Clubmen'; unlamented Allegros lurk behind.

such things were not even in existence until many years after its launch. It therefore calls for some traditional methods to put it together.

Welded by hand

Apart from the distinctive external seams at the front and rear of the car, nothing on the Mini is particularly easy to weld by hand,

owing to the small size of the car. Any assembly job done inside the car, such as fitting the roof lining, is obviously going to be more cramped than on even a 'Supermini' such as a Metro. The first Minis hardly had a lot of spare room under the bonnet, of course, but a modern Cooper now has the addition of fuel injection, an electric fan under the wing as well as the mechanically-driven one, and a far larger screen washer bottle, as well as a brake servo. There is also a good deal more wiring, too. This reduction in an already meagre amount of free space does not make it easy to build the car, however much the powertrain is already built-up before insertion. The exhaust system on the latest Coopers is far more complicated than previously, with extra expansion boxes and catalytic converters to keep the noise and emissions down to stringent modern limits. This makes it harder to fit this latest exhaust system on the car and to ensure that there is no fouling of the bodywork. As for those who write that a Mini is easy for the mechanic to work on, on a post-production servicing basis they either have pipe-cleaner arms and a trained ferret, or have never tried it themselves. The rest of us know all about torn sleeves, grimy shirt cuffs and skinned knuckles!

As a result, the car is made in a distinctly old-fashioned way; appropriately enough, in a listed building. Dating only from the 1920s, it nevertheless has historic associa-

Doors have been fitted, and rough areas sanded off. The body-in-white, still welded to its carrier, is off to the Paint Shop.

tions as many, many aircraft were made there in the Second World War. It is surprising to realise that the Mini has been with us for twenty years longer than the period from the end of the war to its introduction ...

Factory tour

On entering Mini Mecca, the first thing to notice is the relatively large number of people present. The contrast with the nearby Metro and Rover 800 lines is striking; with a state-of-the-art Japanese factory it's staggering. If Cooper production is state-of-the-art 1960 (and no Cooper knew it was destined to be a Cooper until after the body was made - they were selected at random and still are today), the Metro line is state-of-the-art 1980; the Rover 800 line is the only one totally up-to-date.

Longbridge is on the outer fringe of south east Birmingham in the British midlands, and the factory occupies a large area indeed. It is composed of single- or double-storey red brick buildings for the most part, with taller '60s and '70s constructions here and there; the plant is intersected by access roads and there are alphabetically labelled entrance gates around the perimeter, bordered by parkland and inter- and post-war housing. A mile or so away you can be in deep

Newly painted bodies emerge from the Paint Shop to continue their aerial journey to the Trim and Final Assembly lines.

country at the heart of England. Entering the Longbridge plant, you are assaulted by the sound of tapping, knocking and banging echoing through the labyrinthine tunnels of the production halls and open steel galleries: the work area sounds more like a busy railway

shunting yard than a car factory in the 1990s. And there is the ubiquitous din of Radio One played at high volume.

The difficulty is that the assembly task for each Mini coming along the line is not quite the same as the one in front of it (nor the one behind

The body has dropped down onto its engine and suspension subframes, and with drivetrain connected, is receiving its seats and trim.

it). This is because, although the panels that make up the basic shell are - of course - held in jigs (some of which are 30 years old), the manual nature of the welding process precludes the sort of pinpoint accuracy attained with a modern robotised system. Thus, a whole array of dressing and tweaking and bending takes place to overcome each body's little quirks, with appropriate aural accompaniment. The basic way the Mini is actually pieced together is the same as these moderns, in as much as its floor comes along the line, has the front end, sides, wings and rear panels welded to it, followed by the roof to complete the box. When all seams are 'dressed', the body goes off to the paint shop. This is in another part of the factory, almost a mile away. Here it receives its primer, underseal and final paint finish before being conveyed on an overhead elevator - which crosses a dual carriageway at about 50ft - and back into the main plant.

After this the car goes off to for its 'marriage', when powertrain and body are joined. It is at this point that the only fundamental difference (robots apart) between Mini bodywork and all current mass-produced cars occurs. Whereas today all such cars have their subframes carrying engines, front-wheel-drive transmissions and suspensions offered up to the body passing overhead, on the Mini production line the body is lowered 12ft from the line above down on to

these components.

There is a sense of constant progression; nothing is stationary for more than a few seconds. The shells, now complete with front and rear subframes and drivetrain, proceed up aloft again to receive their wiring looms, lamps, wipers, trim and seats.

Changes to body panels
Despite appearances to the contrary, every panel on the Mini has changed since its introduction - except the roof. For example, the sills now have more drainage holes. This may seem to be a small difference, but it still requires an update of drawings, part numbers

The Tahiti is just one example of the Rover special edition Minis, and not dissimilar to the Cooper in terms of its Minilites; German boy racers get macho Revolution alloys on their all-black Minis.

An Associate checks the build sheet to make sure the correct trim has been installed; a variety of special edition Minis go down the line at Rover, interspersed with Metros, so it is crucial that a Cooper gets the right seats, for example.

and so forth. Because there is only one basic shape, however, one might be forgiven for thinking that this would ease the production line's task. Unfortunately, since a basic Mini is not the easiest thing to sell in the 1990s, all manner of special editions are dreamed up to make the punters part with their money. Along with the Coopers, there have been the Rio, Advantage, Classic, Sprite, British Open, Italian Job and so on. Different cars have different specifications, mainly consisting of cosmetic paint jobs, trim and alloy wheels, which means that if the workers (now called 'associates', as are white-collar employees, and even the management) on the Mini track don't keep their wits about them, the line could come to a shuddering halt in a frightful muddle. To prevent this, each identical-looking body has a Vehicle Build Card (VBC) attached to it as it sets off as a body-in-white along its journey down the line.

The VBC tells the the vehicle builder which model has arrived before him, so that he knows what trim to put in, for example. Cars with special trim and higher speci-fication than standard - such as the Coopers, for instance - are not all stuck in at once, but spaced out along the line to avoid any build-up that might occur since a car with extra 'goodies' obviously takes a little longer to complete. This 'seed-ing' of the upgraded models is a strictly-governed procedure, known

as the Sequencing Rules. It is de-cided each day what the ratio of high work content cars to standard models should be. If these rules were not adhered to and a whole dollop of higher-spec models came down nose to tail, the consequent quickening of pace needed to get them all through without a sort of log-jam could see a drop in quality. It is therefore very important to ensure that the sequencing rules are applied. At least this mix of different cars, whatever inherent difficulties may lurk should some-thing go wrong, makes for a higher boredom threshold for those on the Mini line.

Refinements

There is much more emphasis on quality nowadays and the Cooper Mini - being more upmarket as Minis go - as well as being exported to countries like Japan, Germany and Switzerland, has to be generally better made than when it was around in the sixties. It is also more refined, with better sound-proofing and a subframe now rubber-mounted to the body, which helps reduce road-rumble. Much

attention is paid during assembly to preventing squeaks and rattles. 'What was acceptable in the '60s, just won't do in the '90s' was the comment of engineer John Speed. One example of attempts at cutting down unwanted noise on a Mini today is a sort of blanking-strip made to prevent tiny screws falling into places where they'll never be seen again, but may be heard as they vibrate behind the dashboard. Such an apparently trivial noise can drive some owners into a rage.

As this constant striving for better quality goes on, every car is given a brief road-test. But not be-fore it's done a five minute stint on the rolling road. At the end of the line, the completed cars join a traf-fic jam of assorted Rover products. Then a man leaps aboard and takes each one on the rolling road at high speed. I sat alongside for one trip in a left-hand-drive Cooper destined for Germany and contemplated the results of a sudden factory power failure when the Cooper's speedo was registering 70mph ...

After its rolling-road check of emissions at the end of the line, and having been checked for correct

headlamp alignment and operation of wipers, horn, lights, indicators and so on, each Mini is driven about 20 miles, during which the speed-ometer, rev-counter (Coopers actu-ally have them now), fuel and tem-perature gauges are checked. At the same time the car is taken up and down through the gearbox, checking the transmission, and the handbrake and footbrake efficiency are monitored. A speed of 70mph is attained and the car is braked hard to see that it will pull up squarely with no unpleasant clonks or vibra-tions.

Quality control

As yet another way of raising quality, every so often a car is taken at random off the production line and driven for at least 1000 miles. Every item not up to standard is given a certain number of pre-set 'demerit points'. Something that doesn't work - the heater, for instance - would get 40 points. A stone chip on the bodywork scores 20 points and a rattle or squeak 10 points. The current target is a maximum of 35 points, so there is not much leeway. To prevent 'cheating', the cars are not tested by those from the production line, not even from

Longbridge, for they travel over from Canley to carry out this auditing. All this helps to make the Mini Cooper a more refined and far more reliable car than it was during its first life. Unfortunately, because there is not much they can do about updating the way the body itself is built, panel fit is, frankly, still no match for a modern design.

According to Geoff Powell, when a visiting party from a Japanese manufacturer saw the way the Mini was made not long ago, 'they flipped'. It is quite likely, however, that a glimpse at these antediluvian meth-ods may have increased the Japa-nese fascination for the Mini and so prolonged its life. Certainly the la-bour force which works on this line, and the members alternate with Metro production, feel there is a certain amount of cachet to be had making the Ten Foot Wonder.

The Cooper's huge number of competition victories certainly helped to sell many cars, but it also made the workforce very proud. Today, the Mini Coooper may not be quite what it was, but there are no other current Rover products with anything like that competition record and, indeed, never have been. We live in hope.

Another of the reasons for the popularity of the Mini line amongst some of the Longbridge workers is the old-fashioned methods used to build it. 'You can't just throw it together', said one worker, 'It has to be built.' The employees regard the techniques needed for Mini pro-duction as special, saying that 'no particular skills' were needed to build the Metro. Apart from the actual physical task of putting the Mini together, there are other op-erations which require skills not used on a modern computer-de-signed vehicle. Reading good old-fashioned drawings is one.

Many of the drawings made in 1959 are still consulted from time to time. All new developments on the Mini - few though there may seem to be - have to be taken from the original drawings. Should a new bracket be required, say, to mount the second electric fan on the latest Cooper, then out come the illustra-tions from the plans chest, large, faded and folded spreads of techni-cal drawings. It is rather harder to find the exact location of a hole, for example, by these methods than today's, with technology that is sev-eral decades newer. Asked if this reading of drawings could all be a bit tedious, Alan Jones, Chief Engi-neer, Body-in-White, said, 'No, it's actually very convenient because I can use the knowledge and training I was given 30 years ago.' None of the drawings was ever thrown away, so they reckon they can answer almost any question. That said,

another part of the fun is that many of the firms who made the original parts have gone out of business, so removing a handy source of knowledge should a query arise that cannot readily be answered in the factory. Modern methods may make better cars, but many still prefer to work on the Mini. And an electric train may be more efficient than a steam locomotive ...

Sense of history

Because many of the people working on the Mini line have been there for twenty years or more - some since before it began - a sense of history has built up among them. This generates a pride in The Company that can be lacking today, now that it is seen as just one great, sprawling combine. Clearly, those who caused the death of the marques of Austin, Morris, Wolseley, Riley, Healey, Triumph and even Standard, understood nothing about how the workforce would identify with the product they were making and the value of this loyalty. They certainly understood even less about the value of the rivalries that took place, between one make and another. Perhaps this is an inevitable symptom of mergers in the automobile industry, where the actual number of major companies is really very small and the number of specialist marques - specialist sports car firms excluded - is

diminishing steadily.

Geoff Powell, Principal Engineer is still very proud of his apprenticeship indentures: they have 'Austin Motor Company' at the top. 'I never considered that I worked for Leyland when they took us over. They made buses'. At lunch with Pam Wearing, John Speed and Jeff Powell in the lofty works dining room - where there used to be a dining club chairman until ten years ago and now all 'associates' can get their lunches - they related how proud workers were to tell people that they worked at 'the Austin'. To augment this sense of history, many anecdotes are recounted, adding to the folklore of the factory. Apparently, when the Mini was in development it was, of course, top secret, even to many of those at Longbridge. They were told, right up to the last minute, that they were going to build a bubble car. So for many years after they would talk ironically of the Mini line as 'working on the bubble'.

They also talk affectionately of Alec Issigonis. Real engineers are so often genuine, practical people who have to deal in facts and have no need of affected or lofty behaviour. 'He was magic to work for.' was one assessment. Apparently, if he wanted some part to be fabricated, he would always say 'Would you do me that?' He never told the person concerned what to do. If it

wasn't right he never became annoyed, never raised his voice. 'Let's try another way', he would say and, of course, people loved to work with him. They reckoned he was an underrated stylist, often managing to get a freehand curve on a body just right first time. 'He had a brilliant eye' said one who was privileged to have worked with the man. The Mini's lasting visual appeal supports this judgement.

Issigonis was always approachable, as was Leonard Lord, who was often seen around the shop floor, chatting to people. Apart from the good relations that this accessibility with the workforce created, it naturally helped Lord to know what was going on. It is encouraging to report that this sort of attitude is returning to Longbridge today.

Alas, all good things have to end and the Mini cannot go on for ever, although it's a reasonable bet that the Cooper version will take some finishing off. Those who built it have many times in the past been told that production was about to cease, leading to 'much apprehension in the troops'. Further changes in legislation may yet administer the *coup de grace*, even though actual customer demand is still sufficient to warrant continuation of production. This uncertainty may also add to the cachet felt by those still making it, who may very well be there at the end ...

V

PADDY HOPKIRK
PROFILE

Paddy Hopkirk's career ended in 1970 when Donald Stokes axed British Leyland's Competitions Department. Or so we thought. Retrospectives like the Pirelli Classic Marathon, which he won in 1990, and the return of a team of Rover Coopers to the Monte Carlo in 1994, have tempted him back again. Still, it is a measure of his success during the 1960s that, today, Hopkirk's name is still synonymous with rallying. Mention Paddy Hopkirk and anyone of a certain age will conjure up visions of mud-spattered, foglight-bedecked Mini Coopers, invariably doing improbable things, their front wheels at peculiar attitudes. Just as the Mini was the car of the people during the 1960s, Paddy Hopkirk became a man of the people through his successes in international rallying.

While the Scandinavian rally drivers are heroes at home, it's puzzling to note that we don't seem to bestow similar status on our contemporary rally stars. The McRae dynasty is getting there, though, and the BBC's *Top Gear* TV coverage of the RAC rally helps no end. It may be to do with the plethora of motor sporting activities around today; there just wasn't as much going on during the '60s. Also, the world seemed a bigger place; the notion of battling to far-flung destinations like Monte Carlo, Athens, Rome or Vienna seemed truly exotic, and anyone prepared to undertake such a venture was some-

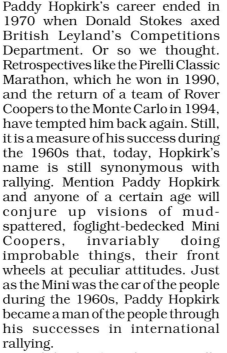

thing of a hero. Nowadays it's taken for granted, going off on such adventures as the Paris-Dakar or the Camel Trophy. Back in 1963, you'd achieved something if the motor got you down to Torquay without boiling over or doing-in a headgasket!

Good times
As Britain struggled out of post-war austerity, there was a need for inspirational figures like Paddy, although he's far too modest to admit it. When questioned about his heyday, he is inclined to be slightly dismissive, as if embarassed by the frivolity of it all. 'Sure, they were great times. Really good fun, right enough,' he drawls in his charming Irish brogue. You just know from his wicked grin that he must have enjoyed himself a great deal. Mini skirts, Mini cars, who knew what was around the next corner! When he cites the late '80s movie *Scandal*, with John Hurt as Dr Stephen Ward, as being a realistic portrayal of how it was in those days, you could be forgiven for wondering just what did go on behind the scenes for Paddy Hopkirk!

Paddy had been active in racing and rallying in a host of competition machinery, from MG TC to Triumph TR2 in his student days in Dublin where he read engineering, to Standard 8 and Hillman Minx for Rootes and Standard-Triumph, and he was hired by BMC in 1962 to drive the works Healeys. In 1963, the Mini Cooper S came out and

Classic shot of Hopkirk giving it his all - or could he be singing - during his run to Monte with Ron Crellin in 1968. They were placed 5th.

Hopkirk's career took off. 'It was a revelation!' said Paddy. 'The Cooper S transformed what, in 1959, had been regarded as a sort of novelty item. Up until then, I hadn't even driven a front-wheel-drive car in anger. It was quite a surprise,' he said. 'We hadn't realised just how good it was. Back then, rallies were generally won or lost on the rough stages, and the Mini turned out to be the right car for the job. It was also very forgiving.'

Left-foot braking

'I had to learn about left-foot braking,' Paddy continued. 'Guys like Carlsson had been at it in the little Saabs for a while, but it was actually quite hard on the transmission. Applying power and brake simultaneously puts a lot of strain on the transmission. And if you use it a lot, like Mäkinen did, you'd knock out your rear brakes as well.' The idea of left-foot braking is that you can go much further into a corner before having to deal with it. Instead of throwing the car sideways, controlling the power by throttle application and correcting the slide of the back end as you would with a rear-wheel-drive car, the direction of steering and throttle pressure are maintained and, at the last possible moment when all seems lost, you hit the brake with your left foot. Hard, and just once. The undriven back wheels then lose their grip because it's a front-wheel-drive car and the back end slides out, using the front end as its axis. You have, in theory, just negotiated the corner!

These were the days when Stuart Turner was Team Manager, and there was always feedback to the production line from competition activities, particularly after the Monte success. 'Anything Turner wanted for homologation was done,' said Paddy. Did the cars get more difficult to drive as different modifications were introduced? 'Not really,' he said. 'The 1275 S was a far better car than the 1098, but when they brought out the 12in wheels the cars got a bit twitchy. And with the limited slip diff, it made them really twitchy. I remember going to the Nürburgring to drive with John Rhodes in a saloon car race. It made it terrible to drive; real muscle-building stuff.' Paddy's and John Rhodes' technique was to place the car deep into the corner, chuck it

sideways with the power full on and allow the rim of the good old Dunlop racing tyre to scrub the speed off. That was certainly one way of burning rubber!

'Another time,' he continued, 'we were tyre testing at Chamroux near Grenoble, trying out the new Dunlop slicks, and I was on full lock when I hit gravel; the right-hand wheel locked under the wheelarch, and I went over the edge! The car slid down the mountainside and came to rest upside down, wedged against a tree. Of course, the doors wouldn't open and I could hear the fuel pump ticking away, pumping petrol onto the hot exhaust pipe! That's when you really start to panic! I put my feet against the windscreen, kicked it out and crawled out that way!' When something like that happens, you realise the special bond which must develop between driver and navigator. Both partners rely on each other in a very particular way: their lives may depend on it. As the major rallies shifted from the public road to off-road special stages, the role of the co-driver became not so much that of map-reader but interpreter of pace notes: just how fast could a particular set of bends be negotiated?

Pace notes paramount

'I always liked pace notes,' Paddy said, recalling blind rallying in the forests. 'That was where the co-driver's skill came in. And as the driver, I could make the most of them by left-foot braking when we arrived at a corner.' Paddy's co-drivers during the Mini Cooper years were Tony Nash, Ron Crellin, Terry Harriman on the Circuit of Ireland and, of course, Henry Liddon. 'They were all good in their own right,' he said. You get to know each other very intimately through all sorts of close proximity circumstances. I have an interest in ocean racing,' he continued, 'and I think that if I could put potential employees in either a rally car or an ocean racer, I'd soon learn what their inadequacies were, what they were really like, and who you could rely on!'

Although he did a certain amount of circuit racing - mostly in Mini-Coopers - Paddy was far happier on a rally. 'I used to do a bit of circuit racing for John Cooper and I enjoyed the long-distance sports car events like Le Mans and Sebring, which I did with John Rhodes; the Tour de France, too,' he said, 'but I think racing can bring out the worst in a person. Some of the behaviour on race tracks is appalling. At least with rallying it's more of an individual sport; you can set a good time over a stage and, at the end of it, find your time is fastest: there's a great deal of satisfaction in knowing you've beaten your rivals on times.'

The current general preoccupation with nostalgia has brought Paddy Hopkirk a lot of publicity in the past few years. He drove the Mini Cooper S to first place in the 1990 running of the Pirelli Classic retrospective. 'It's like old times in some ways. The Pirelli Classic Marathons have been very good fun, although it's a serious event now, and they're pulling in the stars like Moss and Roger Clark. Also, I think as you get older your night time vision gets worse. As always, practice is the thing and I don't have enough time nowadays. I'd have liked to have owned that car, or one of my competition cars,' he said. I asked Donald Stokes if I could buy one when the Comps Department was shut down, but he didn't want to know. I've asked Rover to sell me the very last Mini they make, whenever that comes about!'

Paddy is quite complimentary about rally presentation nowadays. 'The RAC is pretty well covered, and the in-car stuff you get in the Touring Car races gives a good idea of what it's like to be actually doing it.' The TV people have really got the hang of televising motor sport now; the Australians showed them how to do it with the Bathurst race. They've got the cameras mounted everywhere, like in the lights and on the roll cage: you don't miss a thing.'

So what does the rally ace of the '60s have to say about the current generation of rally cars. 'Well, I'd love to have a go, particularly in a Lancia Integrale,' he said. Paddy's current car is a 1.9-litre Peugeot 205 GTi, which he describes as the nearest thing to a Cooper S. 'I just love the shape of them; what makes

Hopkirk and Crellin pose with '64 and '94 Coopers at Gaydon.

me sad is that if Leyland had its act together they could have made the modern GTi Peugeot.' Paddy also runs a Range Rover Turbo and swears by a 2CV for his children, which he describes as 'a bloody good little car!'

Mill Accessories

Today, Paddy Hopkirk has a thriving business at his Mill Accessories factory at Leighton Buzzard. As we sat in his smart modern offices, he exhorted my companion, photographer, Pete Robain, with his bulky camera gear and tripods to 'please mind the paintwork, we've just had it decorated.' In a way this sounded over-fussy, coming from a man who's career was founded on thrashing small cars over rough roads! But, today, there's a different kind of seriousness about him. Paddy's business is concerned with manufacturing and marketing good quality products, and smart presentation is crucial. We were impressed by the tidiness of the operation, confirmed by a tour around his production department and paint booths.

Paddy Hopkirk employs some 200 people. His main lines are roof racks (which are getting quite sophisticated and aerodynamic these days, what with gutterless roofs and so on); he does dog-guards, many for a contract with Vauxhall, and petrol cans, some painted red and some in green. He also owns the Desmo steering-wheel company. The business was founded twenty

years ago, and the Paddy Hopkirk logo in the shape of a car rally-plate is testament to his rallying career. It is an efficient and professionally-run affair, and Paddy makes no bones about the fact that it is founded on the success of his rally days.

However, he admits 'I'd rather people came to regard the products as quality items, rather than buy them just because of my rallying career. I want the Hopkirk name to stand for good quality products.' In view of the success some of his motor sporting contemporaries have made of promoting themselves, it would be surprising if Paddy Hopkirk had failed in some way to capitalise on this. But it has not spoiled him, and he remains a most jovial and modest man, wrapped up in his family and committed to his business.

Going for it again

To mark the 30th Anniversary of the 1964 victory, Rover approved another team of Minis led by Paddy Hopkirk - in the 1994 Monte.

The project was originated by public relations consultant and long time Mini devotee John Brigden who, along with business partner and writer Jeremy Coulter, fired Rover's imagination. Auntie pledged technical support and Hopkirk was hired. Before the event, Hopkirk had this to say: 'It will be fantastic to do the Monte again. It'll be great

revisiting all the old haunts, seeing how stages have changed and getting a taste of modern rallying. It was always a serious business but these days things are a bit different. Myself and Ron Crellin (his co-driver for the event) need to do quite a few miles in the car before we get to Monte Carlo as there is a lot of new technology to get used to. We are all looking forward to the event immensely. It should be terrific.'

Brigden's mechanics, Simon Skelton and James Bilsland, put the cars together. Time, money and homologation prevented Brigden and his team building a really sporty Mini, so the basis for the new Monte challenger had to be the familiar 1.3i Mini Cooper.

'We really have been restricted in what we can do by having to retain the standard cylinder head valve sizes and single-point fuel injection from the road car. Even so we've all been surprised by the power output gains we've made,' said Skelton. At the moment the engine is making about 100bhp, a 40bhp increase over the standard car. It may not sound like much power but it should be reliable. Paddy always said he didn't have the most powerful cars but what power they did produce was dependable. Unfortunately, Hopkirk and Crellin were let down by a broken fan belt, having been running in the high 40s. Some things can never be relied upon ...

44

VI

RALLYING

The funny thing was, nobody really wanted to drive the Mini in a rally. They all wanted to get their hands on the big Healey 3000, which was announced in the month before the Mini. The reason for this is not really surprising, for the previous Healey, the 100/Six, had looked to be the first BMC car capable of actually winning an international rally. The cars that Abingdon were preparing up until that time both for rallying and the odd track race - the MG Magnette, MGA, Riley 1.5, Austin A40 - weren't really competitive enough. The new 3.0-litre Healey was the tool they wanted and nobody was much interested in Mr Issigonis' people's car. Indeed, when the first one appeared at Abingdon, the shop foreman apparently refused to borrow it to go down to the bank, accusing it of being 'too insignificant' to be seen in! It would be true to say that, to begin with, the Competitions Department quite overlooked the Mini as a serious rally-winning car. In a way, this attitude was merely a reflection of the general public's at that time, for it considered the Mini was not a 'real' car, an opinion which had an effect on sales.

International début

The Mini's first international rally was the Viking Rally in Norway in September 1959, very soon after the car's introduction. This lone Mini entry did finish, albeit in 51st place. The very first outright rally win for a Mini came the following month at a local club rally for the Knowldale Car Club. It was called the Mini Miglia and this presumably eponymous event was won by Pat Moss and a chap called Stuart Turner. He can hardly be regarded as 'little-known' even then, for he was about to win the *Autosport* Navigators' Trophy for the third consecutive year. In 1960, he would win the RAC Rally with Eric Carlsson and publish a much-respected book - *Rallying.* As sports editor for *Motoring News,* here was clearly a man 'on his way'. To return further into the past, he and Pat Moss brought home their Morris Mini Minor, registration TJB 199, some 10 minutes ahead of the rest of the field. After this humble success Pat complained the Mini was hopelessy underpowered (it was really too new a model to have been properly 'got at') and Mr Turner spoke of it as being far too uncomfortable. From little acorns ... However, an awful lot of development *would* be required to make the Mini a resounding success in international competition.

Next up was the 1959 RAC Rally in November, an event which, at that time, did not have the importance it was later to acquire. Three cars were entered - as Austin Sevens - and all three retired due to clutch slip, then one of the commonest Mini problems. Since it was the ultimate goal of all rally drivers and rally-oriented car manufacturers around thirty year ago to win the Monte Carlo rally, a rather bet-

ter result was obviously hoped for the following January.

The 'Monte' was then the most famous of all rallies, although now much diminished in prestige on the international rallying scene compared with the '50s and '60s. To win this rally, just as to win the other tough European rallies at that time was - then, as now - a demonstration to the international markets of the reliability and strength of the product. Unfortunately, the highest Mini placing attained in the 1960 Monte was 23rd overall. As six of these tiny cars were entered, this result was rather a disappointment for BMC, if a vast improvement on the Monte result of two years previously when all ten BMC entries retired! In the following Monte of '61, all three Mini entries retired. Many people who, all along, had doubted that such a tiny little car could be made into a rally winner, began to say 'I told you so', but this rather public lack of success helped spur on the development of a more sporting Mini. Although its phenomenal handling and roadholding was clearly evident, the 850cc Mini was much handicapped by slowness. If ever a car cried out at the top of its little lungs for more power it was the early 850cc Mini in a competitive situation.

It is interesting to speculate that it was this desperate lack of straight-line performance which encouraged those who drove the Mini early in its competition life to find ways of taking the corners as fast as possible - and then a bit more so. On a car with towering acceleration there is not the same pressure to take the corners in such banzai fashion. Owners of Fiat 500s, for example, will know the frustration of losing too much speed for a corner and then the agonising delay while the speed slowly builds up again; it explains why all those minute Italian cars are driven so enterprisingly. Thus, with the early rallying Mini, a means of making up for the handicap of a weak engine led to the adoption of the left-foot braking techniques of the Scandinavian rallyists. Mind you, there were other methods, for it is reported that on the 1961 Tulip rally David Seigle-Morris and Vic Elford both drove their Mini at the same time, in as much as one steered and operated the clutch and accelerator and the other the handbrake. Since they finished in a far from disgraceful 23rd place, this tandem-style of driving may have worked! When the Mini got the power it deserved in the S-type, it was near to uncatchable.

The result of these pleas for more urge was, of course, the Mini Cooper. Announced in September 1961, it made its début in the following Monte. Despite the three month gap between these two events, it seems the cars were not sufficiently well prepared, for Abingdon was only given a couple of weeks with the cars before the event started. Nevertheless, Pat Moss and Ann Wisdom won a Coupe des Dames, finishing in 26th place. This was their third Coupe in a row on the event - the first time such a feat had occurred. With only one other works Mini (a standard 'non-Cooper' model) finishing in 77th place, this Monte may have been rather better for BMC than the previous year's, but worse than the 1960 rally to Monte Carlo. Judged on its first appearance, the Mini Cooper had fared no better than the 850 Mini.

It was on this 1962 Monte that Rauno Aaltonen could so nearly have lost his life. He was sharing his first drive for BMC in the Mini Cooper with Geoff Mabbs. They were in second place behind Erik Carlsson when the car rolled on the Col de Turini - the last stage - and caught fire. Bad enough, but Aaltonen was only semi-conscious and the car had come to a stop with the passenger's door hard against a wall. Mabbs had quite a struggle to get both of them out and, although Aaltonen spent some time in hospital, it could have been so very much worse. One would think that this genuine baptism of fire might have put Aaltonen off for life, but racing drivers are not made with the same nervous systems as you or I. As a genre they have always defied their doctors advice and have 'got back in the saddle' with alarming speed. Rauno Aaltonen was no exception and took part in his next rally a few weeks later. He was no stranger to dangerous pursuits, having been Finnish National Speedboat Cham-

pion no fewer than seven times and a member of the country's motorcycle speedway team.

A taste of victory

The Mini Cooper succeeded in winning its first international rally, the Tulip, the following May. Victory was achieved - provided by Pat Moss and Ann Wisdom - thanks to the 'class improvement' system. In the 1000cc class in this event, Minis took the first eight places. The value of this publicity for the factory can scarcely be exaggerated. Home sales were stimulated and exports of Minis received a huge boost. Since over 70 per cent of all Mini Coopers made were exported, a far higher proportion than the bread and butter Minis, the high international profile earned by the Cooper's subsequent rally triumphs should be regarded as worthwhile an investment in time and money as that expended on R&D.

In September, Pat Moss also won the Baden-Baden German Rally, this time with Pauline Mayman as co-driver. This was also thanks to the class-improvement system but, in fact, on scratch they were only beaten by four cars: two Mercedes and two Porsches! This pairing also gained another fine result when, as the lone BMC entry, they came 3rd overall in the Geneva Rally the following month.

The last major rally of the year was the RAC, and this saw the début of another of the 'Flying Finns', Timo Mäkinen. He had already impressed the crowds in Finland, having been sponsored by his employer who just happened to be the Morris importer for the area. Mäkinen was always able to drive just that little bit faster than everybody else. It is quite normal for an ordinary 'road' driver to be absolutely scared stiff during a ride with a racing or rally driver at the helm, but Timo Mäkinen frightened experienced competition drivers half to death as well! John Cooper was one victim and Christabel Carlisle - herself no shrinking violet behind the wheel - wanted very much to get out as soon as possible after a ride with 'The Big Finn' - and this was only on a recce! This amazing turn of speed often put more of a strain on the car, naturally: one of the service crew reckoned Timo could wear out a set of rear brake shoes in ten minutes ...

As yet unfamiliar with the man who was to become the fastest Mini rally driver of them all, one paper had his name as Tim McKinnen and on another occasion he apparently joined Paddy Hopkirk with Irish ancestry: Tim O'MacKinnen! You are reminded of the F1 driver, (Bruno) Giacomelli, whose mechanics nicknamed him Jack O'Malley. Whatever he was called, in this first event for BMC Mäkinen finished 7th, two places behind the Cooper of Aaltonen. Incidentally, Hopkirk and Moss were in Healeys for this RAC Rally and they came home 2nd and 3rd overall. BMC thus gained the team prize and Pat Moss and Ann Wisdom became the European Ladies Rally Champions.

Although 1962 had seen the very important arrivals of the Mini Cooper, Mäkinen and Altonen, it was also the year that Pat Moss left the team. Throughout her time with BMC she was without question the most successful of their drivers, having given the Mini its first rally win, BMC its first international rally win - the 1962 Alpine in a Healey - and the Mini Cooper its first international win earlier that year. She had been competing for Abingdon since 1955, when she drove for them in that year's RAC. Thus, having started and ended on on RAC Rally for BMC, she had been successfully wooed by Ford who offered her more than three times her BMC retainer, as well as other perks. She could hardly afford to turn down such an offer and was sorely missed by all the team, to each of whom she gave a present. Considering her considerable successes, and those of brother Stir-

Pauline Mayman (left) and Val Domleo pause for a checkpoint on the '63 Monte. They were 28th overall and 4th in class.

ling, you may well wonder what Mr and Mrs Moss Senior fed their two children!

Earlier in 1962, Pat's usual co-driver, Ann Wisdom, married Peter Riley, also of the BMC team. When she became pregnant, her place was taken by Pauline Mayman. When Pat left to drive the Ford Lotus Cortina, Pauline moved into her seat to be partnered by Val Domleo. Since Val Domleo went on to marry Don Morley, half of the very successful Morley twins, and since Pat herself would marry Erik Carlsson, the highly-successful

Saab driver, it is pleasing to note that winning rallies was not the only achievement of the BMC rally team.

Monte opener

The first event of 1963 for Abingdon was, of course, the Monte Carlo Rally. This time, the results were rather more encouraging, with Aaltonen finishing third, easily the best Monte result so far. The '63 Monte was also Paddy Hopkirk's first rally foray with a Mini - he was yet another driver who had joined the team to drive the Austin Healey - and he came sixth, heralding the start of a successful period with the little car.

In the absence of the two Finnish drivers, Paddy Hopkirk came home in second place in the Tulip Rally, one position down on the Mini Cooper's previous year's result for this rally, which ran from Holland to the Med and back. Although the S-model Cooper Mini had just been announced, it was not ready in time for this event. Nevertheless, many modifications

Rauno Aaltonen and Tony Ambrose were 3rd overall/1st in class in the 1963 Monte Carlo Rally.

Hopkirk and Liddon brave the verglas in 33 EJB on their way to victory in the '64 Monte Carlo Rally.

were permitted and carried out to Hopkirk's car, including a Weslake cylinder head, raised compression ratio and larger 1.5in carburetters. Running a more standard car in a different class, Pauline Mayman came in 21st. The next rally would see the début of a much more purpose-built car, the 1071cc 'S', which owed its engine capacity to a version built by Daniel Richmond of Downton Engineering and its internals to Formula Junior racing. Really, these S engines were quite exotic lumps in their day.

This car was entrusted to Aaltonen for the Alpine Rally and he demonstrated its superiority by not only finishing ahead of all the 997 Cooper and Healey 3000 entries, he also led the Touring Car category from start to finish, won a Coupe des Alps as well as the rally outright. The 1071 S was as superior in performance to the standard 997 Cooper as that car was to the standard 850 Mini. This really was the start of the Big Time!

Tour de force

No Minis were entered for the Spa-Sofia-Liège Rally a couple of months later, as it was reckoned the little car just wasn't strong enough for this event. However, just to demonstrate its versatility, and to give the far more powerful Ford Galaxies and 3.8-litre Jaguar Mark IIs a serious reason to doubt their virility, another lone 1071 S was entered in the Tour de France

Automobile, driven by Hopkirk with Henry Liddon as navigator. This was a demanding combination of circuit races, including the Nürburgring, Le Mans and hill climbs. At the twisty Pau street circuit near the Spanish Border, Hopkirk actually led for the first 10 laps, before backing off to spare his car. Not only did he come 3rd overall, he and Liddon also achieved this result on scratch. They actually won the handicap category. The impact this had on Mini Cooper (and therefore Mini) sales in Europe was considerable, and in France it was spectacular. Apparently, the BMC dealer in Montpellier took orders for no fewer than nine cars before the rally was even finished and the BMC main distributor in Paris upped his normal quota three-fold.

The final event of 1963 for the Mini Cooper was the RAC Rally. This time it started in Blackpool and ran down to Bournemouth. Two 1071 S cars were entered as well as a 997 Mini Cooper. Paddy Hopkirk was now on a roll, actually being the fastest on more than half the special stages. He came fourth, one place ahead of Mäkinen in the big Healey.

Conquering the Monte

The 1964 Monte saw the finest win so far by the Abingdon-prepared cars. Six Coopers were entered, four being the S types. Hopkirk was driving 33 EJB, the car with which

he had done his giant-killing act on the Tour de France the previous September. Since the Americans had declared their intention to win the Monte and had set a team of Ford Falcons at this target, Hopkirk was once more a small fish in amongst the big ones. Ford had even contracted two Formula One drivers - Graham Hill, World Champion two years before (and very nearly again in '64) and Jo Schlesser. The Dearborn firm obviously meant business.

It cannot be said that the BMC team got off to a good start, for Pauline Mayman and Val Domleo had been involved in a heavy shunt with a farmer's Chevrolet. Pauline had sustained a broken leg and needed 12 stitches in her head, but would otherwise make a full recovery. Next, one of the service crew was killed in a road accident in England on the way to meet up with the BMC entrants at Boulogne. This greatly saddened those behind the scenes, but the news was kept from the competitors until the rally was over.

Although Hopkirk was unable to match the V8-engined Ford Falcons for sheer speed, he managed - just - to win the rally on the handicap system, a marvellous effort considering it had been a relatively dry event which had taken away some of the front-wheel-drive cars' advantage. Hopkirk had to be persuaded that he had actually won, insisting that he'd only won his class, not the rally outright!

Mäkinen came in 4th and Aaltonen 8th. This helped BMC scoop the team prize, which upset the Americans even further. The 1964 Monte had been won by the smallest car in its history and it was also the first British win since a Jaguar in 1956.

George Harriman was so pleased with the performance of the winning duo that each was given a brand new Mini Cooper and Team Manager Stuart Turner received a £500 cheque as a bonus. As this was not far off the price of a new Cooper at that time, it was a generous gesture indeed. Clearly, Harriman could foresee the benefits to be reaped in the extra sales which would result from the win. A resounding party was held in Monte Carlo and Alec Issigonis was flown down to join in the fun. On its arrival back home, 33 EJB even had the distinction of accompanying Hopkirk and Liddon to appear on *Sunday Night at the London Palladium* with Bruce Forsyth. As a top-rating television show in those days - we were easily satisfied then - it represented absolutely first-class publicity for BMC, of course.

In the Tulip Rally of 1964, just one Mini Cooper was entered by Abingdon, although several Mini Coopers were driven by privateers. But this was the famed 1275 S, the use of a long-stroke crankshaft giving the required capacity for this car, otherwise the engine was essentially that in the 1071cc S-type Mini Cooper. Just one of these 1275cc cars, crewed by Mäkinen and Ambrose, was all it took to win the event outright from a Ford Falcon, hot on their heels, in second place. With good placings among the privateers, the Mini Coopers once again beat the giant Fords to the team prize. The winning car was homologated just in time to be allowed entry to the Tulip Rally, so when two 1275 S Coopers were entered in the 1964 Acropolis, for Aaltonen and Hopkirk, more great things were expected. Alas, both these factory entries retired.

Lighter bodywork and Alpine success

There was better fortune in the Alpine Rally a month later, when Aaltonen won a Coupé des Alpes for a penalty-free run. However, both Mäkinen and Hopkirk retired their 1275cc cars. As a matter of interest, Aaltonen's Cooper was entered in Group Three, which allowed it to have a lighter body than the other two, with several panels in aluminium. Pauline Mayman, recovered enough to drive after her accident, was entered in one of the new 970 S cars. She won the Ladies Prize, a most encouraging return for her, and further bolstered her confidence when she finished 20th in the Tour de France in September. Twentieth may not seem much of a position, but it was ahead of Messers Hopkirk, Mäkinen and Aaltonen,

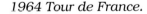

1964 Tour de France.

Now a resident at the Heritage Collection at Gaydon, this is the Timo Mäkinen/Paul Easter 1965 Monte winner, the car with the magic points.

all of whom retired!

It was in this event that Paul Easter made his début as a co-driver, partnering Timo Mäkinen. Although they made a rather sudden exit from the rally when Easter was at the wheel - an accident caused by a local French driver emerging from a side turning - this partnership would go on to prove one of the best. It could be said that Paul Easter was the calming influence that Mäkinen had needed. Until he joined up with Easter, in his twelve previous events for BMC Mäkinen had been accompanied by no fewer than nine different co-drivers. This compares with Hopkirk who had long since settled down with Liddon for all but one of his previous ten starts, whilst Aaltonen was steadiness itself, being partnered by Ambrose on the previous dozen events consecutively. One must presume that the Big Finn's extraordinary car control had taken its toll on the nerves of those who sat next to him, and that Easter - no mean driver himself - was suitably unflappable.

The next event they would contest together would be the 1965 Monte Carlo Rally, certainly one of the most esteemed in rallying folklore. Before that, the RAC in November was something of a fiasco for the works Mini Coopers, with all four entries retiring. BMC honour was upheld by Mäkinen, however, as he came in second in a Healey 3000, despite a trip off into the scenery.

An all time best

The 1965 Monte Carlo Rally provided competitors with the worst weather for many years, and Mäkinen's drive must rate as one of the very best rally performances of all time. Not only were his nearest Mini Cooper team-mates 25 and 26 places behind respectively, but he won the rally both on handicap and on scratch as well. Of the 237 starters, only 35 reached Monte Carlo within the permitted time; less than 15 per cent. Mäkinen arrived in Monte Carlo over eight minutes ahead of the next competitor. The remaining section of the rally consisted of six special

Hopkirk on his way to an uncharacteristically low 26th place in the '65 Monte. Of interest are the heated windscreen, bonnet strap, grille weathershield with lift-a-dot fasteners, sump guard and the use of steel wheels. There are also chunks of ice behind the spotlights. Rauno Aaltonen bought the car from BMC but never competed with it.

stages along the Mountain Circuit. These were of the flat-out variety and Mäkinen was overall fastest in five of them. On the sixth he and Easter suffered a distributor failure.

The heaviness of the snowfalls across Europe made rallying difficult for three reasons. First of all, the designated routes were nearly impassable, with snow roof-high in places; it was to break Mäkinen's windscreen on one occasion. Secondly, the snow covered most of the navigation landmarks. And, thirdly, navigation was further hampered as the constant slipping and sliding did nothing for the accuracy of the distance recorders used against the pace notes. Some crews merely got lost. 'For sure', you say, 'But it was the same for everyone'. This is true, but Mäkinen and Easter were in the only car to finish the journey to Monte Carlo with no penalties. In a way, the terrible conditions merely allowed Timo Mäkinen to show how good he really was.

Those who think that it was more fun in the old days because it wasn't 'ruined by professionalism' should be aware that BMC took more than 500 tyres with them to the '65 Monte. Also, the cars of Aaltonen and Makinen were very highly modified - much quicker than even the ordinary rally-prepared Coopers entered in Group Three, these two cars had lightweight bodies, thanks to alloy doors, bonnet and boot, as well as plastic side and rear windows. Many of the internal panels were drilled full of holes and

resembled a Gruyère and the cars carried no sound-proofing material. The Mäkinen Mini showed 75bhp at the wheels: this must be at least 20bhp more than the non-installed 78 gross bhp of the standard car.

Perhaps the most memorable part of the Mäkinen/Easter effort was not the driving and navigating, but the repairs to the distributor on one of the final six stages. It was remarkable for two reasons. First of all, the duo lost only four minutes getting going again. Since this was the time they needed not only to locate the reason why their car had stopped, but also to replace the very fiddly part - the movable spring-loaded side of the contact breakers. This is the piece with a heel attached which the spring holds in contact with the distributor cam. This was done beside the road in the middle of the night with snow falling, an almost miraculous achievement in the time taken. However, they apparently had Divine Intervention on their side. In changing the contact breaker and its attached spring in the prevailing conditions it perhaps wasn't too surprising that they didn't make a perfect job of it, for they failed to fit the small, circular fibre washer that insulates the end of the blade spring from the distributor base plate. Were contact made, the car would have no spark at the points - and hence no forward motion. But it started and ran happily on to the end of the rally, which it won. An

even bigger party ensued than the previous year's, again with Issigonis in attendance. The man who had not wished to be seen driving the first Mini at Abingdon down to the bank apparently rode a donkey around the tables. There's nowt so queer as folk.

Paladium début

When the winners were summoned to collect their silverware from Princess Grace and Prince Rainier, the winning Mini Cooper refused to go. It took the mechanic some time to realize what had happened and rectify the problem. Late they may have been for the ceremony, but the engine just should not have run at all near the end of the rally without the fibre insulating washer, let alone been driven flat out by an inspired Mäkinen. The two drivers were probably not too upset by this lack of punctuality, even though it concerned the Royals of the Principality. Huge amounts of publicity were once again generated by this second successive Monte win, which included another appearance at the London Palladium. Euphoria does not last for ever, of course, and the BMC competition department came down with a bump when the following month all four Cooper S 1275 cars entered for the Swedish rally retired with transmission failure. The extremely low ambient temperatures had prevented sufficient oil circulation around the differential pinions.

Hopkirk won the Circuit of Ireland for the first time in March 1965 to re-charge the team's confidence-batteries and the next event for the little Cooper car was the Tulip the following month. Things were off to a promising start when Makinen - the only works Mini Cooper entry - was fastest on the first of the 19 stages. This was around the Nürburgring, Timo beating a Sunbeam Tiger with its vastly larger-displacement engine, not to mention twice the number of cylinders. As the rally ended, the Flying Finn was denied any chance of victory by a very strange recalculation of the results, known as the 'class improvement' system. This cannot really be called a misfortune, but Mäkinen's fate in the next rally, the Acropolis, certainly can.

Ordeal by fire
Once again, there was only one BMC works entry and, before long, the exhaust fell off. Continuing without it (or at least without it in the proper place for they put it inside the car), the searing hot gasses under the car ignited the carpets in the front footwell. Paul Easter then took on the job of firefighter as well as co-driver and was to be seen ejecting pieces of smouldering carpet from the car as they flashed along - in the lead, mind. By the time they arrived on the ferry at Patras, the driveshaft

couplings were thoroughly shot and so Timo retired to the bar, obviously believing their rally was over. Paul had other ideas and now became a mechanic, starting to change the knackered universal joints on the boat. As this was done by the expedient method of tipping the car on its side for ease of access, the ferry captain was less than comforted by the sight of the petrol leaking from the tank and finding its way down into the bilges. Having lived for some months with the nauseating legacy of a diesel spillage on a Dutch barge, my sympathies lie with the skipper! However, on reaching land the task was unfinished, so the car was pushed off the boat and turned over again, this time with the help of local donkey power.

The job done, the pair had regained the head of the rally when the rear subframe came apart. A trailing arm bracket had allowed the relevant tyre to wear against the bodywork and deflate. The sump was holed just for good measure. With one stage to go, the service car had caught up - it had crashed around half distance - and the Mäkinen Mini was turned on its side again for a quick spot of welding. Not surprisingly, this time the leaking petrol had more serious consequences than a cross captain; it was ignited by a spark from the welding torch. Despite the car

being ablaze, Timo was to be seen diving through the side window trying to fish his money and passport from the glovebox. As the car was on its side this must have been very difficult - obviously he was being paid well and in cash. With the flames extinguished, they set off again in this now sorry-looking machine. As there were only some 15 runners still in the event, it was hoped that Mäkinen could hold on to his lead. Alas, Lucifer was not bored with his game quite yet and one of the carburetters had been so overheated in the conflagration that the car began to splutter along. When it finally cut out, restarting proved impossible as the bearings had seized, possibly as a result of oil displacement during those occasions when it was rotated 90 degrees from the horizontal. With their car now finally *hors de combat*, Mäkinen and Easter sat disconsolately by the side of the road and watched all the other competitors still running sail past in clouds of dust. They were fewer than sixty miles from the finish. You win some, you lose some. Clearly, the fibre washer miracle had cost them dearly.

Happily, the Geneva Rally provided Aaltonen and Ambrose with an outright and very convincing win the following month. This was followed up by an equally emphatic victory in the Czechoslovakian Rallye Vlatava in July. The goal for BMC was the European Rally Championship, for the minute number of

their cars sold behind the Iron Curtain would not make much sense of entering the rally just as a marketing exercise. Mäkinen drove a Morris-badged car as usual, because of his connections with the Morris dealer in Finland, and Aaltonen was behind the Austin symbol. Apart from this psuedo-difference, the latter's car had Hydolastic suspension and Timo's the conventional (if they can be called that) rubber cone springs. The two cars had low final drive ratios (4.26:1) and very high compression ratios of 11.2:1 (9.75 standard). Aaltonen's Mini caused concern by catching fire the night before the rally, due to an electrical fault, but all went well to give him his fourth win with the team. The next rally for Abingdon was not so successful.

Paddy Hopkirk upheld Mini Cooper honours in the German Rally at Nordrhein-Westfalen, whilst the works also sent out Andrew Hedges in an MGB. Between them, they won every single stage, which was particularly clever as the various controls were often hidden away: at times they thought they were on a treasure hunt. However, the rather dubious handicapping arrangements contrived to award first place to a locally-entered Opel.

Alpine cups compensate

The Alpine did not give BMC a first place, but it was a close thing. Mäkinen, driving the only non-Hydrolastic works Cooper of the four entered, missed out on victory by less than two seconds. Nevertheless, the team collected no

fewer than 27 major awards from its 100 per cent-finisher record, including four Coupes des Alpes, Paddy's award winning him a Coupe d'Argent for three non-consecutive penalty-free performances. (The Coupe d'Or is for three consecutive ones.) Pauline Mayman had come out of a sort of retirement to try and win the Ladies Prize - the Coupe des Dames - for the third time in as many runs. She and Val Domleo, her co-driver on the other two occasions as well, achieved this ambition. Victory for them was particularly sweet as their car's engine seized after boiling away its water because of a slipping fanbelt. They apparently scooped up sufficient of the now precious fluid from a nearby stream, using the screenwasher bottle. They were

The works Mini Cooper with the distinction of three outright victories in 1965: the Circuit of Ireland, the Polish, and the Three Cities. Now belonging to Alastair Vines, development engineer at Rover, the car is still fully competetive and a Pirelli Classic entry. A ride in it is a boneshaking, almost deafening experience, prompting the thought that the heroes who crewed these cars really earned their money.

driving DJB 93B, supposedly the car which had enjoyed great adventures in the hands of Mäkinen and Easter during the Acropolis. Presumably, Pauline and Val were not superstitious! It was one of Abingdon's most successful rallies in its history, with the Minis winning the Team Prize.

The Polish Rally was next, and was only entered to help Aaltonen on his way to the European title. He won the event, despite managing to scald his arm quite badly when he was checking the radiator level. Careless, but who hasn't turned that cap just a little too far themselves? He managed second place behind Mäkinen in the following rally, the 1000 Lakes, and Hopkirk took 6th place in this event, which was a very fine performance for he beat several strong Swedish entrants. These results brought BMC the Manufacturers' Team Prize once again. Aaltonen did his title quest a power of good with a win in the Munich-Vienna-Budapest Rally, otherwise known as the Three Cities. It was, for once, a fortunate win, since the leading Lancia had engine failure merely 30 miles from the finish.

The final event in 1965 was the RAC, held as usual in November; every year we are caught out by early snows, especially in Yorkshire, and this time was no exception. As Mäkinen was the biggest threat to Aaltonen's chances, he ran in a different class, in a Healey, as did the Morley brothers, while the rest

of the team were Cooper-shod. As it happened, the only other person in the running for the title, Réné Trautman in his Lancia, withdrew just before the start of the rally. Aaltonen was thus assured of his championship and he and Ambrose found themselves in DJB 93B, the car bearing the registration from the Mäkinen/Easter Acropolis frolic. The event turned out to be a classic duel between Rauno Aaltonen and Timo Mäkinen.

Yumping for joy
The weather presented the competitors with much snow and ice, and Mäkinen's driving was inspired in the conditions. At one point he led the rally by five minutes from the second place competitor, who happened to be Aaltonen. The slippery conditions helped to throw Timo off the road in Yorkshire and should have put him out of the running, but his super-human car control - with help from Easter who spent some time on the Healey's rear bumper trying to assist traction - saw him regain the lead by the time the rally reached Wales. With most of the other competitors left well behind, it was peeling down to the wire between the two Finns. The deciding territory was snowy slopes in Wales, and a front-drive car is at a distinct advantage in such conditions. Whereas a rear-drive car will start to slide sideways as more power is applied on an icy incline, to the point where there isn't enough road left, forcing the

driver to lift off and therefore slow down, a front-drive car can just keep on scrabbling upwards, without the need for such drastic throttle-lifting. In these conditions, Rauno gained nearly a minute on Timo, a lead which he held to the finish.

It was a shame that Mäkinen didn't win the RAC Rally after his extraordinary drive and perhaps a shame that the Big Healey did not win it on this its last try, after no fewer than four times as runner-up. Nevertheless, having won five of the team's eight rallies in 1965, Aaltonen was a deserving European Rally Champion - the first time the championship had been won in a British car. The next rally would be the '66 Monte, one that would provide BMC and the Mini Cooper with the best publicity they had ever had, although not exactly in the way planned.

A dazzling performance dimmed
The 1966 Monte Carlo Rally is remembered in the UK as the one where the Mini Coopers finished in first, second and third places. That the organisers of the event tried their damndest to disqualify them - and eventually succeeded on a trumped-up infringement of lighting regulations - does not really take away the belief that the Minis managed a clean sweep on what used to be the most important rally in the calendar. Perhaps it is not entirely a coincidence that the Monte ain't what it used to be.

Mäkinen/Easter in their 1275 S battling through the elements to take first place on the 1966 Monte, only to be disqualified - along with several other Brits - for alleged lighting infringements.

It all began when the international rally regulations - Appendix J - were made available in June the previous year. The only important change in the rules was to the requisite quantity of cars that had to be manufactured in the previous 12 months prior to the start of the rally. Homologation for the two categories in which the 1275 S Mini Coopers usually competed - Groups II and III - now required 100 and 500 units respectively to have been produced: no increase in Group II and up from 100 in the previous year's Group III. The largest change was in Group I - pretty well standard production cars - which had gone up from 1000 to 5000 units, but this wasn't relevant to the Abingdon effort. However, in November, the Monte Carlo Rally regs were issued and these made it obvious that only a car entered in Group I would stand a realistic chance of outright victory, so harsh was the handicapping system to be in Groups II and III. It is generally felt the organisers did not reckon that 5000 Cooper S models could be built in the stipulated period and, because of the handicap system, the Coopers could not win in those categories where fewer cars were required to be homologated. In fact, 5,047 1275 S cars were made, thanks to a step-up in production instigated by Stuart Turner.

These regulations, as well as containing a number of ambiguities and unclear passages, were rather late in being issued. Then three revisions were issued in the last few weeks before the rally, creating a lot of extra toil in the workshops at the Abingdon Competition Department. This, of course, created considerable difficulties for all competitors, so much so that Volvo and Saab gave the whole thing up as a bad job and did not submit their entries at all. Stuart Turner and his counterpart at Ford, Henry Taylor, flew off to the FIA in Paris in the December to try and sort out the muddle. They had no less than 100 points to raise which needed clarifying. They returned satisfied that the cars were in accordance with the regulations in every respect. They never brought up the fateful headlamp question, simply because they never saw a problem there in the first place. There was no question of trying to get around the regulations, since they reckoned that this year the rules were going to be very strictly applied in the first place. To add to the confusion, the final draft of the Appendix J regulations did not arrive at Abingdon until Hopkirk's Cooper S had been sent off to Poland for his Warsaw start.

At the beginning of the rally, some of the team were dining in Monaco when the Anglophile head waiter told them he happened to know that it had already been decided victory would go to a French car - somehow it would be fixed. When BMC's Competitions Press Officer went to Rally Headquarters before the start he was pointedly informed that BMC mechanics must be ready for scrutineering when the rally finished. This is normal, but it was unusual to be reminded of it before the rally had started. Also, the French press was very antagonistic towards the British, and allusions about 'exposing cheats' were appearing in the papers. It seems the French just could not believe a genuine Group I car could be so fast on the special mountain stages. The hostility increased as Mäkinen went quicker. On the icy bits he was faster altogether than some of the hot Group III cars. As it was the previous year's Monte winner who was again setting the pace, the French must have already forgotten how fast the man could drive.

Quartz iodine bulbs

At the end of this 900 mile Monaco-Chambéry-Monaco section, some teams were requested to attend scrutineering in the morning - an odd time in the middle of the rally. It was the lamps that the Monégasque officials were after. All the works Mini Coopers (and some other cars) were fitted with the then new-fangled quartz iodine bulbs. These were of the single filament variety and so were the two fog

lamps mounted between them. Because these headlamps lamps could not dip, the foglamps were arranged as dip beams, so that when the driver switched to dip, the headlamps went out and the foglamps came on; these foglamps could also be operated as well as the headlamps. Alternatively, the headlamps could be dimmed, by passing the current through a resistance.

In the *parc fermé*, the lights were checked by the officials with the latest in hi-tec equipment: a cardboard lid taken from an old hat-box. Later on, a notice was put up in Rally Headquarters stating that some cars were not complying with International Highway Regulations: strangely, there was no mention of the Rally Regulations. On the list were the names of the cars which had these supposedly irregular lighting systems and a description in each case of the system used. It was also stated that the acceptability of all these lighting arrangements would be decided after the rally - during final scrutineering. All attempts by Stuart Turner to get a clarification of this rather curious notice produced nothing, despite promises.

With this rather unpleasant cloud in the air, the teams set off for the final fling, a night run of nearly 400 miles. Mäkinen put up another superlative performance. Although in the dry he was well down on speed in his Group I car, he managed to be in the top five on the last

test, which was more slippery. In the early morning, they awaited the results on Radio Monte Carlo. Timo Mäkinen in GRX 555D was the provisional winner, with Aaltonen second and Hopkirk (just managing to overhaul a pair of Lotus Cortinas driven by Roger Clark and Bengt Soderstrom) taking third place. Abingdon could hardly have wished for a better result. However, the organisers clearly had a different one in mind.

Scrutineering was ludicrously rigorous. All told, it lasted for nearly two days - far longer than usual. The engines were stripped right down and internals measured and weighed. For the weighing, the scrutineers had brought along more of their scientific apparatus - some bathroom scales. They weighed the wheels after removing the tyres and even checked the output of the dynamos. All the while the BMC mechanics were standing by to ensure things were being carried out fairly. At one point the scrutineers found a discrepancy in engine capacity, until it was pointed out to them they they were checking against the specification sheets for a standard 848cc Mini. While this was going on, John Cooper spoke on the telephone to George Harriman, telling him that the French were determined to find something wrong with the winning cars. 'You're not worried, are you?' asked Harriman. 'Yes I am, actually' replied Cooper candidly. 'Well, we won it, didn't we?' was Harriman's ebullient re-

sponse. He wasn't wrong, really.

Perhaps the best bit was when the scrutineers decided the Hopkirk car had a front track some 3.5mm too wide. This vitally significant detail (a measurement of a whisker more than one eighth of an inch) was announced to members of the French press who crowed delightedly. However, the track was measured with people sitting on the bonnet and when their weight was removed and the car raised to its regulation height it was grudgingly admitted the track lay within the correct limits. (Since a Mini's rubber cones would always settle somewhat in use, especially after a 3000-mile ordeal such as it had just completed, the track would change at the same time because the front wheels must move through an arc as they go up and down). The accusation was withdrawn, although unaccompanied by an apology. At this point the team of works Coopers believed their positions were safe. After all, nothing had been said about the lamps during this final scrutineering. Nevertheless, when the results were pinned up the three Coopers, plus other British cars - the Lotus Cortinas and Hillman Imps - were nowhere on the list. First place was awarded to a Citroën.

Hopes fade

More than one hour elapsed - it must have seemed an awful lot longer to some - before a reason was given. The disqualifications were made because the cars' lighting

(*i.e.* dipping) arrangements did not conform to Appendix J - not the Highway Regs which were originally mooted. A total of 32 protests were put forward by Stuart Turner and other team managers. The organisers rejected them and so appeals were lodged with the Automobile Club of Monaco, with the same result. The FIA, the governing body of international motorsport, was the next target. All protests were to no avail. Finn Pauli Toivonen, the driver of the Citroën DS now awarded first place, felt his win was undeserved and he failed to appear for the prizegiving in protest. It would probably be fair to say that the British had not been ruled out to let a French car win, but because the organisers believed the *Rosbif* must have cheated somehow and therefore had to be punished. It would also be fair to say that although it has been claimed many times the Coopers' new lighting arrangement gave no gain in performance, this cannot be true. On the night sections of the rally the great increase in wattage must have been of more than marginal benefit.

Meanwhile, the French press had become insufferable and was making suggestions that Timo's car was nothing like the ones in showrooms - an odd assumption after the marathon scrutineering binge. Stuart Turner had something of a brainwave. The leading French sports newspaper, *L'Equipe*, had at least been open-minded as regards the notion of entering non-standard standard cars, so BMC suggested they conducted a run-off between Hopkirk's 'third-place' car and a brand-new 1275 S from a French showroom. Taking a suitable car from the Wright Brothers' Riviera Motors BMC dealership in Monaco, the cars were to be driven alternately by Mäkinen and French journalist-cum-racing driver, Alan Bertaut. The course used was some steep and twisting streets at the back of the Principality and the cars were timed by stopwatch. Whether Mäkinen or the Frenchman drove, the showroom model was the quicker of the two. (This was hardly surprising since all the 'blueprinting' in the world carried out on the rally car's 'standard' engine could not help to offset the weight handicap of sumpguard, rollover bar, extra lamps, extra instruments, extra tools and so forth.) The result was given to the press the following day.

Unfortunately, this enlightening demonstration did not alter the decisions of those dealing with the appeals. In a final act of churlishness, the rally organisers refused the disqualified drivers a share in the prize fund, the richest in rallying, and even denied them their official plaques for finishing the rally. The whole sordid episode did, however, gain BMC and its Minis even more publicity than they would have managed had the French admitted they had won. The disqualifications in the 1966 Monte were an embarrassment to the true French motorsport enthusiast. Paradoxically, the French have been particularly fond of the Mini ever since.

Disqualification - again

The 1966 rally season did not continue with much more success for BMC than the Monte Carlo opener. In the Swedish Rally in February, both the Finns were entered and both retired. At the same time, Hopkirk and Tony Fall were doing their best in the San Remo 'Flowers' Rally. Paddy's 15th place proved to be the better effort as Fall was disqualified in the same Group I car that Paddy had driven in the previous Monte; he had removed the carburettor air filters to get a bit more urge. This was not a good idea so soon after the Monte débacle. His disqualification at a spot-check was a fair cop this time, in strict contrast to Vic Elford's winning Lotus Cortina which was ruled out because of a discrepancy between the car's specification at scrutineering and the homologation form. The trouble was, the particular item of specification which ruled him out was a misprint.

In April the same pairings were used both in the Circuit of Ireland, where Fall won, no doubt watched by a rueful Paddy who had retired with more than dented pride, having rolled his car three times, and for the Tulip Rally. In this, a Group I and a Group II Cooper were to be entered, but neither of the Scandinavian stars wanted the

more standard Group I car. The indecision went on until it was decided by the toss of a coin with Mäkinen drawing the short straw. As a result, Aaltonen won this Dutch rally outright and his team-mate managed to win the Group I category from Soderstrom's Lotus Cortina, coming 9th overall. This was perhaps a good result, since the Cooper started to burn oil at an alarming rate and Easter was kept very busy pouring the stuff in and changing the plugs. Hopkirk and Fall were entered in the Alpine, with the Irishman winning. The Englishman retired after swiping a pile of logs during an 'off', so this result was therefore the opposite of that for the rally in Ireland.

With three outright wins for the team of Mini Coopers since the Monte, much was expected at the important Acropolis Rally, also in May. Three cars were entered for the three established BMC stars. All three cars used Hydrolastic suspension and were also kitted out for the well-known rigours of this Greek event, with all manner of underbody protection for the sump, exhaust, brakes and battery. The driveshaft couplings were of the latest stronger design. The main rivals were anticipated as the works Ford Lotus Cortinas of Elford, Roger Clark and Soderstrom. With hindsight, it might have been more accurate to write that their chief opposition was from the organisers.

The battering to which cars on this rally were subjected soon caused a rear trailing arm bracket to fracture on Mäkinen's car, in turn causing rear-end steering. This would have been the end of their rally, but one of the ex-rally Coopers (it had won the Circuit of Ireland the previous month) was encountered with a couple of journalists on board. A quick swap over of components took place. With this bracket fitted - and the donor car immobile - they set off again, eventually to retire with head gasket failure during the final circuit race. He and Paul Easter were still classified 10th, nevertheless. Aaltonen also had engine problems which led to his retirement, while Paddy Hopkirk went on to win - or so the team thought.

Not cricket

With but four minutes of the hour remaining in which to place official protests, the organisers decided that the Hopkirk car had arived some 14 minutes too early at a control and had been worked on inside a control area, near the official service area. This dropped him to third, behind two of the Fords. The problem had arisen because the large number of spectators had caused a parking problem in the service area, but permission had been obtained from the control official to service the car there, because of the lack of space. Apparently, only one wheel of the Hopkirk Cooper was in the trespass area and the card was stamped without penalty at the time. Protests were made to the organisers, to the National Board of Appeal and to the FIA, all to no avail. It seems odd that several cars were worked on inside this control area, but that only the rally leader's car was demoted. That sort of thing just ain't cricket, is it?

Some comfort was extracted for the team by Tony Fall now having his turn, from the next rally on the calender, the Scottish. The winning Cooper was DJB 93B, the infamous 1965 Acropolis car, so presumably its gremlins were now fully exorcised with this, its second rally win. In the Geneva Rally, Paddy Hopkirk led until his gearbox broke, leaving Fall to come home second to a Lotus Cortina. Because of the high placings of a couple of private entrants, the Mini Coopers won the team prize, which helped a little for not winning outright. Back in Blighty, Fall was entered in the London Rally in - you've guessed - DJB 93B. He led all the way to near the end when he totalled the car. The stage on which this happened caught out so many competitors it was subsequently declared too dangerous and closed.

In the Czech Rally Mäkinen and his fellow Finn team-mate took it in turns to lead. At the end, a flat-out gallop around a street circuit in Prague saw Timo in first place when a rocker broke - a very unusual failure for these cars. Aaltonen thus won this stage and the rally. Timo managed to limp over the line and claim third place overall. With fourth place in the event being taken by the Polish Champion, Sobislaw Zasada in another Cooper on loan from BMC, the Minis took the Team Prize. Altogether a good result.

It was not a good result from the next rally, the German, though, where competitive performances from the Coopers of Fall and Hopkirk came to nought when both cars retired with piston failure. This occurred while they were taking part in the ten lap sprint around the fast but dull Hockenheim circuit. Upon stripping the engines down, it was found that both had suffered gudgeon pin seizure. Once again, this was a rare form of breakdown for a Cooper engine, especially so with both cars going out of the rally in this way.

Beating the handicap

Driving a 970cc car this time to help beat the handicap system, Tony Fall did just that to win the Polish Rally in August. Mäkinen came in second in the regular 1275 car, which operated less favourably under the handicaps, but even he was comfortably ahead of the rest of the field. In the Welsh Rally Fall was not so fortunate, for he was forced to retire. Next was the 1000 Lakes which, unsurprisingly, Mäkinen seemed to enjoy, having come 4th in '64 and won outright in '65. This time around he was again successful, with Aaltonen third and another works Cooper sixth.

Four cars were entered in the Alpine rally, driven by BMC's four stars, Mäkinen, Aaltonen, Hopkirk and Fall. Mäkinen was first out in this hot and dry event with head gasket failure while in the lead. Hopkirk was next with differential failure and Fall the last go with that Mini Achilles heel, driveshaft failure. That left Aaltonen, who carried his team's honour to the finish in third spot behind an Alfa Romeo GTA and a Lotus Cortina. He was actually disputing the lead with these two and a Porsche when he, too, was nearly eliminated when his car experienced a total electrical shutdown on the final stage down to Cannes. Henry Liddon did some makeshift wiring which got them their placing, but they missed a Coupé des Alpes by a mere 20 seconds.

Mäkinen it was who finished first in the Three Cites Rally - Munich-Vienna-Budapest (you may wonder if it will ever become Four Cities with Eastern Europe in such turmoil). This lifted him to within just four points of the European Rally Championship, won the previous year by his fellow countryman, Rauno Aaltonen. To bolster Timo's chances, the factory (now British Motor Holdings, one of many corporate aliases to be adopted over the next few decades) entered no fewer than eight cars in the RAC Rally, its largest entry for a long time.

Stars hired for RAC assault

All the cars were Cooper S models. To the usual four driver line-up were added two more Finns, Simo Lampinen and Marjatta Aaltonen, Rauno's sister. It was not the first time that a woman whose brother was already a very famous driver had driven for the Abingdon team and Marjatta was no stranger to rallying, having experienced success at home. The other two new recruits for this national rally were Harry Kallstrom from Sweden and none other than Graham Hill. This last choice was in retaliation to Ford, who had landed Jim Clark. The appearance of these two generated a huge extra surge of public interest in the rally: a similar thing happened when Nigel Mansell raced a Ford Mondeo in a touring car race at Donington late in 1993. The BMC driver line-up for the 1966 RAC Rally now consisted of five Scandinavians, two Englishmen and an Irishman: sounds like the start of a good yarn!

First of the above drivers to leave the event was Graham Hill, his car's sump oil leaving a significant trail as he crashed along. Closer inspection revealed a hole in the diff casing which had somehow been punched through from the inside. A temporary repair to the hole with plastic metal was just that, although the car made it from Somerset to the Lake District. The going must have been fast and furious, as both Fall and Aaltonen, R, visited some ditches. Lampinen, however, went one better on the Dovey stage in Wales when he rolled right out of the rally. Simo makes an interest-

ing comparison to his countryman Timo. Lampinen had suffered from polio as a child and, as an adult, found walking slightly awkward, even uncomfortable. Mäkinen suffered from bouts of eczema which covered most of his body - a truly unpleasant complaint and one which caused him extreme discomfort when at the wheel. So often, when the very high achievers in this world want to do something, they are not deflected from their purpose one jot by difficulties which would have the merely mortal among us surrendering long before ...

Clock watcher

Mäkinen was in his element, meanwhile, setting a string of fastest times on the stages. The times of one earlier stage had to be cancelled as Aaltonen had managed to set off with the stage timing clock hooked onto his car's door handle. This must have been an attempt by him to match Mäkinen, by an unusual method of making the fastest time on that stage! Paddy Hopkirk's effort came to an abrupt halt in the notorious Kielder Forest section when a driveshaft disintegrated as he was reversing back to an overshot junction. Alas, all these mishaps to the team could not match that which befell the leading Finn, for Timo's engine expired, along with his hopes of the Championship, close to home on the Yorkshire Moors. Some consolation to the team, if not poor Timo, was that Harry Kallstrom

came in second behind a Lotus Cortina. Aaltonen and Fall were fourth and fifth, so at least the Mini Coopers made a clean sweep in their class.

The last big news of 1966 was that Stuart Turner was leaving his position as Competitions Manager to join Castrol but, before departing, was to have a last go at supervising the '67 Monte.

Tyres bring sweet revenge

After the 1966 débâcle, the team's desire to win the Monte had never been stronger. Unfortunately, as the Mini's original design became older, this task became harder - just as it was becoming more difficult for the Mini Cooper to win any rallies. BMC knew this and, on the basis of safety in numbers, a very strong team of five cars was entered: Timo Mäkinen/Paul Easter, Rauno Aaltonen/Henry Liddon, Paddy Hopkirk/Ron Crellin, Tony Fall/Raymond Joss and Simo Lampinen/Tony Ambrose.

This rally was about tyres, for the organisers had invented two new categories. The first was as before, where a car could use as many tyres as necessary, but would be penalised 12 per cent on times. The second was a restriction to eight tyres for the Common Run and the Mountain Circuit, these being the most hard-fought sections of the rally. Stuart Turner calculated that the first category

was a non-starter, so to speak, and there then existed the problem of selecting suitable tyres that would give the required combination of grip and longevity. Dunlop worked for many weeks on this problem and much testing was carried out. Because four tyres would have to be carried in the car, the weight penalty would be a problem due to the Mini's relatively marginal lack of power, compared to the works Porsche 911's, for example. Also, because only two tyres would go into a Mini's boot, the prospect of carrying them on a roof-rack was not considered ideal because of both the increase in frontal area of the car and the unfavourable change in the centre of gravity. The first problem of the tyres' weight was solved by the Minilite wheel, cast in magnesium alloy and now *de rigueur* for the serious Mini Cooper restorer. The second problem was solved by carrying two of the tyres on the back seat, held in place by a quick-release clamp. With both the new wheels and the rear-seat mounting of the tyres squared up with the organisers, the cars set off for their respective starts.

When the cars had returned to Monte for the final bash around the Mountain Circuit, Timo's was the leading one of four Minis, all behind the Porsche 911 of Vic Elford. Less than one minute covered these first five cars in the Rally, for it was a damned close-run thing. The Minis

were helped by judicious selection of the tyres permitted, after advice from the recce crews who had discovered that much of the snow was only a very thin surface layer - thus obviating the need for full-studded tyres. On the Mountain Circuit, the first part was dry, which did the Minis no favours at all as the more powerful cars could use more of their power. Happily for the team, it began to snow harder, enabling Mäkinen and Aaltonen to set the pace.

Alas, Timo's luck deserted him for the second rally in succession, when a sizeable boulder rolled down the mountainside in front of the car, smashing the starter motor, distributor and oil cooler. This was the end of the competition for LBL 66D's crew but, had the rock gone through the 'screen, it could have been more than the end of just Mäkinen and Easter's rally. As it was, they were classified in 41st position. With the snow continuing to fall, Rauno Aaltonen managed to finish just 13 seconds ahead of a Lancia. Paddy came home in sixth place, Tony Fall tenth and Lampinen 15th - all fine results. The officials gave some anxious moments - as if anyone had forgotten the previous year - when they counted and recounted the times, taking several hours to put out the official results.

In the Swedish Rally the following month, the two Finns, Rauno and Timo were the BMC entry, but Mäkinen only got as far as the second stage when a brake caliper broke. Aaltonen did rather better than this, which was surprising in view of the rather dramatic accident that occurred. Hitting a bank of snow, the car rolled end-over-end, during which many of Aaltonen's and Liddon's belongings flew out of the suddenly glass-free rear window. The car landed back on its wheels and the pair managed to retrieve some of their personal effects - which entailed quite a long walk. Finding the Cooper still driveable, they finished in third place. This was the first time a Mini actually lasted the distance in the Swedish event. In the next rally, the Sanremo Flowers, a second place was attained, thanks to some ingenious lateral thinking.

Roadside repairs

It was a rally of attrition - the San Remo Flowers - in which Hopkirk found himself in the lead, thanks in part to other cars failing in the harsh conditions. As the finish drew nearer he was being outpaced by a Renault Gordini, although holding on to a slight lead. Less than one mile from the end of the last special stage, a driveshaft U/J disintegrated - a common reason for rally roadside repairs to a Mini. Unfortunately, despite a shove from a local tractor over a small hill which enabled them to reach the service point, there was neither the time nor the room to make the repair. This would mean the loss of a placing - let alone first - just 20km from the finish in San Remo. However, it just so happened it was downhill all the way from the service point, with one time control about half-way...

With the service pair giving them a hefty shove when necessary, they made it to the time clocks and, feigning drastic clutch slip by dint of plenty of artificial revving noises (from the engine), Paddy rolled off down the incline out of sight from the officials. With yet more pushes and an extraordinary trip along a coast road crowded with people and cars, where the nudges from the Vanden Plas Princess R were somehow undetected by anyone that mattered, they were now within yards of the final control, which was situated at the exit of a tunnel. Gaining quite some speed in the tunnel, the support car braked hard at the last possible moment, propelling Paddy into the daylight - a Mini missile. Not content with merely arriving in a normal fashion, he actually did a hand brake turn around a traffic island and coasted into the finish. The level of skill required to pilot a car at some speed on a tortuous route with no power of its own, suggests

Paddy Hopkirk raises the dust during a finely judged drive to first place in the 1967 Acropolis Rally.

that Paddy really deserved that second place. It must be the only time a Mini has finished a competition with Rolls-Royce power! Had this stunt occurred and been found out during the 1966 Monte, you can bet the crew would have been tumbrelled off to the guillotine.

The next event was a strange departure for a Mini Cooper: the East African Safari must be one of the most unsuitable rallies that a Mini could possibly undertake. Despite an extensively-modified car with all manner of tweaks, mostly in anticipation of deep water because the '67 Safari was one of the wettest ever held, Aaltonen went out through a combination of recurring overheating and, finally, mud clogging the air filters. In the same month, Paddy Hopkirk was set at 'his' event, the Circuit of Ireland, which he won comfortably from a non-works Cooper S in second place. In the Tulip Rally the Porsches were expected to win at a canter, but at the finish Vic Elford found his 911S less than one minute ahead of Timo, whose engine had

fractured a piston, necessitating large quantites of oil being poured in at every available opportunity. With Rauno Aaltonen third and some good placings by privately-entered Coopers, BMC won the Manufacturers' Team Prize.

The Acropolis always seemed to be a rally too far, with the Abingdon-prepared Mini Coopers either leaving the rally when in first place (three times) or being disqualified from that place (1966). This year was different, although it must have looked as if the Greek event was proceeding true to form when Aaltonen met a non-competitor coming the other way when the road should, of course, have been closed to the public. The errant

It's 1967, and Tony Fall charges along the Highland forest tracks on his way to a second Scottish Rally victory. Co-driver is Mike Wood.

63

driver was actually a doctor who, having seen another competitor plunge off the road, had jumped in his own car to render asssistance. He never got there. In the ensuing collision Aaltonen was hospitalised with concussion. Mäkinen took up the leading position but was sidelined with a cracked rear subframe and a wilting gearbox. This left Hopkirk, the driver disqualified the previous year, out in front. The culmination of the rally was a circuit race at Tatoi, the result of which would not affect the final placings, although it was essential to finish. After a spirited drive where he was mixing it with a Lancia and the now ubiquitous Lotus Cortina, Paddy's car ran its bearings on only the fourth lap. To carry on would have meant certain terminal engine failure, so he wisely coasted around to just short of the finishing line. At the sight of the chequered flag of the half-hour race, he started the engine and drove gingerly across the line to take a very well-judged victory. It was a most popular win.

In the Scottish rally the Swede, Lars Ytterbring, had the use of a factory 1275 S, in which he came second. The Geneva Rally which followed was chaotic. It seems the organisers decided to make two rallies of their event; one for Group I and III cars, the other for the rest. This meant that the Minis of Fall and Julian Vernaeve, the Belgian, were awarded first and second places in the rather meaningless 'Criterium de Crans-sur-Sierre', whilst Vic Elford was deemed to have won the Geneva Rally proper in his 911S. An interesting point was that both the works Minis in this event were trying rear anti-roll bars for the first time.

Visual handicap

Tony Fall crashed out of the London Rally in July and, in the same month, Rauno Aaltonen made his exit from the Danube Rally in very novel fashion. At the Hungarian border he was categorically refused entry without a visa: a good example of small-minded bureacracy which flourished under 'the system'.

Neither lack of visa, accidents or any other competitors could stop Mäkinen from winning 'his' event, the 1000 Lakes. This rally turned into a three-way tussle between the Saabs, Lotus Cortinas and the lone works Mini of Mäkinen. He won despite the gearbox remote control coming apart - a fairly regular happening - and the much-publicised result of overheating, which caused him to drive some 10km to the end of a special stage with the bonnet wide open. It had not been fastened properly after a lightning removal of the auxiliary lamps to try and lower the engine temperature. Despite this extreme visual handicap, Timo was only 19 seconds slower than the fastest car on that stage. With that kind of driving, perhaps his win - the third in a row there - was almost a foregone conclusion. But it was to be the last BMC rally win by this fine driver.

Under the circumstances Paddy Hopkirk managed a superb win in the Alpine Rally in Setember. The Mini Coopers were really hardly competitive by now, there being several faster cars around: the Mini was now in its 9th year in production, after all. The Lotus Cortina, Alfa Romeo GTA, Porsche 911 and the little Alpine Renault A110 Berlinette were some of the cars giving the Mini a very hard time in this event. However, while his teammates did not finish - Mäkinen and Aaltonen suffered mechanical woes and Fall fell off - Paddy drove steadily along in seventh place or thereabouts. When fog shrouded the event, some inspired use of superbly-prepared pace notes by Ron Crellin enabled Paddy to overtake several cars on the run to the finish. With the expiry of the leading Alpine, Hopkirk achieved a splendid victory which would turn out to be the last by a Mini Cooper in an international rally. The final two rallies of the year were the Corsican and the RAC. Unfortunately, both were to prove enormous let-downs.

Injected eight-port head

Because the Mini Cooper was beginning to struggle for want of power, the factory had come up with a rather fetching eight-port head with fuel injection. The Tour de Corse was entered and the recce car for this event was fitted with this new weapon to give some idea of its behaviour under rally

conditions. Two Mini Coopers were entered in Group 6 which had several mods, including knock-on Minilite wheels, larger radiators and alternators. Alas, these tweaks didn't help the cars much, for Hopkirk and Aaltonen were both out within a short time on the very first stage, with slipping fanbelts which caused flat batteries and, more seriously, overheating. That both belts came from a faulty batch did not spare the blushes.

The disappointment over the RAC Rally was that it was cancelled, because of a national outbreak of foot and mouth disease. The fuel injection car was to have contested Group 6 as the new induction system had yet to be

homologated. Three other Coopers with carburetters were entered. An interesting aside was that one last effort was to be made to get that elusive RAC win for the big Healey. A car was prepared with an all-alloy engine with triple Webers. Alas, it remained unrallied. The days of the supremely competitive Mini Cooper were now fast running out. 1968, however, might just have provided yet another win on the Monte, but for the weather.

Last shot at the Monte
The 1968 Monte turned out to be the last try for the BMC Mini at that most publicised event. And they made a very strong attempt at victory with extensive tyre testing

which resulted in over 700 being taken along, plus new Downton gas-flowed heads and some new carburetters. These last were nearly to prove the undoing of the team before the rally even began. As it happened, it wasn't so much the scrutineers that beat them, or even the increasingly formidable opposition. They were beaten by the weather - or lack of it.

Studded tyres from Finland
Timo Mäkinen had brought more than one tweak back from Finland with him. Studded tyres, for example, which were at one time more advanced over there than Abingdon realised; a new design of sump guard was another. Not long

Tony Fall bends the Cooper's tyres among the Provençal pines; Mike Wood busies himself getting them to Monte Carlo in 4th place - second Cooper home.

before the new year, he showed the Competitions Department a pair of modified Weber 45 DCOE carburetters which he had seen a Mini competitor using back home. These were tested by the works and found to be preferable to the previous set-up, giving over 90bhp at the wheels for each car. The decision was taken to use them on the 1968 Monte in Group II, which meant that the car's original manifold had to be retained. To get the Weber to mate with a manifold more used to the trusty SU carburetter, a sort of flange was welded to the Weber. Fine, although the FIA were not over-enamoured

with the new set-up, saying that the flange was a non-permissible intermediary device, whilst the Competition Manager, Peter Browning, argued vehemently that it was an integral part of the carburetters. It seems that the other modifications to the Webers in question meant they could be regarded as prototypes and so Browning won his argument, not before threatening to withdraw the whole works team. There was a proviso to the Mini Coopers being allowed to start the rally: if another competitor protested, the organisers would reconsider their decision.

The weather proved a bigger

problem than the Sporting Commission, for there was almost no snow on the special stages, therefore wiping out much of the Minis' advantage. This had the effect of encouraging the drivers to go absolutely flat out with the consequent extra strain on the cars. Timo's was the one that wilted - is this a surprise? - when the crankshaft pulley came loose. This meant the fanbelt slipped wildly and the water pump and alternator ceased to keep up with the engine's needs, so to speak. Upon making it to the next control, Paul Easter swears that, on arrival, the engine was red hot. Nothing new in that statement, but the en-

gine in ORX77F really was glowing in the dark! Hampered by the freakish dry weather, the other three Minis of Aaltonen, Fall and Hopkirk came home 3rd, 4th and 5th overall, beaten only by two Porsche 911s.

Scrutineering was not a very relaxing affair, not least of all because the bod in charge also officiated in 1966. The carburetters were totally disassembled and practically viewed under microscopes, but this time the all-clear was sounded and the Minis' placings were official. The Coopers also won the Touring Category and the Team Prize. This was as good a result as they could ever have achieved under the circumstances. Had it snowed normally - for a Monte - it may not be fanciful to suggest that the three crews would all have moved up a couple of places. We shall never know ...

With both Minis retiring with mechanical woes on the San Remo Flowers Rally, it was becoming clearer that the cars were not getting the development they needed to compete favourably against, for example, the Porsches. Part of the problem was that a great deal of time was being channelled into preparation for the London to Sydney Marathon. Nevertheless, some good results - although no more outright wins - were still obtained.

On the Circuit of Ireland, despite having a Group 6 car with lightweight panels and the new Weber carburetter set-up, our man just could not keep pace with Roger Clark's new Escort Twin Cam. Suffering first from overheating and then differential failure, he was eventually out, joining his team mate, Ytterbring, who had crashed out earlier after striking a bridge. An ex-works Cooper came in second, however.

On the Tulip Rally, both Mäkinen and Vernaeve had Minilite wheels with 5.5 inch rims, almost a sixty percent increase on the original 3.5 inch Mini rims. Vernaeve came in 3rd behind two Ford Escorts, but Mäkinen had a rather extensive 'off' which dropped him almost to the end of the placings.

Flat-out stuff

One Mini was entered in the Canadian rally, known as the Shell 4000, to be driven by Hopkirk. Much of this was flat-out stuff and the Irishman's car started to overheat. The service crew then fitted the car with an auxiliary radiator and it was promptly disqualified. In the rather more important Acropolis event, the two Finns were once again finding the going tough against the Ford Escort and the Porsches. Mäkinen went out with overheating which eventually turned into head gasket failure - or was it the one that caused the other? This was to be the last time he drove a Mini Cooper for the team. Aaltonen also had engine cooling problems but brought his car home in 5th place. His co-driver, Henry Liddon, reckoned that their car, RBL 450F, was the best one they'd driven yet, so, apparently, some progress was still being made at the Abingdon Competitions Department!

In the following month a single works Mini was entered in the Scottish for Lars Ytterbring, who gained second place to the now ultra-competitive Escort Twin Cam of Roger Clark. In this event, the Cooper was fitted with an auxiliary radiator in anticipation of the now common cooling difficulties which were a result of coaxing more and more power from the engines: more power produces more heat. On the Mini this was more of a problem than usual, thanks to the siting of the radiator.

The last rally of 1968 to be entered by a works Mini Cooper was the TAP Rally in Portugal. Hopkirk was the sole representative and he was leading until almost the end when he was overhauled by the winning Lancia. This only happened because he had the wrong tyres for the last special stage; the service crew arrived too late - due to fog - to fit the right ones.

Most of the rally team had been given their cards at the end of the year, as rallying was to be a low priority for the works Minis now that Leyland was the name on everyone's lips. Hopkirk was retained for 1969 and a decision taken to enter the cars in several rallycross events. Undoubtedly highly entertaining to watch - hence the strong TV coverage - these mudfights were perhaps rather demeaning for the

cars which had triumphed in the world's toughest rallies. More interesting was the fact that the newly-formed Leyland régime could and would now openly enter the Mini Cooper in circuit races.

Works Mini Coopers were entered in only two international rallies in 1969. The first was the Circuit of Ireland, where Paddy tried 12in wheels with 6in rims for the first time, but complained of a loss of stability and so reverted to the 10 X 5.5in wheels and tyres. He finished third despite a misfire which took some time to trace, followed by suspension troubles.

In the Tour de France, really a sort of road race with token rally hillclimb bits thrown in, fuel injection reappeared for Hopkirk's car, whilst the second Group II car for John Handley ran on the Weber set-up. Brian Culcheth's Cooper was entered in Group I. The event was full of dramas and ended with Paddy fourteenth overall, winning his class, despite several problems. Handley went out after bumping into a wall, apparently after a pace-note misunderstanding. This was a shame as he had been lying in sixth place at the time. Brian Culcheth came second in his class, only beaten by another Mini Cooper, the privately-entered car of Julian Vernaeve.

With the Mini Cooper now no longer a serious contender for winning the important rallies, just two minor ones were entered in Australia at the end of 1970. These were the last two events contested by works Mini Coopers. Culcheth contested both the Southern Cross Rally and the Rally of the Hills in Australia. He finished fourth in the second event but retired in the first, along with Andrew Cowan who was entered in a Clubman.

End of the Line

This may represent the end of the line for the works participation of Mini Coopers in rallies, but many, many circuit races had already been won by these cars with both covert and overt factory support. Many more would be won by privateers after 1970. What is remarkable is that the works Coopers outlived a succession of other war-horses campaigned by the factory: in the late '50s there were Riley 1.5s, A40s, Sprites and, of course, the big Healeys, which carried on into the '60s; the few MGAs were replaced by MGBs, which spanned the decade, with MGC GTs eventually superseding the gallant old Healey 3000s, albeit as circuit racers. The Austin and Morris 1800 'Land-crabs' were successors to the earlier oddball Wolseley 6/90s, and Morris and MG 1100s were tried on occasion; Triumph 2500s were taken on long-distance marathons. By 1971 a RAC rally, the factory weapon was a 1.3 Marina, but a couple of years later the Dolomite Sprint was in the ascendant. Nothing came close, however, to matching the Cooper's consistency and competitive staying power.

Postscript - reflections from the driving seat

Tony Fall, another member of the works rally team in the mid to late '60s, maintained his competition career after the Abingdon closure in Ford Escorts, Datsun 240Zs, Lancia Fulvias, BMW 2002s, Peugeot 504s, and subsequently partnered by Jimmy Greaves' on the London-Mexico Rally in an Escort Mexico. He was the leading light behind the Opel Dealer Team in the early '70s, and for 15 years was GM Europe's head of Motor Sport. Today he owns Safety Devices, manufacturing 75 per cent of the roll cages used in international competition, as well as supplying Land Rover with parts to equip its US-spec vehicles.

'It was such a shame when Lord Stokes went and put the kibosh on it,' reflected Tony. 'If you look back at the Mini, it could have gone on winning for another five years. It may have been disadvantaged by the size of the wheels, but being only ten feet long made those roads very wide! OK, it wouldn't have won everything, but you'd still have achieved significant results with it.'

Tony continued: 'Even in the days of Abingdon, there was none of what you'd call scientific engineering; we modified things because they broke, and we did it by durability testing. We'd take the cars to Santa Florida Abbey in Wales, thrash them round the hills, and if something broke we'd find a way round it. Nobody actually sat down and said, we'll put the tyres on the road here, make a contact patch and work our way backwards through it all. In fact, I never saw a drawing board at Abingdon: it all tended to be...well, Timo wants this, Rauno's got a brilliant theory," and somehow it all came together. There was no real development strategy. Someone said let's put 12in wheels on; but Timo didn't like them, so we didn't bother with them. He happened to be the only one of us to test them, and they didn't suit, so that was the end of it!'

Tony recalls that probably a lot of opportunities were missed. 'They were a lot more honest in those days about the regulations compared with how they are now. Today, they look at a car and consider how they can get away with the tweak they want to do without being caught, or they interpret the regs in a different way. But in the old days, the amount of cheating was virtually nil. Even something like an odd extra spot weld was considered a risky modification.

He recalls the most gruelling event was the Marathon de la Route, effectively four days and nights spent on the 14-mile old Nürburgring circuit. 'At Abingdon in '67 and '68 we did the Nürburgring 84 Hours, and in '67 we were second overall in a 970 Cooper S. I was with Andrew Hedges and Julian Vernaeve. That was a killer of an event - 84 hours round the Nurburgring makes all these long distance racing drivers at Le Mans look like a load of cissies. The next year we did it in an MGC GT and we were leading until the brake pads got stuck and we dropped to fifth. I had to do umpteen laps without any brakes at all and they had to stop it in the pit lane by throwing jacks underneath it. The following year - '69 - I actually won it with a Fulvia. Going from a Mini to a Fulvia was like stepping into a tank, even though it's a tiddley car. The 504 was a barge by comparison.'

Mini Cooper

VII

RACING

On the basis that anything is possible, one could - eventually - list all of the circuit races won by Mini Coopers. Unfortunately, the research for this task would take forever and the resulting publication probably be bigger than the car itself. Certainly many of the Minis which won track races were Mini Coopers, but many events were won by modified Minis before, during and after the Cooper's introduction in Autumn 1961. Indeed, in the last 20 years or so, the Minis that have won races have hardly been anything at all like the production model, let alone a Cooper version. This presents a reviewer of track performances of the Mini Cooper with a problem. With rallying rules being what they are - even if they didn't always go in the Mini Coopers' favour - we know what performances the Mini Coopers achieved, thanks in great part to the well-documented official works participation. With racing, the distinction between a modified Mini and a Mini Cooper has become very blurred.

Angry hornets
When privateers began to race their Minis, taking corners three or four abreast like swarms of bees and individuals behaving like angry hornets, the race-going public began to take more notice of saloon car racing. Many a spectacle was

provided by the likes of drivers such as Tony Lanfranchi, Bill Blydenstein, John Aley, Gerry Marshall, Bill McGovern, Vic Elford, Sir John Whitmore, Doc Shepherd, Ken Costello, Steve McQueen and Christabel Carlisle, to name just a few. McQueen would go on to buy several Mini Coopers and would probably have enjoyed an illustrious racing career but for the stifling insurance requirements of the US film companies. Christabel Carlisle, apart from upsetting many male egos, added more than a little glamour to the events in which she partook. Having been given one of the new Austin Sevens for her 21st birthday present in 1960, Christabel Carlisle entered a few rallies without resounding success. Some friends talked her into entering a club race at Silverstone where her raw speed made her something of a crowd-puller. When some kindly BMC mechanics on a test session at the Northamptonshire circuit replaced

Trailer mounted French Innocenti looks more like a concours candidate than a serious racer.

70

A lapped Riley 1.5 takes a wide line to avoid the train of Minis speeding into Goodwood Chicane in 1963.

Warwick Banks in no. 211 is the meat in this Mini sandwich, with an Anglia hanging in there at Druids bend, Brands Hatch.

Christabel Carlisle gave the boys a run for their money - and frequently beat them.

A hairy moment at Goodwood Chicane during a saloon car dice in 1963. An Austin Cooper takes avoiding action as a Morris Cooper goes awry ahead of an Anglia and Giulia Super.

a fan belt on her Mini, an association was formed between Abingdon and Miss Carlisle which included the occasional loan of a car, as well as help with the tuning by racer Willy Griffith. Later, her car would be prepared by Don Moore. When Stuart Turner arranged a test session in the new MGB at Sebring in 1962 on a very wet track, the times surprised him more than a little:

2m 15.2s Paddy Hopkirk
2m 16.8s Christabel Carlisle
2m 19.8s Elizabeth Jones
2m 26.8s Pauline Mayman

In a race at Brands Hatch in 1961 on 1st October, Christabel was thoroughly embroiled in a stirring dice with five other Minis, which included some notable (male) drivers. She led for most of the race but was finally passed by Vic Elford. The racing was so close it was reported the commentator was almost apopletic at the finish (shades of Murray Walker). Although the Minis had provided easily the best entertainment of the race, they still finished well behind the far more powerful leading cars. Neverthe-

less, it was a surprised winner, Mike Parkes driving a Jaguar 3.8, who found three of the Mini pilots - Elford, McQueen and Carlisle - climbing up to join him on the victory podium, much to the delight of the crowd. Apparently, much kissing then took place, most of it landing on Miss Carlisle (that's a relief!). After this, all four did a victory lap of the circuit to the accompaniment of the traditional horn-honking salute from the spectators parked on South Bank.

You'd be forgiven for wondering what Christabel Carlisle's occupation was, given her fearless performances behind the wheel, where she could - like Pat Moss - take on and beat 'the boys' who, apparently, would sometimes gang up and box her in on the straights to stop her getting ahead! (Odd that in almost all other sports, women compete separately: tennis, golf, athletics, cricket, for example.) No, she was not a riding instructor, a pilot, or even a lion-tamer; Christabel was a piano teacher. She is now Lady Watson.

Major attraction

It was drives like the one at Brands

that began to arouse great interest in saloon car racing; whereas before, the saloon car race, although popular enough, was not the great crowd-puller it is today. When the Mini Cooper appeared on the race tracks, the actual possibility of a Mini win was an added bonus to the entertainment of close Mini racing. This was especially true on the twistier circuits, where the giant-killing performances of the Coopers would attract even more spectators. Saloon car racing entered the Big Time with the Mini, generating a level of interest that is still healthy today.

Before the works began officially in 1969 to try its hand at entering Mini Coopers on a grand scale in circuit races, the Cooper Car Company had been racing them since 1962 with backing from the factory. This support could be quite variable as regards the financial side, depending, it seems, on how much cash BMC deemed it had to spare at a particular time. Nevertheless, in 1962, John Love won the British Saloon Car Championship, driving a Mini Cooper entered by Cooper's team. The following year, their other '62 driver, Sir John

Lurid slides at Silverstone 1963, with Salvadori's Mk 2 Jaguar leading various Coopers and a Sunbeam Rapier.

Whitmore, was runner-up in the title race, only beaten by a Ford Galaxie, a car about four times the size of the Mini and driven by Jack Sears (who may, somewhat indirectly, be the person responsible for the imposition of the UK's current 70mph speed limit - testing AC Cobras on the M1 at warp-factor speeds was not approved of on high). Also, in the 1963 season Cooper provided a car on an occasional basis for Paddy Hopkirk.

The success of these Mini Cooper goods, scarcely two years on sale, had tempted competition into the market place, in true free-trade tradition. In 'Europe' - a place the UK apparently didn't geographically belong to in those days - a Cooper with an engine tuned to such good effect by Downton Engineering had propelled Rob Slotemaker - the original Flying Dutchman? - to the 1300cc class of the European Saloon Car Championship. At home Ralph Broad entered a Cooper, modified to his own specifications, driven by John Fitzpatrick. It seems that Fitz went so well, sometimes beating the Cooper Coopers, that certain feath-

ers were ruffled in BMC high places, especially when it was known that Broad's Birmingham business was hardly big-budget stuff. Building his team up from two to four cars - for John Fitzpatrick, John Handley and the less well-known Jeff May and Peter Tempest - it became obvious that 'Team Broadspeed' was

now a serious competitor to the BMC/Cooper team, even if the factory's involvement with the Cooper team was not widely known.

European Touring Car Champion
The result of Ralph Broad's success was that Fitzpatrick was pinched from them for the Cooper team in

European Touring Cars in their infancy, with Warwick Banks leading a tiny Fiat Abarth at the Nürburgring in 1964.

1964, when factory support for this Surbiton outfit was placed on a more secure basis. John Cooper contested the home events and Ken Tyrrell entered two cars in the European Touring Car Championship for Cooper, to be driven by Julian Vernaeve, the Belgian, and Warwick Banks, who would earn his living as a pilot. Banks also drove Tyrrell's FJ Coopers as well as the 970cc Mini Cooper, which he reckoned had 'a little jewel as an engine'. He describes it as closely resembling that in the FJ cars with which he and Jackie Stewart cleaned up that year. Banks would win the European Touring Car Championship outright for Tyrrell in 1964, and Fitzpatrick the 1300cc class, plus second place overall in the British series for Cooper.

Loneliness of the long-distance racer

Warwick Banks recalls some interesing moments racing the Mini Coopers, such as when he and John Whitmore took 1.5 minutes off the class record in the Mont Ventoux Hillclimb. At the Nürburgring during a six-hour race, he lapped the 970S in 10m 40s. This 1964 time set by a little saloon car would have put him onto the grid for the 1957 German Grand Prix! He recalled

with rueful humour how, at Monza in a single-handed, four-hour race his team manager, Ken Tyrrell, 'wouldn't let me out of the car ... for anything!'

The following year, Banks drove for Cooper in the up to 1.0-litre class of the British Saloon Car Championship. He was victorious in eight out of ten races in his class - which he won, of course, and was at first awarded the Championship, only to have it taken away and

handed to Ford, after its successful protest. This stemmed from an incident at Crystal Palace when a 1275 Cooper shunted his 970 car up the bootlid at the first corner. Apparently, the driver of the car which used his as a brake told him he shouldn't have been in front as his was the smaller engine. When this driver reached the pits, John Cooper 'came close to flattening him ... with good reason as it turned out', added Banks.

Greedy for oil

In the Spa Francorchamps 24-hour race partnering John Rhodes, sharing stints in the 1275S, Banks

Two drifters: John Fitzpatrick heads Warwick Banks at Club Corner, Silverstone, July 10th 1965.

The Mini Cooper Maestro, John Rhodes. Nobody did it quite like him.

remembers that the circuit could be negotiated by the Mini 'virtually flat' [out], with the exception, naturally, of La Source hairpin. He thinks the lap speed must have been close to 100mph. Trouble was, the car developed a greed for oil and, because replenishing could only be done after a certain distance had been covered, 'about an hour after each pit stop,' they had to drive each corner 'in chunks,' sort of threepenny-bit [12-sided old British coin] fashion, to stop what oil was left from falling away for too long from the pump's pick-up pipe. He was taking a nap when Rhodes woke him with the news that the engine was now redesigned, 'with its crankcase split from one end to the other'.

All-told, Warwick Banks calculated that he has driven around 10,000 racing miles in Minis. Like Rhodes, he says they were golden days and that they were lucky to have experienced them. 'Just think', he muses, 'superb music, cheap petrol, fast, unsophisticated cars usually with no brakes [this is enjoyable?] no speed limits and no

breathalyser. How DID I survive, I often wonder?' He accurately reflects, sadly, that many didn't, explaining that was one of the reasons he retired in 1965 - for 24 years, anyway. He will always cherish, he says, the memories associated with driving works Minis for for two years, as well as the company of 'some formidable and able motor racing personalities', a type

Rhodes in typical tyre-smoking attitude; he claims to have discovered the technique by accident the first time he was given a run in a works car.

Rhodes with left shoulder up and lots of lock applied as the Cooper is thrown into a corner.

he thinks may not exist these days. He reckons that as the competition became ever fiercer and the cars became more and more modified, so driving tactics deteriorated and attitudes were born 'that are still being used today in the BTCC. They do no one any credit'. You would have to talk to a lot of people today to find someone to disagree with this last comment.

Initial success
At the end of 1964, Ralph Broad was having a tough time. He had been given favoured status from the factory, as regards updated specification tweaks and stronger gearbox internals, for example, but

his financially challenged state saw him in need of help. Since, despite the lack of cash he had managed to beat the Tyrrell cars across the channel on more than one occasion, BMC awarded him the European race contract for '65. John Fitzpatrick returned to Broad's team alongside John Handley, and John Terry was also called in as a relief driver. Cooper still had Warwick Banks and acquired the services of John Rhodes. (If at this point the reader has noticed there are so many drivers mentioned whose Christian names begin with 'J' - let alone called John - it must be a legacy from Formula One, where the World Drivers' Championship

was won 13 times out of the 17 seasons to 1966 by drivers whose names started with that letter! A and N have been *de rigueur* since 1980.) Anyhow, this driver Rhodes was no spring chicken, being 38 years old in 1965, but this advancement in years compared to his Mini Cooper-driving contemporaries was no handicap: he was faster than all of them.

Rhodes defines the technique
He joined Coopers, he claims, as 'team leader, chief cook and bottle-washer'. The second thing he remembers on arriving at the Surbiton premises was a Renault Dauphine with a Coventry Climax

Rhodes is hard at work earning his keep for the Cooper Car Company at Goodwood. The contortions needed to make the Mini Cooper do what he wants are quite incredible!

engine in the back; the first being the young lady serving petrol on the forecourt! He was there to help assemble some Formula Junior single-seaters, known as Auspers. These were quite successful cars owned by the Midland Racing Partnership. Many of the tricks put into practice on the engines in these cars would find their way into the Mini Cooper units. Thus, Formula Junior racing was used, if you like, for Mini Cooper engine development: after all, it was the saloon car which earned the money! Rhodes describes Cooper's workshops as an 'Aladdin's Cave for a motor enthusiast, with rows and rows of Formula Junior, Formula Two and sports cars being built.' The Cooper Formula One team was just across the road and he regrets, he says, 'not having the cheek' to go and gaze at them. Nevertheless, he describes how racing drivers, team managers, and 'titled folk' would stroll in and out of the deep but small frontage garage. He assembled the Formula Junior cars alongside Denny Hulme, who would become Formula One World Champion before the decade was out, and tells of pushing part-completed cars out of the workshop and into a pub car park in order to avoid the official from Customs and Excise. This was done because if skilled labour was used to assemble cars, a duty had to be paid: only when assembled at home by an 'amateur' was the tax avoided. (This turned out to be one of those daft, unenforceable laws.)

Above: John Rhodes and his son Tim inspect one of his old cars at a historic meeting at Silverstone.

Left: John Rhodes and Warwick Banks are chums today, and both active on the sporting scene. They are together here at Castle Combe.

Despite his successes in Formula Junior - he won the FJ Championship of Ireland in 1960 - he did not rate himself as a driver of single-seaters. He would qualify a distant last in the 1965 British Grand Prix and he claimed that saloon cars were easy to drive fast, but that anyone who could conquer a single-seater 'could drive anything'. After competing in these 'pure' racing cars, he said he found the Mini Coopers so slow that he couldn't frighten himself in one, so drove it flat out all the time. This is rather a modest way of assessing his unquestioned talent, but is typical of his self-effacing manner. Many describe him as a complete gentleman - until he got behind the wheel of a racing car, when he apparently sprouted horns. This Jekyll and Hyde tendency is reminiscent of Jimmy Clark, also.

John Rhodes tells us that his unique cornering style was arrived at by accident, when being given his first try in a Mini by Ginger Devlin, the shop foreman and team manager at Cooper's garage. 'I flew into the first corner (having just dismounted from some quick laps in Bob Gerard's Cooper) far too fast - Mini Cooper brakes were a joke. Throwing it sideways, it just flew round in clouds of tyre smoke. I had arrived! Before the tyre war and stickier compounds, that was the fastest way to drive. Flat into the corner, slight lift to throw the back end out, and flat out again. Wonderful!' Not only did his adopted driving style - or did it adopt him? - entertain the crowds, it often confused other competitors who had less experience of the 'Smokey Rhodes' technique. Seeing him disappear sideways into a cloud of rubber fumes, they would assume he was currently occupied with the beginning of a great big prang. Not wishing to be involved, they would lift off and Rhodes would pull out a few more yards. Rhodes believes his style of driving gave Dunlop 'a real headache', his tyres often getting 'hot enough to boil an egg'. On one occasion, he and team manager Ginger Devlin were tyre-testing with Ian Mills, Dunlop's competition manager, in attendance. Because of the heat generated, the tyres were throwing off chunks of rubber after ten laps when they needed them to last twenty. Rhodes overheard Devlin telling Mills that it was a good job Dunlop weren't going into the manufacture of prophylactics ...

Ralph Broad, meanwhile, was not finding the 1965 season in Europe too successful, largely because of his financial situation which caused him to have to skip some of the races. When he entered races at home, Broadspeed-prepared Coopers often beat the Mini Coopers prepared by the Cooper team. This was not in the script and BMC did not renew his contract for 1966. Not over-thrilled, Broad defected to Ford to prepare and race Anglias, taking John Fitzpatrick with him. Broad presumably forgave the factory for their fancy footwork, for he did return to help develop the Triumph Dolomite Sprint, which was successful, and the Jaguar XJ-12 Coupé which, despite Broad's best efforts, wasn't. The problem with this car was one traditionally associated with Jaguars - it was too heavy. 'If it weighs more than a ton(ne), don't race it' is sound advice which will never apply to a Mini.

With Banks now plumping for single-seaters, his place in the Cooper team was taken by John Handley, who did not follow Fitzpatrick and Broad to Ford. If all this should sound a trifle fraught, it resembles a chamber music recital at the vicar's when compared to the dishonourable shenanigans rife in today's Formula One.

Factory sponsorship

The 1966 season saw the Johns Rhodes and Handley in the Cooper team, which was to be the only one with factory sponsorship. The cars would now have engines prepared by Downton Engineering, instead of those prepared at BMC Engines Branch by Eddie Maher. Don Moore would now contest European events, with Paddy Hopkirk as driver. The following year, with Rhodes and Handley still in the team, they were up against the Superspeed Ford Anglias of John Young and Chris Craft, and the Broadspeed Anglias of Fitzpatrick and Anita Taylor: despite running their homologated fuel injection

Steve Neal - Cooper S driver - drove the British Vita cars in the late '60s.

Oulton Park and Rhodes has pushed the hapless Lotus Cortina into a serious error; although the Cooper's raised left wheel suggests Rhodes is going left, he is actually avoiding the rolling Cortina and about to go into a right-hander.

engines they were often outpaced. Reliability was on their side and the championship went all the way to the last round, with John Fitzpatrick just winning the title from John Rhodes.

Earlier in the year in March, the factory entered a 1275 Cooper, the '66 Polish Rally winner GRX 309D, in the 3-hour support race at Sebring, driven by Paddy Hopkirk and John Rhodes. The competition was rather feeble. Apparently, there were no fewer than 70 cars on the grid and for many the starter's flag was out of sight: Paddy, starting from the rear, had passed roughly half of the cars before he reached the start/finish line! The car ran like clockwork and led its class, despite some refuelling problems which caused a hasty last lap refuelling stop, which necessitated a bit of rule-book waving by the BMC team manager to secure their class win.

In August, two 970 Mini Coopers were entered by the factory in the Marathon de la Route, a much-corrupted version of the once awesome Spa-Sofia-Liège Rally which now took place at the home of the German Grand Prix, the Nürburgring in the Eiffel mountains. These cars were running in Group 6 and were lightened with alloy panels and perspex windows. Also added were an auxiliary radiator - to counteract that overheating tendency again - and an extra oil tank with an electric pump, which was operated from the driver's seat. (You would have thought the driver might have had enough enough on his plate with Nürburgring's 176 corners.) The cars had three-man teams for this 84-hour event, comprising Vernaeve/Fall/Hedges and Poole/Enever/Baker.

The Minis were the two smallest cars in the race and, after the first day, were lying 3rd and 4th, helped somewhat by wet weather. One car had a throttle cable break and repairs incurred a severe time penalty. The driver who took over, Alec Poole, was instructed to go flat

Gordon Spice drove Cooper-Britax-Downton cars in 1968.

out but instead went off and inverted, after mistaking one of the corners for another in the fog. This is very easy to do at the 'Ring, even in good visibilty. The other car screamed on and when Elford's leading 911S Porsche broke a brake disc, it actually led for a while. Then it was the Mini's turn for a gremlin to strike and a wheel bearing collapsed, with the hub taking a while

to remove. Nevertheless, the Cooper finished in second place overall - a more than impressive feat after 5500 miles around the 'Ring. It also won the award for the shortest time spent in the pits - a marvellous tribute to reliabilty.

In 1968 the British Vita team got BMC factory support alongside Cooper's and would contest the European races in the one litre class, with John Handley and Alec Poole. The Cooper team retained the amazing Rhodes, now partnered by Steve Neal, and contested the British events in the 1300cc class. The British Vita team won their championship with Handley, more thanks to reliability than speed, for the Mini was now out-powered by its competitors - even in the same class, that is. Rhodes missed out on the main title again but won the 1300cc class. There had been much support from Abingdon for its various teams in 1968, but in 1969 this would all end as the company was being stalked by Stokes.

Rallying was not a great favourite of the new régime and was drastically curtailed as it was considered to be too expensive. Racing

was on the new menu - as well as the hybrid rallycross - now with a heavy emphasis on winning. This was not going to be easy in the case of the Mini Cooper as it was really now rather ancient in competition terms for international events, fought out by rival teams with full factory-backed teams. Although the Competitions Department at Abingdon was sceptical about the Mini's chances of regular success, the alternative was no Competitions Department.

The two drivers were to be Rhodes and Handley, who were paired in the '67 Cooper team. Cooper, no longer receiving factory support, would join up with Downton and form the Cooper-Britax-Downton team with Steve Neal who had partnered Rhodes in the '68 Cooper team, and Gordon Spice. The first race that Leyland would contest with the Mini Cooper was the Guards Trophy saloon car race at Brands Hatch in March, and a new development seen on the cars was the 12 inch wheel.

One of the problems with having such tiny wheels is that they go round more often. The 15 inch

wheels on the Jaguars that ruled the racing roost at the time of the Mini Cooper's introduction would make about 40 per cent fewer revolutions than the 10 inch wheels of the small car over the same distance covered. The 'extra' rotations of the Mini's boots tended to cause the tyre temperatures to be critical, and tyres that are overheating wear out too fast which translates into a reduction of grip. This problem became progressively more difficult to cure as the Minis in competition - both racing and rallying - were given stronger and stronger engines.

One way of lowering the temperatures is to change the 'rubber' compound, but this method had already been tried several times as the cars became ever more powerful. Another way was to increase the contact patch - the part of the tyre that touched the ground. This means that the weight of the car is distributed over a larger area, thus lowering the pressure of the tyre on the ground. There are two ways of increasing the amount of tyre on the road, the obvious one being to widen it. However, this was at the time when tyres generally were ex-

Left: No longer, in 1968, enjoying works backing, John Cooper joined forces with Britax and Downton with Steve Neal and Gordon Spice driving. One of his cars harries the Abingdon-prepared car of John Handley. The cars now used 12 inch wheels.

Right: A quartet of 'hot' Ss chase the Escorts at Silverstone, 1969.

panding very rapidly and, as the Mini in competition had already gone from 3.5 inch to 5.5 inch rims, there was no room left under the wheelarches for wider tyres because the bodywork could not be extended without homologation difficulties, where applicable. Otherwise, the cars coming off the production lines into the showrooms would all have to have flared arches. Then, as now, flares were out.

The other means of increasing the contact patch was to increase the diameter of the tyre - and this was the method that was chosen at the beginning of 1969. After much consultation it was decided on a 12 inch tyre, that is to say, a tyre to fit a 12 inch wheel. This two-inch increase in wheel diameter meant one inch had to be taken out of the sidewall of the tyre, to avoid altering the cars' gearing. These shorter sidewalls brought with them less flexing and therefore a further reduction in heat generation. Less flex also meant quicker response. The first tyre was too responsive, too nervous, as a result of having sidewalls that were too stiff. The second 12 inch tyre was of a softer compound with slighlty altered carcass construction, the combination of which gave a little more grip as well as being more controllable.

Leyland days

The first race for Leyland, in March 1969 at Brands, would go down as 'one of those days' which turn out in such a way that staying in bed

might have been a better idea. On the way to the circuit the transporter had clutch failure on a hill in Henley. The race was very wet and John Rhodes was put out on the grid in a start-line shunt. John Handley had nearly reached the end of the second heat when he flew off in the murky conditions and totalled his car as well. To round off a less-than-perfect day, the truck that replaced the transporter got bogged down in the mud in the paddock. The team's two cars - what was left of them - weren't the only red items that afternoon!

The next race was better. Held the same month at Silverstone, it did not give Abingdon much time to prepare two more cars. Nevertheless, the cars both finished, in 10th and 11th places overall and 4th and 5th in class, splitting the two cars in the Cooper team, driven by Spice and Neal. Unfortunately, they were outgunned by the Broadspeed Escorts - no doubt to Ralph's great satisfaction. More races produced very similar results: the Britax-Cooper-Downton cars were hard to ,beat, the Broadspeed Escorts impossible. The engines in the Leyland 1300cc works-entered, Mini Coopers were now giving nearly 130bhp. 3rd and 4th places in May at the twisty Crystal Palace were the best results so far.

At Hockenheim the following month, overheating was a problem

in the hot June weather and engine temperatures were kept manageable by the simple expedient of keeping the heaters full on, therefore acting as auxiliary radiators. The cars finished 5th and 6th, no match for the Alfa Romeos, but what the drivers thought of the comfort levels of their cars in the prevailing summer weather is not recorded. More rather average finishes followed until the 6-hour race at the Nürburgring in which both cars retired with broken rear trailing arm pivots. Obviously, the new tyres were managing to generate new levels of side-loading which, coupled with the Nürburgring's arduous layout, proved too much for these components.

In the Spa 24-hours Touring Car classic - four times longer than at the 'Ring - the offending suspension parts were suitably modified, but the two cars both succumbed to engine failure. They had been fitted with the extra oil tanks and driver-operated pumps, but these were thrown out at scrutineering. Whilst the Rhodes/Mabbs car lasted less than two hours, the Handley/Enever Cooper had less than 90 minutes to go when a connecting rod elected to ventilate the block. As it was leading its class, this failure - not common on the A-series engine - was particularly galling. Talking of engines, in the next race , the Gold Cup at Oulton Park,

Frantic stuff with both cars well over the kerb at Crystal Palace; Rhodes makes the grass cuttings fly as he holds off Fitzpatrick in a Broadpeed Escort.

the Rhodes car had a very special unit, thanks to the work of Harry Weslake, a man who knew more than most about cylinder head design. A capacity of 1299cc from an almost 'square' bore/stroke ratio and titanium conrods still left it outpaced behind the Fords, finishing twelfth.

It must be remembered that the Mini's biggest handicap was its engine/gearbox configuration, which meant that these two rap-idly-ageing, basic parts always had to be used together under the prevailing rules. It must also be remembered that circuit racing for the Mini was new stuff for Abingdon who may have comprised the best rally team mechanics in the world, but racing and rallying aren't identical disciplines and they were taking on teams who already had considerable experience and skill. In the circumstances Abingdon simply could not have done better.

In the last race of the year - and the last for a works Mini Cooper (not Clubman) - the Salzburgring Saloon Car Race in October, the results achieved by the two Johns turned out delightfully unrepre-sentative of the Leyland Mini's rather uninspiring season. After a tussle with the Alfas, Rhodes and Handley finished comfortably ahead of the entire field. The celebrations afterwards were memorable, but perhaps weren't actually remem-

The Works cars were used latterly in televised Autocross events; here is John Rhodes in the mud at Croft, Yorkshire, in February 1969.

bered too well the next morning. Both the factory team and Cooper's failed to win the championship title. Entering 1300cc cars to try for outright wins was the main reason, although Abingdon had no alternative. The title was won by the canny Jim Whitehouse of the Arden team who entered his driver, Alec Poole, in the one litre class.

More space under the bonnet

After 1969 the Clubman was more popular for racing, mainly because the longer bonnet allowed more room for crossflow heads with fuel injection that many were now using, as well as a front-mounted radiator. A growing number of strange devices would appear, most fitted with enormously wide tyres which may have enhanced the Mini's cornering grip, if not its looks, and with all manner of engine conversions from a 1660cc A-series engine - don't tell Sir George Harriman - to Richard

Longman's BDA-engined device, huge V8s shoehorned in, and even cars with more than one engine.

Twinny for Targa Florio

Not many people know this, but before John Cooper's now famous attempt to kill himself on the Kingston by-pass in such a contraption - described elsewhere - the factory asked Downton to enter a two-engined device in the 1963 Targa Florio. This circuit makes the Nürburgring seem like one of those tedious American ovals. At 44 miles to the lap, it was very dangerous and the two who were to drive the 'Twinny' were John Whitmore and Paul Frère, the journalist and racing driver. Aside from 100 miles-to-the-set-of-tyres consumption, overheating dogged the rear engine which was eventually switched off. Not fitted with an engine ejection device, the car struggled on to the finish, carrying this formidable

ballast in its rear. Interesting this may be, but this car, as with many Minis raced since the end of the sixties, wasn't really a Mini Cooper at all, any more than a Metro 6R4 is a Metro. Nor was it the only twin-engined Mini. A man in Hertfordshire has recently made an exceptionally professional job of putting two A-series units in one. Around in the mid-1960s, I seem to remember, was a car called a 'Twin Jag Min' which had two Jaguar engines in it. Either its creator was intrepid or a madman. Take your pick.

The truly golden days of the Mini and Mini Cooper were gone, although one must not forget the many, many successful drivers who started their racing in these little un-aerodynamic boxes. The irrepressible late Formula One World Champion, James Hunt, started out on the tracks in a modified Mini, whilst both the sadly posthu-

Leading club racing Mini exponent, Terry Harmer, harries a fat Anglia at Brands Hatch - a typical scene from the mid-60s.

mous 1970 F1 champion Jochen Rindt and fellow Austrian and three times F1 champion, Niki Lauda, opened their accounts competing in hillclimbs in Mini Coopers. Considering it was designed purely as a people's car, its competition record is fabulous, in the true meaning of the word.

A trio of French racers; Coopers have a cult following in mainland Europe too.

VIII

SUPER COOPERS: COOPER SPECIALS & SPECIALISTS

As a rough guide, here are some performance figures, given as averages from properly conducted road tests, from the standard Mini to a Cooper highly-tuned by a specialist tuning firm. All were taken during the Mini Cooper's heyday, during the first half of the 1960s.

is generally inversely proportionate to its longevity. A good example of this might be the Formula One qualifying engines of recent history, some of which produced maybe 1400bhp from a turbocharged 1.5-litres. Nicknamed 'grenades', they lasted fewer than half a dozen laps ... It

	0-60mph (secs)	Top speed (mph)
Standard Mini	28	72
997 Cooper	18	85
998 Cooper	16	90
1071 Cooper S	13	93
1275 Cooper S	11	97
Broadspeed Cooper 'S'	8	120

Since the 1960s car performance has changed more than we realise, perhaps; it's a sobering thought that a modern Skoda will outpace all the basic Mini Coopers, and a Fiat Tipo diesel all the S models. The 1965 Broadspeed, one of many Cooper Minis you could buy at the time which were faster than the standard product, was something else and really a road-racing car, being somewhat 'nervous' and probably not as durable as the less highly-stressed factory products. There is no doubt that BMC could have extracted far more power than it did from the production Mini Coopers - consider the Formula Junior outputs - but the specific power output of an engine

would hardly have made sense for BMC to sell to the public cars which had engines (Triumph Stag apart) that needed overhauling every 6 months.

Variations on the theme
While the Mini Cooper was in full swing, the factory obviously wondered from time to time about variations on the theme. One very interesting example was ADO 35, a very pretty Pinifarina Coupé, designed for the factory in the early 1960s, which Mini enthusiast, Richard Howard, found in a garden in Birmingham in 1988. Although these styling studies were meant to be destroyed if not used, this one - bodyshell only - seems to have been

Here is one that might have been a serious production car. Code-named ADO 35, it is an alloy bodied Pininfarina-designed coupé, featuring an MG Magnette grille but based entirely on Cooper S running gear. Owner and Mini afficionado Richard Howard is renovating this car but will probably have to have screens made specially.

The upmarket Mini that never was: Richard Howard's stylish MG Mini has comprehensive dash and Webasto roof.

What was clearly designed as an MG Mini does not have a hatch or boot lid; fuel tank is visible through the number-plate panel. The 1961 Mini parked alongside is a Hooper conversion, belonging not to Alan Whicker, but to Margot Fonteyn; it has clocked just 15,000 miles from new.

spirited out by a Longbridge employee. In traditional fashion, it lay untouched in his garden for over 20 years, suffering from the usual 'It's not for sale, I'm going to rebuild it' syndrome. Many a fine car has passed away because of this lazy attitude. Not this one, which already has been given Mini Cooper running gear under its gas-welded aluminium bodywork. Richard reckons the body was built by two people who didn't speak to each other, as each side is slightly different. In fact, this was done to try out different styling details on the same car. The proud new owner intends to rally his unique and asymmetric car, providing he can find the wherewithal to pay for a windscreen, which is of obscure Fiat origin and will have to be specially made. He also owns an MG Mini, again with Cooper running gear, which is endowed with a very

much more classy interior than the cars wearing Cooper badges. A one-off, it could be considered a sort of cross between a Mini Cooper and a Riley Elf.

There were a couple of exceptionally fine high-tech variations on the theme in the late '80s; the ERA Mini and the Sprintex super-charged BAC M-30. Another variation on the Mini Cooper script, which

ERA, a famous name from Britain's motor racing past, produced the turbocharged and luxuriously appointed M1 in the late '80s. Every car carried a numbered plaque. Maximum speed was claimed to be 115mph with the standing start quarter mile covered in just 16.6 seconds.

1993 Checker Mini - built to order by Marcos at Westbury, Wiltshire - has an authentic period feel, offering real performance at a realistic price.

could be considered a modern equivalent to the Broadspeed Cooper S, is the Checker Marcos Mini, a car made to look far more like the original Coopers than the latest Rover Phoenixes. It is made by Jem Marsh's Marcos Cars Ltd at Westbury in Wiltshire, England.

To extend further the Checker's '60s personality, Marcos has provided a central instrument binnacle, customised door furniture and period-style seats.

In 1976 the rights to the Mini Marcos were sold to Harold Dermott, who produced the Midas, seen here in 1988 guise. There was also a convertible. The body was made of injection moulded GRP and finish was of an extremely high standard. Running gear was ex-Metro, with hydragas front and rear trailing arm suspension. Sadly, the Corby factory burned down in the late '80s and efforts to revive production have so far been unsuccessful.

Originator of the Mini-Marcos and Mini-Jem, frog-like fibreglass devices with Cooper running gear, Marsh is perhaps better known as the purveyor of some of the hairiest-chested sports cars around in the Marcos Mantula and Mantara. The Checker Marcos Mini has a 1300cc engine with two 1.5in SU carburetters, an original-looking dashboard and interior, and even sports period racing mirrors - the chromium-plated, cone-shaped variety that we all used to put somewhere over the top of the head-

A Downton-tuned engine, worked over by Carlow Engineering in a 1275 Mk 3 Cooper S. This was the best way to get power with tractability in the '60s.

According to Jem Marsh, the ideal donor for a Mini Marcos is a Mini van, as it shares the same wheelbase. Cooper running gear will provide appropriate performance.

At Le Mans in 1967, a Mini Marcos was timed at 141mph on the Mulsanne Straight. It was running with a standard factory supplied Cooper engine and, a year earlier, a Marcos was the only British car to finish the gruelling 24-Hour race.

lamps. This car further differs from the new Cooper in being an accelerative match for almost any modern hot-hatch - just as that Broadspeed might be - thanks to some clever engine work by Richard Longman. However, this car is entirely docile and doesn't fidget about on any black top more uneven than a surface-plate. It was inspired by demand from Japan where it is selling very well. It can be bought here to special order, for less than ten grand.

Downton Engineering
A myriad of firms have gone in for Mini tuning. This is no surprise, since the early Mini's abundance of handling and roadholding ability was entirely counterbalanced by its lack of power. Agility without urge is manna to a engine tuner who needs a project to test his skills. In the Mini Cooper's competition heyday, the two most famous specialists were Downton and Broadspeed. It is generally reckoned that the boss of Downton, Daniel Richmond, was the first person to tune a Mini.

Downton Engineering was based in Downton, Wiltshire. It had been going for some while before 1959, but the Mini appealed to Richmond and he modified a car to such effect that it is now held in the Rover Heritage museum. Richmond was a quiet man, whose favourite pastimes - when he wasn't making Minis go faster than anyone else - was drinking Krug champagne and

fishing. Often, he would combine the two. The business side of the concern was successfully managed by his wife, Bunty, who made up for Daniel's reticence. Richmond's skills were such that he was a very frequent visitor to Longbridge and Abingdon, rubbing shoulders with Alec Issigonis, George Harriman, Alex Moulton (the rubber suspension and Hydrolastic suspension guru), Stuart Turner and John Cooper. He used to say his power outputs were arrived at by attention to detail and hard work - not by magic. It is notable that his workshops were always spotless; this is certainly a rare thing in the trade. He undertook special conversions for those who wanted the ultimate Mini Cooper. Steve McQueen, the Aga Khan, Dan Gurney and Enzo Ferrari were among his customers. Since these people could afford the best, one must assume that they went to the right place. Richmond's cylinder head modifications were eventually used exclusively in BMC's Group II 1275 engines. Apparently, they were virtually unchanged throughout their use by BMC until the Mini Cooper was put out to grass by Leyland in 1970.

Several now well-known people worked for Downton's. Jan Odor was a Hungarian refugee who seems to have been semi-adopted by Richmond. After a disagreement over company policy, he left to set up Janspeed. Gordon Spice and Richard Longman also were involved at one time or another. Sadly, Dan-

iel Richmond died in his mid-forties. A few years later his wife killed herself.

In a 1965 test of a Downton-modified Cooper, which quite happily reached 8000rpm, the power output was found to be improved by more than 20bhp, the top speed up by about 12mph and the time taken to reach 90mph was down by more than 15 seconds. The extraordinary thing about this improvement in outright power was that the 1275 Mini Cooper's famed top gear flexibilty was by no means sacrificed. In fact, even the maximum torque and its delivery characteristics were slightly improved into the bargain. Obviously, it took much longer to achieve such results than BMC could spend on every production engine, and this meant money. However, as this particular road-test car would reach 60mph less than one second slower than the E-type Jaguar, which was King of the Road at that time, Downton clients were well pleased, no doubt.

Broadspeed Engineering
Ralph Broad's activities in the early 1960s are covered in the chapter on racing. His company, Broadspeed, in Birmingham, England, also offered a tuning service for customers' Mini Coopers in 1965 one of his modified Mini Coopers was given a going-over in a road test. The particular car examined was really a Group II racing machine, less civilised than the Downton car. Having been

The Mini-based Deep Sanderson 301, built by Morgan racer Chris Lawrence (of Lawrencetune), has strengthened steel chassis with fibreglass body. It cost £750 in kit form in 1963, The Cooper engine was mid-mounted and the engine cover hinged backward (i.e. the whole back end of the car).

Transverse, mid-mounted Cooper engine installed in the Deep Sanderson (1963) with special manifolding and huge, side-draught carburettor.

overbored by 'twenty thou' (0.020in), giving the now well-recognised 1293cc and spinning to 8500rpm, it produced almost 120bhp, which gave a top speed of just over 120mph. It was said it would have gone 10mph faster were the final drive ratio a bit higher (*i.e.* numerically lower). Modern performance figures, indeed, but you wonder what a current motoring magazine would make of the oil consumption - 75 miles to the pint.

Taurus and Speedwell

Other tuners whose Coopers were fed to the public at that time were Taurus and Speedwell. Taurus had premises near Ladbroke Grove, West London. Like Downton they were pretty quick off the mark, offering a useful increase in performance on the first of the Coopers before the model was one year old. With only a Stage One conversion, the Taurus-modified 997cc car would have very similar performance to the 1275 S Cooper. When they turned their hand to this model, once again they achieved useful, if not startling, improvements in acceleration, but with complete tractability. If also a

David Ogle's automotive design firm was trendy in the early '60s, with styling carried on by John Ogier and Tom Karen after Ogle's death in a road accident in 1963. Projects included a study on the Daimler SP250, and the Reliant Scimitar and Robin became a reality; there was an Ogle Aston Martin show car at the Montreal Show in 1972. The Ogle Mini of the mid-60s was a rotund coupé with Cooper running gear.

With fibreglass body and Cooper mechanicals, the curvaceous Ogle possessed an excellent power-to-weight ratio.

Stage One conversion, this did not cover balancing and, on the 1275 engine, this was more noticeable an omission than on the smaller-engined car.

John Cooper

Perhaps one should not really add John Cooper's firm in south-west London to the list of tuning specialists, as his company was inextricably bound up with the parent car maker. However, he *was* responsible for that daring contraption, the Twini. With a fuel-injected Cooper engine in a (front) subframe at each end, it had 175bhp. Since each axle was being driven separately, in theory, the top speed would be similar for a single-engined car of half the power. However, acceleration was improved thanks to superior traction, but not by as much as a 175bhp Mini with all that power coming from one output shaft. Whatever, it was fast enough. Flying along the Kingston by-pass one night, the bracket on the rear set-up that held a steering arm steady - making it, in effect, a wishbone - detached itself from the subframe, thanks to some corrosion around the weld. The ensuing end-over-end cracked Cooper's skull and frightened a following motorist into a nervous breakdown. That the motorist tried (unsuccessfully) to

sue, sounds very *avant-garde* for those days - perhaps it was an American? Any possible plans the factory might have had to develop this layout for racing were promptly knocked on the head by Harriman.

Lawrencetune

Some months before this mishap, another firm based in west London, Lawrencetune Engines Ltd of Acton, was building a twin-engined (2400cc), fuel-injected Mini Cooper-engined single-seater. With attention from Daniel Richmond, the total engine power was around 200bhp and the device was to be driven in hillclimbs by Reg Phillips. Chris Lawrence, the proprietor, closely linked with Morgans as a tuner and having co-driven a Plus 4 to 13th place at Le Mans in 1963, also built a Deep Sanderson 310 Coupé with a highly-tuned, mid-mounted Mini Cooper engine, and this car was accepted for the '63 Le

Mans. Another attractive, low-slung, mid-engined sports racer of the early '70s using Cooper S motivation was the Unipower.

Many Mini owners of the 1960s could not, of course afford the Cooper version and some had budgets that would not run to a trip to one of the tuning firms to fettle their own car. But they still craved a Cooper. Rob Giordanelli, once a proud hot Mini owner and now a leading Alfa restorer, says that when you saw a Cooper badge whizzing towards you in those days, you swivelled your eyes around as it passed to see if it had brightwork around the side windows. 'They would change the badges, the grille and spray the roof,' he explains, 'But they never bothered with the window frames'. No chrome equalled fake!

Later on, as people generally became more affluent, all manner of tricks were performed on the

A German owner's rainbow paint job brightens up the day; but was it conceived as a hangover cure or could he just not decide on a colour?

The 'Hot Rat', seen at the Dutch International Mini Meeting at Terwolde, 1992; after such a lavish paint job, you wonder what happened to the wheels ...

Mini and Mini Cooper by owners in search of more performance. Using the A-series engine, the maximum capacity with the standard stroke is around 1293cc. Stunts such as offset-grinding of the big-end journals will yield up to 1385cc displacement. It is generally reckoned Richard Longman - who must have won as many races in Minis as anyone - has the current A-series record at 1660cc, using a highly expensive crankshaft. Given that maximum bore size, it must have a stroke equal to the old Jaguar XK

Mini Sprints were low, but this Nostalgia takes roof lowering to extremes; even the bonnet - ex Morris Minor - has been lowered to expose the engine.

Looking more like a box than a Cooper, the 1990 Maguire has broad, one-piece extensions front and rear with extravagant air scoops for brake and engine cooling.

Neat frontal treatment of 1966 Radford 1000 has driving lights set in the grille.

Luxurious Radford de Ville 1300 used the 1275 S engine, and was popular with the late '60s glitterati.

As sumptuous as a Cooper could get in the '60s, this Radford de Ville has leather seats, wood-rim wheel, walnut door trim cappings and a comprehensive, rationalised dashboard.

engine! Running on methanol, it has around 150bhp at the flywheel. However, you cannot make a Stradivarius from a railway sleeper and the A-series engine is now eclipsed by younger designs. There is a perfectly refined and docile Honda 4-cylinder cooking family-car unit which manages 170bhp from 1797cc, without forced induction. This is a higher specific output than the Longman bomb. More and more Mini owners, it seems, are turning to other engines for their thrills.

As with the pure racing cars when the rules began to change in the 1970s, many of the modified road cars have long since ceased to be Mini Coopers - if they ever were - but some are intriguing, nonetheless. There is currently a car with a three-cylinder Daihatsu turbo-diesel engine under its bonnet. Intriguing enough, but that it all fits in with its in-line gearbox and front-mounted radiator without resort to a Clubman front-end is even more so. Performance is about equal to the 1071 S Cooper, except that fuel consumption is around half that used by the Cooper, at 60mpg average. Driving it is even more fascinating when the absence of transmission whine is noted, apart from the strange engine sounds inherent in a three-pot turbo.

Another brave soul has intro-

Rear treatment of Radford de Ville hatchback shows interesting way of handling the numberplate location; rear seat folds away to provide considerable luggage space. The Radford 1000 alongside looks positively tame by comparison.

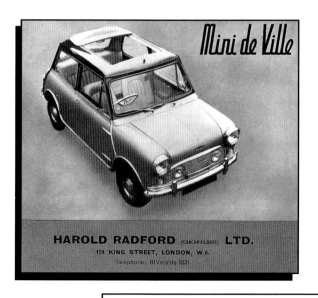

Mini de Ville

HAROLD RADFORD (COACHBUILDERS) LTD.
124 KING STREET, LONDON, W.6.
Telephone: RIVerside 8831

luxurious
comfort
in a
MINI *way*

THE MOST LUXURIOUS SMALL CAR EVER OFFERED FOR PRESTIGE MOTORING IN BUSY TOWN TRAFFIC

As one of the few remaining craftsmen coachbuilders we have developed three super luxury versions of the amazing Mini range. These cars have been fitted with every imaginable extra and retrimmed to the very highest standards of comfort and luxury.

MINI de VILLE "GRANDE LUXE" ON AUSTIN OR MINI COOPER £1,088. ex works

MINI de VILLE BEL AIR
Slightly reduced specification but retaining all the most desirable adaptations. Car plus £223 (all Mini models). ex works

MINI de VILLE—De Luxe
This car has the accent on limousine comfort but retains most outward features of the ordinary Mini. Car plus £87-10-0 (all Mini models). ex works

Modified cars can be supplied based on any one of the Mini-range or customers' own cars modified to specification or personal requirements.
Basketwork optional on all models.

HAROLD RADFORD (COACHBUILDERS) LTD
124 KING STREET, LONDON, W.6 Telephone: RIVERSIDE 8831
Officially appointed Specialist Coachbuilders to Rolls-Royce and Bentley
ILLUSTRATIONS BY KIND PERMISSION OF "THE MOTOR".

MINI DE VILLE
SPECIFICATIONS

MINI DE VILLE "GRANDE LUXE" - Based on Mini-Cooper Car

1. Car completely re-sprayed and retrimmed to customer's choice from wide range of colour schemes.
2. Front seats remodelled for additional comfort.
3. Electric windows on both doors.
4. Swivelling front quarter vents on both doors.
5. Walnut finish fascia panel with wooden door fillets.
6. Full "Motorway" Instrumentation - Speedo, Rev. Counter, Ammeter, Oil Guage, Clock, Parking Lights, Headlamp Flasher, Map Reading Light, Individual Side Parking Light Switch, Cigar Lighter, Volume Control, Revolving Ash Tray, Automatic Light to Cubby Hole Door.
7. Grab Handle - Passenger Cantrail.
8. Nylon rugs, front and rear. Matching carpet on door kicking panels.
9. Webasto roof.
10. Padded visors.
11. Laminated steering wheel.
12. Passenger reading light.
13. Parking/Winking lights.
14. New grille with two recessed spot lights - spread and long beam.
15. Recessed reversing light under rear bumper.
16. Badge bar.
17. Distinctive headlamp cowlings.
18. Chrome exhaust extension.
19. Rear window demister.
20. Radio, Speakers front and rear. Roof Manual Aerial.
21. Extensive sound insulation.
22. Front seat extension links.
23. Door night caution lights.
24. Two horns.
25. Arm rests to Front Doors.
26. Box Arm Rest between front seats.
27. Chromium Body mouldings.

Price **£1,088 ex works**
including Mini-Cooper Car

MINI DE VILLE "BEL AIR" - plus any Car of the Mini range

1. Front seats remodelled for extra comfort. Extension links on front seat mounting.
2. Combined glove-box and centre armrest.
3. Door armrests.
4. Ash trays, both doors.
5. Wind down window, driver's door.
6. Webasto roof.
7. Basket work, side panels, doors and quarters.
8. Radio - Roof Manual Aerial.
9. Distinctive headlamp cowlings.

Complete Conversion Price £223 ex works

MINI DE VILLE "DE LUXE" - plus any Car of the Mini range

1. Front seats remodelled for extra comfort. Extension links on front seat mounting.
2. Door armrests.
3. Ash tray, both doors.
4. Wind down window, driver's door.
5. Distinctive headlamp cowlings.
6. Grab handle - Passenger Cantrail.

Complete Conversion Price £87. 10. 0. ex works

Harold Radford (Coachbuilders) Ltd. _____ 124 KING STREET, LONDON, W.6. Telephone: RIVerside 8831

Radford Mini conversions were purchased by many famous names in the Swinging '60s. This original brochure shows what you got for £1088, which included the cost of the Mini Cooper.

MINI de VILLE

APPROVED OPTIONAL EXTRAS

1. Trimming in leather instead of P.V.C.
2. Webasto Roof Deflector
3. Wing Mirrors.
4. Winding Type Windows.
5. Ash Trays to both doors.
6. Wicker Look (Basket Work) English or Italian Cloth.
7. Arm rest to rear squab.
8. Dog Venetian Blind.
9. Demister Panel to rear glass - stick on type.
10. Brooks Retractable Straps.
11. Underseal.
12. 1 set (4) Ace Rims.
13. Lucas Screen Jets.
14. Fire Extinguisher.
15. Engine :- Speedwell Conversion. Extra for brake-lining & Servo.
16. Frankfurt F.M. Radio Set ultra short-wave.
17. S/F Extra Tank.
18. Change tyres for inner tube preference.
19. Kenlow Thermostatic Fan.
20. Special sliding and reclining seat to match P.V.C. Hide extra.
21. White walled tyres.
22. Twin air horns.

Harold Radford (Coachbuilders) Ltd.
124 KING STREET, LONDON, W.6. Telephone : RIVerside 8831

duced a Lancia twin-cam and its five-speed gearbox into the bonnet space of his Mini. Nicknamed 'Mincia', the performance is hectic, although the radiator on this car now has set up home in the boot, so it isn't really a practical road car. The usual American V8s have appeared in Minis, but mainly for drag-racing - in a straight line: the handling of a Mini can be affected with the addition of a cast-iron lump weighing half as much as the whole car! Several other adventurous owners have emulated Longman and used BDA Ford Cosworth units, and so forth, on top of the Mini gearbox, but although a 'box can now be had with five forward speeds, thanks to Jack Knight, the basic item is not the most reliable gearbox in the world, especially when asked to accommodate large increases in torque.

Jack Knight Developments

Jack Knight Developments has been offering a five-speed gearbox for Minis for several years now. Jack Knight ran a small reconditioning business, also in south-west London, and built a Formula 500 racing car in the late 1940s, getting to know John Cooper (and, presumably, Issigonis) in the process. He went on to make transmission parts for Cooper and competition ones for BMC, going on to manufacture the internals to make a five-speed 'box for the Mini. Unlike more modern units, including the current JKD one, it retained the 1:1 top gear ratio, having four extra ones squeezed in, where there were three before. Unless the owner changed the final drive ratio, his top speed - even if he also found a useful power increase, that is - would be the same for the same revs, so no drop in engine speed and noise on the motorway either. The modern five-speeder from Jack Knight Developments now has an overdrive 5th ratio and is made in road and competition guise. A six-speed is under development. At least this configuration makes sense on a relatively low-powered vehicle like a Mini. The current crop of 500 horsepower, megabuck superbarges with six-speeds are just being silly. JKD have also built a twin-cam head, for sale in Japan. Very compact, it is not cheap, however, but should eventually become available in the UK. five-speed transmissions for Minis are also being supplied by Minisport, a Lancashire-based company. For both this unit and the new JKD one, the buyer will need a touch more than £1000. Machining always was one of the most expensive of manufacturing processes.

Janspeed

Another successful tuner of Minis who has survived from long ago is Jan Odor, who set up Janspeed Engineering after leaving Downton in 1962. Based in Salisbury, no more than four miles from his old employer, he now operates from a 30,000 sq ft factory which used to see production of Spitfires in the war. Now employing nearly 100 people, Janspeed has mainly made its mark with its free-flow exhaust systems, which can be purchased for almost every make and model of car from Minis to Porsches. It also supplies carburettor kits, modified cylinder heads, camshafts, turbocharger conversions, uprated suspension and brake components. Janspeed has a whole department given over to Mini conversion and competition parts, and is a leader in the go-faster market, where so many other firms from the 1960s just never survived. Jan Odor's son Keith - curiously styled O'Dor now - is a front-runner in the British Touring Car Championship these days.

Kent Automotive Developments

A more recently-formed company is Kent Automotive Developments, which was established by Gary Oldfield in 1988. Already a well-respected R&D engineer, Gary worked for Weslake and Piper. From a partnership formed with Colin Woolard in 1990 has evolved a rather beautiful twin-cam, 16-valve cylinder head which fits on to the A-series block. In its mild form it produces around 110bhp and the torque figure is positively mouth-watering at 115lb ft at 3600rpm - all this from making use of the 1275cc underneath. It isn't cheap, of course, but as somebody famous once said 'The quality will still be

One owner's neat solution to the dash panelling of a left-hand-drive Mk 1 Morris Cooper.

enjoyed long after the sting of the purchase price is forgotten' - or something like that ...

David Vizard

It's time to mention the guru of the A-series. David Vizard made his name showing people how to tune Mini engines during the 1960s. He's done more development work on these engines than possibly anyone else; especially - he would have you believe - the factory, and the difference is that David has passed on his research through his book *Tuning BL's A-Series Engine*, a work which sets the standard for tuning manuals.

An apprentice aerospace engineer in 1960 at Smiths Industries, Cheltenham, David was busy with such projects as the world's first automatic landing system and, in his spare time, running around in a Sprite-engined A30, when he discovered the Mini. To be precise, he found a couple of pals with Minis were blowing him off on the corners; soon the attraction was irresistible and he, too, became a Mini owner. He'd built his own workshop flow bench by 1962 from two second-hand vacuum cleaners and,

by 1965, was in the Mini tuning business.

Few people were familiar with engine dynamics and, during the late 1960s, Oselli lent him dynamometer space. 'I went to Tecalemit Jackson at Plymouth, too, which was the same dyno as Richard Longman used.' says David. By 1970 when his flow bench operation had been developed to British Standards, David had a substantial advantage in the tuning world. 'The most powerful engines are built by people who don't have access to a dynamometer,' he jokes, meaning that, without this facility, claims for power output are worthless. People who don't believe in flow benches are those who don't have one and have never used one!'

By 1975, though, his health had taken a downturn, mostly, acording to his doctor, as a result of grinding too many valves and skimming too many heads. It was the lungs. No-one hangs around in a cold, damp climate if they can help it, and David moved to Tucson, Arizona, where it's hot and dry, moving to his present home at Riverside, California, in 1980. He has a $500,000 workshop at Riverside

which, he says in a West Country burr unchanged by a decade of West Coast living, 'would make most racing teams green with envy!' Here he has a computerised dynamometer, computerised flow bench and a research and development capability on performance testing which few can ever hope to match. 'Five years ago, I could do tests in the workshop which even GM couldn't handle. The difference is that professional race engine builders have to develop their engine during the winter, then freeze that design and sell it to whoever's going to use it during the season. I'm on a twelve month development schedule with my work. And, at my place, I can do in one week what it takes six months to do on a regular dyno.'

What has this to do with the man who's name is synonymous with tuning Minis? Well, it seems he's managed to do more work on the A-series engine since he's been in the US than during the preceding decade. 'I've been having a crusade on cams,' he explained. 'I can point the finger at Rover and accuse them of using cam designs which are at least 20 years old. The 649 cam was actually designed in 1958 and, 30 years on, they're still selling the same cam! Recently, we've been looking at a concept which has been tried before: the 'scatter pattern', where cam timing differs on each cylinder, and we've picked up 4bhp on it. Leyland lacked the ability to put glamour into sport,'

he went on,'they should have brought out a new cam every year and marketed it as the latest tuning mod.' Like the Ford Rallysport operation.

Dave was always a competition enthusiast, having campaigned a 1275 Cooper S in 1970-71, with notable success at the Prescott hillclimb when he was faster even than F1 machinery. He raced an Avenger with works support from 1973 to 1976, with conspicuous success, and Vizard-tuned engines regularly produced more power than class rivals. He returns most Summers from the States to keep an eye on the British scene.

'Not many people are aware of the philosophy of popular engine trends', says Vizard, referring to the marketing of performance tuning. 'The most easily tuneable engine is not necessarily the most popular. The A-series engine had the greatest margin for tuning, whereas the Ford twin-cam which succeeded it as the popular motor in the sixties was difficult to modify without a budget and much more hard-core engineering know how. People who tuned the A-series engines often weren't any good after that engine died away. There's a formula for the popular engine,' he continued. 'Availability, cost, know-how and results. You have to have these in order for an engine to be widely used and, of these factors, common know-how is crucial. This accounts for the popularity of the Chevrolet lump in the US, when the Ford V8 is almost the same engine. The Ford is a successful engine, but there's no common know-how about tuning it. Ford do market tuning equipment, but they need to educate the school-leaver, say, about how to use it. After all, someone who grows up with hotted-up Fords will most likely be buying top-of-the-range Fords in twenty years' time. As it is, they'll never challenge Chevrolet in the States. They need me to write a tuning manual!'

He is very proud of his A-series tuning manual. 'The book allows me to build people's cars for them by proxy,' he says 'They do it themselves, my way. I sponsored my daughter Samantha's drag racing 1275 Mini GT - it's less dangerous than road-racing - and the drag-strip is totally related to engine performance. Her Mini is good enough to regularly shut down V8s and 3.0-litre Capris, and if anyone says they can beat her in a similar car, they're welcome to prove it. In fact, here's my challenge. If anyone can beat 14.07 seconds, 99mph, at Long Marston, with a minimum weight of 1556lb, less driver, then I'll pay £200 against the official RAC clocks. And we'll put them up at Riverside and they can show me how to build a drag race engine. If not, they can buy my book!'

In actual fact, Dave Vizard has by now probably done more work on Chevrolet engines than Mini engines. Other titles he's written since being in the States include *How to Rebuild Your Small-Block Chevy*, *How to Modify Your Pinto*, *Nitrous Oxide Injection*, and *How to Build Horsepower*. He also holds some 45 patents on everything from fuel additives to silencers. 'I give the customer a guarantee,' he says. 'If it's not the best there is, the customer doesn't pay.' It's mostly consultancy jobs now for the man who doesn't work for a living. 'I've done research for all the major speed companies.' he says.

However, it seems Dave Vizard is still very much remembered over here as the 'Wizard' of the Mini engine. He was technical editor of the script of a one hour video for the Mini's 30th Aniversary party, which shows to what extent Minis can be tuned. Filming was done at Jan Odor's Janspeed workshops, with input from John Cooper and Paddy Hopkirk. 'The script is heavily reliant on my book, saying 'refer to page so-and-so for a full description.' Everything is fast moving, so the viewer is pointed in the right direction if he wishes to know more,' says Dave. 'I've enormous respect for Jan, and the video was a good opportunity for renewing my aquaintance with him.' The video will be available from August Bank Holiday. Any Mini fanciers out there keen to see-off the Cooper S had better go for it.

Oselli Engineering

Those who don't wish to throw away their A-series heads, whether down to cost or originality reasons, should pay a visit to Oselli Engineering in

Oxford. This is another 1960s company that has managed, like Janspeed, to survive into the nervous nineties. Founded in '62 by David Oldham, Oselli are sometimes called the 'A-series Supremos', such is their experience and expertise, much of the groundwork for which was learned preparing cars for rallying.

Minisprint Engineering Developments

The company MED, acronym for Minisprint Engineering Developments, is a little newer than Oselli, having been started up in 1981 by Steve Witham. Based in Leicester, MED also works wonders on the old A-series engines, to such good effect that it supplies many of the top names in the tuning business. In other words, wherever you buy that super new engine from, it may have parts in it - crankshaft, block, head, perhaps - that came from MED in the first place.

There are many other places to chose from for improving the performance of your Mini. The Avonbar Performance Centre in Weybridge, Jonspeed Racing at Nuneaton, Green and White Mini Spares, Mini Spares Centre in London, N11 and Keith Ripp's Ripspeed at N18, are all specialists for the A-series engine. Many of these companies can also supply suspension and braking system improvements to help take care of the extra power generated. Of course, this is not a definitive list of all the firms available with expertise in tuning the Mini. The owner of this car is truly spoiled for choice.

Mini Cooper

IX

COOPERS
ANCIENT
AND MODERN

The Longbridge PR machine is a little understaffed: Pam Wearing handles things virtually single-handed, as far as I could tell, so there was a slight hiatus in getting my factory excursion cleared and even longer to get hold of a Rover Cooper to try out. Don't get me wrong, this isn't sour grapes; in my position of humble writer I was receiving privileged treatment, anyway: the instant response is reserved for journals interested in covering current production models as opposed to people like me doing retrospectives on a 30-year-old car like the Cooper. Pam pulled out all the stops once I was in the system. When the car was delivered - how's that for service? - I was not disappointed; a pristine Cooper in red with white stripes to play with for a few days. And it had only 1200 miles on the clock.

It certainly is a lot of fun to drive; a positive breath of fresh air, in fact, especially for anyone who normally drives a modern car. It's

The test car was delivered by Longbridge's PR people, and provided the author with a few days of motoring thrills.

The regular Cooper steering wheel has always been reminiscent of that of a double decker bus, but the modern cars have a good leather rim wheel; dash is walnut veneer, instruments are grouped in front of the driver.

so small you feel you can reach out and touch each corner, which is actually not far from the truth; you're almost clipping apexes with your own body, which makes it the closest thing to a go-cart besides, well, a go-kart. Because this is a new car, everything is very tight and responsive; a restored car feels looser.

Childrens' favourites

There are slight frustrations about the ergonomics of the new Cooper. Because the front seats have headrests, the back of the seat doesn't tip fully forward, becoming trapped against the roof. This makes it virtually impossible to get into the back, and getting a baby into his seat meant kneeling on the front seat and placing him over the top. This struggle was overcome by our four-year-old, now a Cooper devotee,

Mostly because of its four-speed gearbox, the Cooper is not the best of motorway cruisers; far better to pick the fast A and B roads.

for Superperformance!

AUSTIN MINI SALOON COOPER

KEL 236

Left & centre: This original brochure from the early '60s emphasizes that the Austin Cooper is very much a car for the enthusiast.

has become a highly-civilized environment. There are still a number of storage spaces which were heralded in the 1959 promo film where family luggage, most of it in tidy rectangular boxes, was stashed away: under the back seat, in the door pockets (where in Mini folklore you were invited to guess how many milk bottles would fit in each), in

AUSTIN MINI SALOON COOPER *...for the enthusiast!*

with a spot of in-car mountaineering. But however popular it might be with the kids, today's Mini is not the family car of BMC's 1959 advertising.

On the other side of the coin, the front seats themselves may appear to be bulky, but they are a huge improvement on original Cooper equipment; neatly upholstered in leather and padded in the right places to provide support for

sides, thighs and the small of the back. They are also more comfortable!

With the upmarket touch of the walnut dash, the Cooper's interior

1993 Rover Cooper's plugs and electrics are protected from moisture by a plastic shield; injection engine with ancilliaries makes for a pretty crowded under-bonnet environment.

104

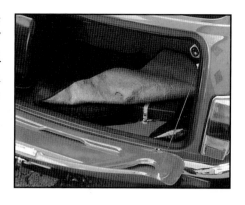

The modern Cooper's boot space is somewhat compromised by the fuel tank, left, the wide spare tyre, and battery box. A pushchair would not fit, so it's not exactly an ideal family car.

cubby-holes either side of the back seat. Different is the glove locker in the dash, which would have been fresh air in the days of the central speedo binnacle.

You get a good Rover-branded radio in the new Cooper, although the radio is an anachronism. Instrumentation is still minimal, but for this you could read 'refreshingly unpretentious'. Elsewhere in the dash is a clock, mounted over in the centre where the speedo used to be; the rev-counter and speedo are in front of the driver and there are fuel and temperature gauges.

It's on country lanes that the Cooper is a real pleasure to drive - you can happily swoop around bends and don't seem to loose any speed on a cross-country journey. Its progress is so seductive that you soon get to feel there's no need to slow down for bends. Or is there? Perhaps that's the one flaw with Cooper driving in the '90s, because these days there's vastly more traffic on the roads than there was in the car's heyday which means hazards around every turn. The temptation to exploit the Cooper's handling may be just too great, behaviour which might have been all very well in the '60s when there was every chance of a clear run. Although the use of only four gears on a B road is not a problem - only rather unusual in this day and age - there is a temptation to avoid changing down for a bend because you know the revs will soar and the engine scream. Ratios are quite

widely spaced and, although a reasonable compromise, the gearbox cries out for five gears when so much of today's motoring takes place on motorway-standard roads. You could relegate the Cooper to the rôle of second car for weekend pleasure use, which is fine if you can afford it. On a long run the four-speed box could become a serious drawback because high engine revs will be wearing, for you as well as the motor. It's a mark of how accustomed one has become to the five-speed box that after several days' use, I still found myself looking for fifth in the Cooper. If you want to achieve high speed, you have to use the revs to the full in each gear, building speed as the revs soar, and this is especially true when overtaking. Turn-in to corners is beautifully neat, and if you find you're getting oversteer, the slightest slackening of the accelerator will bring the nose back in line.

The years have been kind to the Cooper. There is no suggestion of unwillingness to start, unlike the cars of friends in youthful years which needed pushing. This unerring reliability is no doubt due to the fuel injection, and the engine is also quick to warm up. The starter switch is on the steering column, rather than on the floor where it once was.

Striking a pose

It didn't take long to find my ideal driving position although the seat was fully back on its runners, and I still had to adopt the splayed legs

posture. Somehow this was acceptable in a car the Cooper's size, whereas it wouldn't be in an Alfa 75 (my regular transport these days). On a cross-country run you're too busy hustling it around the corners to notice the driving position much anyway. It is interesting to reflect on the Cooper's proportions. When it came out it was thought of as a small car, of course, and was judged against the big cars of the day, like Crestas and Jaguars. Now, those cars are no bigger than the middle-ranking family-sized cars, yet the Mini endures as the archetypal small car. Even so, appreciating it as a family car against something like a Saab 900 is difficult to swallow; it doesn't really rate as a family car at all except on shortish jaunts. We're back to ergonomics again. The boot won't accommodate a baby buggy now, because the space is taken up with the single petrol tank and spare wheel. The boot floor cover resembles a child's papier mâché fort as it has to accommodate a bulkier spare wheel. Carrying capacity is thus severely compromised; but then the Cooper was never conceived as a load carrier.

Third World edge

Although the modern Cooper is far more refined than its ancestor, you can still tell its origins are back in 1959 when you notice the crinkles in the metal of the bonnet edge where it curves. Today, it looks

The Cooper's small size and agility make it a key player to have in your arsenal when motoring in the city.

Bus driver's steering wheel and central instrument binnacle were features of this 1964 Austin Mini Cooper. (Courtesy Andrew Morland)

Crammed engine compartment of the same car. (Courtesy Andrew Morland)

*Beautifully preserved
1964 Austin Mini Cooper.
(Courtesy Andrew
Morland)*

*Superb 1964 Morris Mini
Cooper pictured at Brit-
ain's Silverstone race
circuit. (Courtesy Andrew
Morland)*

CHOICE OF E

Specially develop

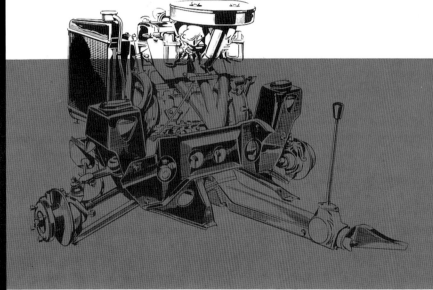

The amazing success of the incredible Mini-Cooper 'S' saloon is exceedingly well known. Outright winner of the 1964 Monte Carlo Rally, its versatility is now even further enhanced by the availability of 970 c.c. or 1275 c.c. power units.

Vital to any competition car is an efficient braking system. The power to stop quickly is inherent in the 'S'-type saloon. The 7½ in. (0·19 m.) disc brakes on the front wheels are a further development from those successfully designed specially for the Mini-Cooper.

There can be no lack of confidence when motoring at high speed because safety is a built-in feature of the 'S'-type Mini-Cooper!

Emphasis is definitely on the instrument panel in competition events. And there is no difficulty in deciphering what is happening in the 'S'-type Mini-Cooper. The instruments are contained in a centrally placed oval nacelle, the speedometer contains a fuel gauge, and separate gauges are provided for water temperature and oil pressure. Concealed illumination is provided for night driving.

positively third world.

When it comes to ride, things are firm yet compliant, which means you bounce along on an undulating surface. You have to hang on when going flat-out under those circumstances although it doesn't affect the car's ability in corners; you can still toss it in and it still goes round. You could even say it's user-friendly in that it seems to relish being driven in this way.

The view from the driving seat

The cabin of the Mk 2 Austin Cooper S was a decidedly austere environment; bakelite wheel, lonely instrument binnacle, sliding windows and deep door pocket was all you got.

This original sales brochure celebrates the 1964 Monte Carlo win and offers two engine capacities for the Morris Mini Cooper 'S.

is mostly road and scenery, but what little you see of the car is aesthetically pleasing - the rounded shoulders of the front wings present an amiable shape. The particular shade of red of this car seemed to turn heads - or was it that the Cooper itself commands attention 30 years on? Some people were actually surprised that the Mini was still in production, let alone that you can still buy a Cooper.

At speed you're bounced around in a way that you wouldn't be in a long-wheelbase car. At 85mph there was beginning to be a build-up of

wind noise from the A-pillars; and at 4500rpm it was doing 90mph, with more to come. The brakes were excellent, hauling it down to pedestrian levels efficiently and with no dramas. Just what you'd expect from a new car, but perhaps not necessarily from a 30-year-old design. You have to rivet your right foot to the floorboards to keep it all going as fast as possible. Speed is built by getting the revs up, backing off, pressing on again and repeating the process until the desired velocity is achieved, then it's lift off for the corner - a confidence

lift almost, and begin all over again.

Ancient and modern

It's easy enough to evaluate a modern Rover Cooper with its contemporaries. But what about a classic Cooper S with a modern hatch? Recently I had to perform this task for *Performance Car* Magazine using a Citroën AX GT and a 20-year-old Cooper S.

Shouldn't be too difficult, I thought; after all, they were both 'state of the art' models in their particular market segment, at the time of their inception. On paper it

FOR SUCCESSFUL RALLYING TODAY'S CAR IS A MINI

MOTOR week ending January 22 1966

14 outright wins for Mini in 1965

Fourteen outright wins for the fantastically successful Mini-Cooper 'S' in major international events. In 1965, too, the European Rally Driver's Championship was won in a BMC Mini-Cooper 'S'—the first time it's been won with a British car!

Here's 1965's record sequence of wins:—

* MONTE CARLO RALLY (2ND SUCCESSIVE YEAR)
* BASCO-NAVARRAIS, SPAIN
* FLOWERS AND PERFUMES RALLY, FRANCE
* CIRCUIT OF IRELAND (3RD SUCCESSIVE YEAR)
* BODENSEE-NEUSIEDLERSEE RALLY, AUSTRIA
* GENEVA RALLY
* CZECHOSLOVAKIAN RALLY
* POLISH RALLY
* RALLY OF 1000 LAKES, FINLAND
* MUNICH-VIENNA-BUDAPEST RALLY
* HUBERTUS RALLY, GERMANY
* FLANDRES-HAINAUT RALLY, FRANCE
* PETROLE RALLY, FRANCE
* RAC RALLY OF GREAT BRITAIN

Get the feel of success! Test-drive the rally-winning Mini-Cooper 'S' today!

AUSTIN/MORRIS
MINI COOPER'S'

THE BRITISH MOTOR CORPORATION LIMITED, BIRMINGHAM AND OXFORD. OVERSEAS BUSINESS:
BMC EXPORT SALES LIMITED, BIRMINGHAM AND 41-46 PICCADILLY, LONDON W.1.

BMC advertisement from Motor *magazine of January 22nd 1966 capitalises on the Cooper's competition success in 1965.*

looks as though the AX could well be the modern equivalent of the Cooper S because, unlike the other car often cited as the modern day equivalent - the Peugeot 205 GTi - the AX has carbs.

In truth, though, it's more complicated than that, for lurking at the back of your mind is the fact that, three decades on, they're still making the Mini and it isn't just a question of addressing aesthetics, ergonomics and performance and saying this one's got vinyl seats, the other's got electric windows and so on. The AX has a cd of 0.32, and there's hardly a wind-resisting facet to be seen. The little old Cooper has

those jigging seams up its roof pillars and looks positively dumpy, cute, even, beside it. No, you have to get behind the wheel to assess the true character of both cars and their relationship to one another.

The pair I tried were a brand new AX GT belonging to journalist Peter McSean, and the Mini Cooper

1966 original sales brochure emphasizes Cooper S features and reminds potential purchasers of the 1965 Monte Carlo win. You, too, can be a rally star!

S of Mini Cooper Register PRO Philip Splett. The AX was not yet run-in and therefore not in a position to be fairly matched performance-wise with the Cooper S, but was nonetheless sufficiently representative of the breed. Splett's car was a Mk III 1275, built in 1972 and owned by him since 1974, when it had only got 4000 miles on the clock. Even now, it shows a mere 33,000. Philip explained that it began its life by being sent straight from the factory to Downton Engineering, where its suspension was converted back to the original 'dry' rubber cone specification. It was fitted with a stage 3 head, which endowed it with 1.48in

The Mini Cooper 'S' - back to the future

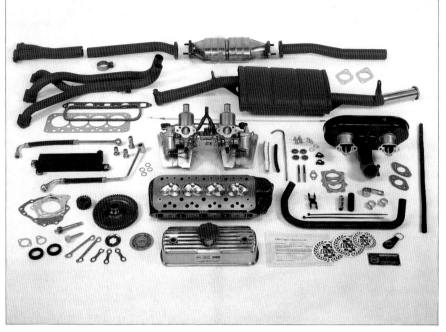

The Mini Cooper legend was created by John Cooper, whose mechanical career started in a small BMC garage in Surbiton. It was here, during the late 1940s, that Charles Cooper and his son John founded the Cooper Car Company to design and construct racing cars.

Their first car, the Cooper 500, was an amazing racer with its 500cc motorcycle engine.

With drivers like Stirling Moss at the wheel, the Cooper 500 achieved wide acclaim and won many championships.

Cooper Racing Cars were exported to all parts of the world, and were raced successfully by all of the great front line drivers - Brabham, McLaren, Fangio, Hawthorn, Salvadori, Surtees, Stewart and Rindt. Cooper Cars soon became the World's largest manufacturer of pure-bred racing cars, and achieved the remarkable feat of becoming Formula 1 Champions of the World in 1959 and 1960, with Jack Brabham as driver.

The birth of the Mini Cooper was brought about by a combination of this experience, ingenuity and determination. The Mini's designer was Alec Issigonis, a man with real genius and innovative flair. Going into production in 1959, the Mini, with front wheel drive and independent suspension, was well ahead of its time and a design forerunner of many cars of today. John Cooper's tuning and racing experience allied to a long standing friendship with Issigonis, prompted him to fit the Mini with a 1000cc Formula Junior engine. Essentially an uprated version of the 'A' series Mini power unit, the Mini Cooper legend was about to be born.

Soon after the launch of the Mini Cooper work was well under way for an even more powerful version and in 1963 the Mini Cooper S was launched, going on to enjoy success in nearly every rally and circuit of the era. It won the European Rally Championship outright, the European Touring Car Championship and the British Saloon Car Championship, as well as becoming three times winner of the Monte Carlo Rally.

With this string of victories the little car with the Cooper badge was in popular demand. Distinguished owners included such celebrities as the Beatles, Peter Sellers, Enzo Ferrari, Steve McQueen and Lord Snowdon. The car even became a star of the big screen in the cult film "The Italian Job".

Now these precious gems from the 'sixties are valued and sought after collectors' cars, remembered with fond affection.

With Rover reintroducing the Mini Cooper for the 1990s and the 'S' performance pack from John Cooper - the legend continues.

The John Cooper 1275 'S' Pack

The 1275 'S' Pack from John Cooper gives you all the thrills & excitement of the original Mini Cooper S. It's the perfect complement to your new Mini Cooper by Rover.

Like its famous predecessor, our 1990's Mini Cooper S captures all the panache of the original classic. With the 'S' Pack fitted you will be driving a car powered by an 78 PS Performance Engine, capable of accelerating from standstill to 60 Mph in under ten seconds and on to 100 Mph (wherever allowed of course). This achieved running on unleaded fuel and retaining the exhaust catalyst.

As soon as you lift the bonnet, the similarities between the Mini Cooper S of old and new are immediately apparent. The traditional twin 1¼" SU Carburettors sit neatly on a gas flowed inlet manifold fitted with an updated high performance air intake system.

At the heart of the conversion is a new exchange cylinder head, developed by John Cooper & Janspeed Engineering, offering a performance straight out of a race engine Tuner's handbook. Its specially shaped combustion chambers, gas flowed inlet and exhaust ports, all polished and balanced by hand, provide smooth power delivery and watch like running.

A freeflow, long centre branch exhaust manifold, plus a high performance exhaust system, retaining the original equipment exhaust Catalyst, ensures the match for power and of course emits all the right noises. As with the original Mini Cooper S a complete oil cooler kit is also included (original equipment on the limited edition Mini Cooper).

To complete your new Mini Cooper S an alloy rocker cover is included together with Cooper S side & boot decals. Each conversion comes with its own commemorative numbered chassis plate, this together with a certificate endorsed by John Cooper prove your car's authenticity.

The John Cooper 1275 'S' Pack may be ordered and fitted by John Cooper Garages or through your local Rover Dealer. The 'S' Pack may be fitted on any new or nearly new Rover Mini Cooper and comes complete with full warranty.

---

inlet and 1.15in exhaust valves, a 12:1 compression ratio and a very healthy 85bhp. It has 1.25in SUs and a 288 degrees dwell steel cam, as used by Ken Tyrrell when he ran the F2 Coopers.

You can get into just about any modern car and make it go reasonably quickly, and so it is with the AX. The PSA 1340cc unit is very willing and the gears are light and easy to use. But the steering felt very sensitive, almost as if there was too much air in the 155/65 x 14 Michelins. This allows the AX to be whizzed around with quite superb agility and its relatively high specification makes it a far more desirable proposition for coping with contemporary traffic situa-

tions. Like all front-wheel-drive cars, the Citroën has that 'lift-off for oversteer' characteristic, which makes it superbly responsive in corners.

You sit rather higher up in the AX than in the Mini, in comfortable, body-hugging Recaro-style seats, as opposed to the small and unsupportive vinyl seats of the Mini. As Philip Splett pointed out, you can, of course, fit after-market seats in your Mini; he's a biggish chap and could use something more comfortable, but on this car he's stuck with the standard seats for the sake of originality.

Being a passenger in a classic Cooper S is not that much fun. The ride is hard, the legroom poor and

the seats are, let's face it, abysmal. However, driving it is a different matter. It demands to have its performance exploited and in a particular way which the enthusiast cannot fail but appreciate. The Cooper S engine loves to rev and makes all the right noises. It pulls well through the gears, although its not possible to say quite how well, because the Cooper never came with a rev-counter; that was always an 'extra'. It seemed to achieve an easy 50mph in second gear and the ratios are very well spaced. Learning where the knotches are is easy enough, but engaging first and reverse is a knack. The way it hangs on around the bends is still pretty impressive, thanks to its stiff

112

suspenslon and wider-than-standard 165/70 x 12 Michelins on 6in Minilites. It feels very sure-footed, and you can place it very accurately in a corner and drive through on the throttle. Compared with the AX, there's very little change in attitude when you lift off, and applying the power provokes only minimal understeer.

There's no way of comparing these cars directly. It's horses for courses, really, because the two cars are like chalk and cheese. Even a modern Cooper would be difficult to compare directly with the AX because that would boil down more to a matter of taste. If you're old enough to have grown up driving cars in the '60s, then you won't feel lost in the Cooper. The Cooper S would be my choice if I lived in the country. But despite its good tractability for an 18 year old car, its competitive feel and urgent need to exercise itself would be somewhat lost in the city: on a long run you'd be deaf and crippled by the tlme you reached your destination! The Citroën, on the other hand, felt insipid to drive by comparison, but there's no question which one you'd rather be in while sitting out a traffic jam or, short of taking the train, you'd do the long-haul in.

Two decades on, it's obvious that small passenger cars have come a long, long way in terms of creature comforts and efficiency but, in fact, no distance at all as far as thrills and sheer driver enjoyment are concerned. Depends on where

Der Neue ist ganz der Alte.

The new Cooper is everything that the old Cooper was, according to this Austrian postcard brochure.

Philip Splett's Mk 3 1275 S, fifth from last of the series, and the car which the author used to compare old and new against the Citroën AX; the Cooper got the vote for good character.

you live and what you need a car for, I guess. Both cars provide similar economy at around 40mpg if driven reasonably, and with twin tanks, the Mlni Cooper's range is about 450 miles. There's not really

that much difference in price, elther, for the AX costs £7900, while Philip reckons the Cooper to be worth £8-£l0,000 on the classic market. I'd say go for the Cooper S and put a smile back on your face.

X

BUYER
BEWARE!

The Mini Cooper Register has published a really useful booklet called *The Mini Cooper - A Buyer's Guide*, compiled and edited by John Parnell, which describes in a concise, comprehensive style the evolution of each model and catalogues important change points in the production history. I have to say that it provides a lot of information about the cars which I wasn't previously aware of. It also warns potential owners what they should look out for when out Cooper shopping. The reason for exercising caution when buying is simply because of the increasing number of bogus Coopers on the market. Unscrupulous souls hang all the special Cooper trick-bits on a standard Mini, come up with a fake provenance and the unwary punter is conned. The early '90s recession lopped perhaps as much as a couple of grand off the price of a Condition 1 1275 S which, in 1989, might have fetched £7000 in the UK. However, with more people strapped for cash, there was just as much incentive to try a rip-off. It comes down to authenticity in the end, because if you want a Cooper, there are plenty of proper ones to choose from and there's no reason to be palmed off with a car that's not the genuine article.

As a fan of the engine swap myself, having dabbled in this way with an Anglia and an Alfa Romeo, I can see the attraction in fitting a bigger engine in a standard Mini to augment the performance. But I never tried to pass off either car as anything other than a big-engined Anglia or Alfa Giulia. The spoof Coopers are less likely to be advertised in the specialist press, of course, because of the danger of the perpetrator being rumbled, but it's worth bearing John Parnell's advice in mind.

There are four principal ways of faking up a Cooper. Firstly, it may be a Cooper S created from a regular Mini shell supported by the V5 logbook of a scrapped car. Alternatively, and more simply, it may be a bog standard Mini with Cooper or S cosmetics and no attempt to switch documentation. Or it may be a genuine Cooper purporting to be a more powerful and more valuable S. The MCR booklet warns against Mark 3 Minis fitted with the 1300GT unit posing as Cooper Ss: spot check - the latter had the removable tappet chest covers, the 1300GT didn't. If looking at a right-hand-drive Innocenti Cooper, make certain the rhd conversion has been done well; there were no factory-made cars with rhd and there are other factors such as right- and left-hand dipping to bear in mind.

Coming more up-to-date, it might just be worth someone's while getting up a regular Rover Cooper to look like a limited edition RSP Cooper. Avoiding such forgeries is relatively simple once you are aware they exist. The first thing to do is to swot up on everything to do with the chosen model, from production dates to specific trim options. Hav-

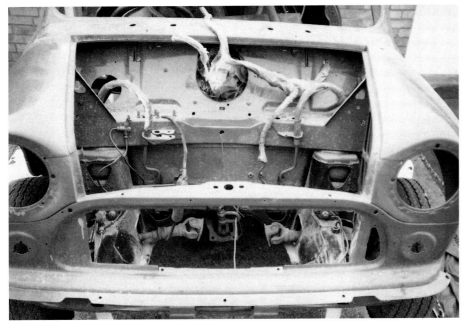

Complete engine/transmission change is relatively easy in a Mini, so beware of swopped engines when buying what you believe is a Cooper.

ing identified a possible car, get the registration, chassis and engine number details from the vendor and have them verified by the relevant Registrar before getting more involved. Find out why the owner wants to sell and watch it if the description given of the car's history is at odds with your own research. It goes without saying that one should always go for the car with low-mileage, well documented service history and continuity of ownership, which will naturally be top dollar but better value in the long run.

The most dlfficult forgery to spot is the 'Cooper' built from a shell and using a logbook from a wreck. A restoration may mean that it's had just that, and whether that's acceptable depends on the level of authenticity you seek. But be suspicious if it has just had extensive restoration and there is no documentation or service history. In the UK virtually all genuine Coopers would have been registered with the DoT Swansea computer in the '70s, so be wary of a very recent date on the V5 logbook in the 'Number of Former Keepers' section. It may also be possible to check original registration details in other countries. If the chassis plate with machine-punched em-

bossed letters looks as if it has been replaced by something different, ask why. Do the coded numbers on the window glass specifying when it was made tally with the date of the car's manufacture? There is a formula, simple when you've figured it out, which establishes in which quarter of the year the glass, either Triplex or Indestructo, was made, and the Triplex code even gave the month. Otherwise, check for a respray and be concerned if the most recent colour is the one recorded on its Heritage Certificate (a certificate of authenticity issued by the British Motor Industry Heritage Trust); this could indicate a reshell job. Although it is no proof of authenticity, if no Heritage Certificate is forthcoming, there may be something to hide. If in doubt, the relevant model register might well be able to sort out any queries or uncertainties surrounding a prospective purchase.

XI

RESTORATION

Course of action

If you're set on buying a classic Cooper, there's a fair chance it will need restoring, unless of course the job has already been done, and done recently. In any case, the most economical approach is to buy one which someone else has already spent the money on, because restorations invariably cost a great deal more than you initially estimate for. The only thing to be sure of is that the work has been done correctly, and this is something you can be more in control of if you are commissioning or carrying out the work yourself. By now you'll know that the Mini Cooper Register is the most reliable source for a cared-for Cooper, so taking out a membership subscription and assessing the market place is clearly a good move.

So assuming you're up for a restoration project, or a basket-case lands in your lap, where do you start? With a decent workshop, naturally, and preferably with a hoist and a pit. Then assuming we're talking about a comprehensive rebuild, you gut the car totally, removing trim, carpets, seats and soundproofing. Get any mechanical work done at this stage, as it saves possible paintwork damage later, so clearly, you'll need to dismantle the drivetrain and send away whatever needs reconditioning as appropriate.

Some cars are complete basket cases although Philip Splett's 1966 Mk 1 Cooper is not quite in that category. Be sure what you're buying is the real thing ...

This car needs work on doors, A-panels and inner wheelarches.

Middle: The shell has been rubbed down and filled. The areas around headlights and indicators are especially vulnerable to decay.

Vulnerable points

This isn't intended to be an intensive 'How to' guide, but simply to indicate those areas where the cars are likely to succumb to corrosion. This is a legacy of a thirty-five year old design, with all its attendant moisture traps and lack of protection - which just wasn't an issue back then. Working from front to back, examine the areas around the headlights, and the panel-join with the front panel. The front panels will have been peppered by stones, and unless touched up, rust spots will have formed on the outside. But it's underneath where the real problems start. Mud thown up by the wheels sticks on the inside of the wheelarches and the associated corrosion sets in. By the same token, the inside front of the inner wings and the damper turrets are also vulnerable. The bonnet itself may rust along its turned down edges. Behind the front wheelarches and ahead of the doors are the triangular apex panels, and because of moisture being trapped behind, these will almost certainly have incurred rust damage. They are crucial to the car's integrity because the door hinges are located here, and if their mountings are compromised, the doors will drop.

At the front of the roof, the tops of the 'A' pillars either side of the windscreen have been known to rot

Despite appearances, the interior trim on this car was complete and in good condition. New carpets were needed.

Door bottoms rot so new doors are fitted, along with hinges and A-panels. An entirely new front end was considered the most economical solution for this particular car.

The shell is gutted before serious body restoration work begins.

out, allowing water to drain inside the car's bodywork. This is caused by condensation in the foam underneath the roof headlining, although it can be set up by untreated corrosion in the roof gutter. Remember that rust isn't content to attack the place it starts in - it affects adjacent panels pretty quickly as well. In the area at the base of the screen, water collects on the closing panel beneath the scuttle, and the evidence is displayed around the seams where it meets the front wings. These are favourite places for the bodger's art to have been practised; as are the sills. It's more than likely that your car will already have received a new pair - inner and outer, and original-pattern ones with any luck. (You can check this by looking for four drainage holes instead of the six in modern versions - and make sure the jacking points have been fitted too.). Water collects in the sills, having found its way there from the scuttle and damaged subframe mounts, and inevitably, they will dissolve, most obviously towards the rear.

Drainage problems are the main cause of rust in the Cooper's doors. At the top of the main door section is a channel in which water collects if the plastic drainage pipe is blocked. This pipe should be connected with a drain hole at the base of the door, and if the arrangement comes adrift, water can swill around in the door bottom, setting up the usual rust scenario, manifest in orange blisters all along the foot of the door.

Rust doesn't confine itself to the exterior panels; you have to look inside the car as well, firstly at the areas behind the front wheelarches. It's small consolation that corrosion in the floorpan will be easy to spot. The main cause is damp carpets; and if you suddenly find the seats listing to one side, it's probably because the cross-member they're mounted on has rusted through. To assess the next area of structural importance, you still need to be inside the car. Either side of the rear seat are storage bins, and a glance in them will reveal how badly the rear subframe mounts and their adjacent box-sections have been attacked. You might also see bubbling paint on the outside of the car ahead of the rear wheelarches, but that's just the tip of the iceberg. The root of the problem lies within, at the rotten subframe mounts. The well below the rear seat squab butts up against the subframe, and the felt insulation pads which have got damp will promote rust, which attacks from the inside.

Within the boot, problems can occur if water has seeped in through old and faulty seals, or a poorly fitting lid. First casualty is the battery tray, suspended below floor level. Next to go are the corners below the fuel tank (or tanks if it's a post-'66 S), where water collects, and in some cases, the spare-wheel well. The lid itself may show traces of iron oxide around the lower rim, and double-skinned versions from late Mark 1s and Mark 2 cars are more difficult to restore. If there is no hinged number plate and you have a genuine Mark 1 or 2 bootlid, it must have already been mended - but with a later lid or unorthodox repair. And down below, mud deposits build up in the small box sections at either end of the rear valance, and the tin worm gets to work here too.

Specialists

It's no surprise that a number of expert restorers specialise in Mini Coopers, and every metal component is available, so no car is beyond redemption. Certainly, the

Now in etched primer, small defects in the surface can be seen and rectified.

Below: The finished car, pictured at the Norwich Union Classic Concours at Bath where it took first prize.

body is the Cooper's weakest area, because mechanical parts, from engine and gearbox to ancillaries and suspension, can be replaced, as indeed can all brightwork, which may be bought new, and trim acquired from specialists.

There is always an element of doubt about which route to go with the restoration, and it may boil down to economics in the end. Common sense will prevail if the choice is between a revitalised bodyshell for around £5,500 from Mini Machine or a whole set of new panels - circa £1,500 - for your basket case, with a specialist's labour rates on top. You may well be doing yourself a favour to opt for the restored and painted shell. The hacking out and surgery required to remove the rotten sections and weld in the new panels will involve hours of graft. There is a purist argument in favour of this avenue which assumes that your car is going to be more 'original' with its existing shell, however much it is re-panelled, than transferring its identity to a different shell. Whichever way you go, you'll probably have to cover the same ground with any car, so if you're bent on a restoration project you may as well buy the cheapest Cooper you can - provided it's genuine.

A selection of the leading UK specialists can be found in an appendix.

Mini Cooper

XII

COOPER
COMEBACK

Rover revival

To mark the 30 years of Mini production, Austin Rover brought out a 'Racing' model, finished in either red or green with a white roof. Cooper team cars were green, the works racers red. In 1989, John Cooper brought out his own retrospective model to celebrate the Mini's 30th anniversary. The traditional sporting colours were retained and white go-faster stripes ranged along the flanks rather than the bonnet, and round white decals on the back next to the number plate read *John Cooper Garages 30th Anniversary Model*. There was a run of just 500, and to make the whole process of recreating something approximating the original cars easier, the gearing was left untampered with at 3.1. Wheels were 12in Minilite replicas, shod with Pirelli Cinturato CN54/145 70 SR12 tyres. The dashboard was the same as current generation Minis, now laid out before the driver and including a rev-counter. Under the bonnet, Coopers had installed a Janspeed cylinder head, which contained polished ports, big valves (1.2in inlet, 1.1in exhaust), plus steel inserts to prevent valve seat wear when running on unleaded fuel. Twin 1.25in-SUs were fitted and the Janspeed head gave a

To commemorate Paddy Hopkirk's victory in the 1964 Monte Carlo rally, Rover brought out a 'rally pack' for fans to decorate their cars; the battery of lights looks impressive.

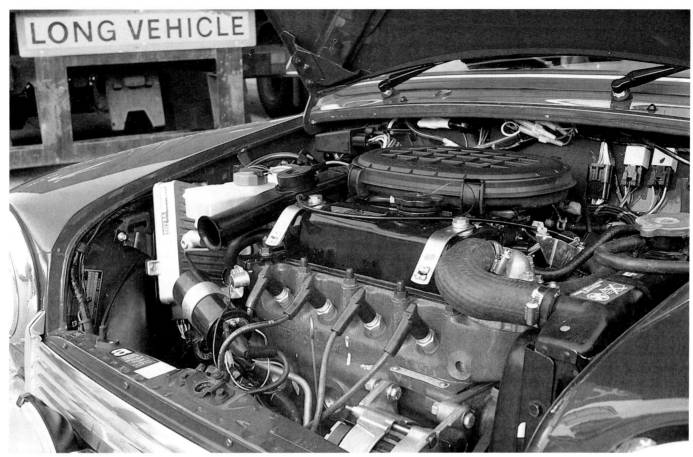

Engine of the 1994 Rover Cooper 'Monte' which has the splash guard removed to reveal red painted head - the poor man's Testa Rossa?

compression ratio of 9.75:1. It was topped with a chrome rocker cover, an oil cooler was fitted and a twin-box exhaust system provided the finishing touch. It was red-lined at 5800rpm, although the 64bhp maximum was attained at 6000rpm. Flexibility was the key with this model and to achieve anything approaching genuine Cooper S performance required the use of maximum revs. In 1992 John Cooper brought out a special 'Si' pack for the latest run of fuel-injected Mini Coopers, now extended to oil cooler, uprated fan pulley and belt, high-compression (10.5:1) polished head and a new

Modern Rover Cooper with optional Minilite wheels has timeless profile; the graffiti plague is a more recent phenomenon.

exhaust box. There was now an alloy rocker cover.

Nearly twenty years after its demise, the Mini Cooper has made

something of a comeback, although many people will only have eyes for the Real McCoy - and who would blame them? John Cooper had been

A beautiful replica with lowered suspension, built for a Japanese enthusiast by John Cooper, and much admired by young enthusiasts at Silverstone.

The first ever Cooper replica, created on a 1071 Cooper S in 1975

exporting his Cooper conversion kits to Japan for some time and they were proving very popular. The Japanese had been buying 300 standard Minis a year and the president of Austin Rover Japan, Cedric Talbot, saw a demand for something extra special and asked Cooper to put a 1000cc MG Metro engine in a Mini Mayfair and ship it out. This was done and the Japanese loved it. Talbot then requested AR to make 1000. Type Approval was a problem and Musgrove deemed it not worth the effort for what was, to a manufacturer like Austin Rover, a trickle of cars. Perhaps they failed to see the interest this would generate in their other products?

This oriental interest in the cars would not lie down, of course, and after successfully exporting several of these 'John Cooper Conversion Kits', Cooper decided to bring out a 30th Anniversary' Cooper conversion for the home market. The idea

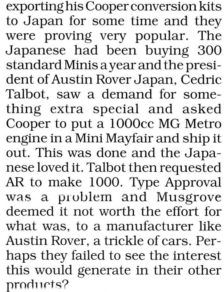

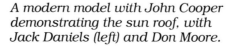

A modern model with John Cooper demonstrating the sun roof, with Jack Daniels (left) and Don Moore.

was to take one's Mini to John Cooper's base in Ferring, England, and pay a sort of eponymous 1275 pounds sterling to have it breathed on. Rather obviously these Cooper conversion kits were offered in 1989 and a run of 500 was planned.

To the 998cc engine was added twin-carburetters and a Janspeed-reworked head producing 64bhp - some 9bhp more than the original one-litre Cooper units. It was not, however, endowed with all the fancy materials of the Cooper S engines of yore and the emphasis was more on refinement with performance rather than the other way around, as was the case with the original cars which, after all, did have better sound-proofing and interior trim than the basic Minis at that time. This 1989 model also had rather higher gearing than the early cars, since to change the final drive would have entailed removing the engine. Although it blunts acceleration, this gearing made for more relaxed motorway travel, in lieu of a 5th gear to drop the revs when speeding along. Since there were no motorways at all in the UK when the Mini was announced - well, not quite! - the low gearing would not have seemed so tiring as it does today. That said, the gearchange action was highly praised as was - surprise, surprise - the handling. Unfortunately, the ride was found to be full of sharp vertical movements, although road imperfections did not throw the car off-line.

The success of these John

Morris Mk 1 1275 S of Porsche expert Nick Faure and photographer-journalist Chris Harvey awaits the start of the 1988 Pirelli Classic at Tower Bridge, London; there is no chrome around the windows.

Cooper conversions made the factory take notice and it took one of them away and tested it for some 20,000 miles. With a positive evaluation of its reliability, it gave the go-ahead to allow dealers to fit the Cooper conversion kits themselves, with full factory warranty, thus considerably stepping up the number that could be converted. The success of all this prompted the factory to gain the necessary Type Approval and make a Cooper of its own.

First to appear was the RSP (Rover Special Products) Cooper Limited Edition, in June 1990, around 1050 of which were sold. This was the car that was bedecked with twin white bonnet stripes which were, with impeccable bad taste, emblazoned each side with a magnified version of John Cooper's signature. 'Looks a bit Promenade Percy', commented the man himself. This car featured a derivative of the A Plus engine, being by this time a Metro motor. It had a single carburetter, oil cooler and a catalyst. Producing 61bhp, it somehow managed to display all the standing-start acceleration of the original 1275 S car, although most certainly not that car's top gear acceleration, nor maximum speed. Perhaps the 1960s Coopers' horsepower figures were a trifle optimistic? They have certainly proved to be so with other makes. Bonnet-script apart, it certainly looked the part with its replica Minilite wheels, tinted glass, driving lamps and - of course - white roof.

Metro's injection

Rover followed up the RSP very shortly after with a mainstream production model, in the autumn of 1990. This car had the same motor as the Limited Edition but no oil cooler. Bonnet stripes (without signatures), Minilite wheels and driving lamps were now all optional. Apart from a few other details, it was the same car as the 'special introductory' model which appeared a month before. One year later, fuel injection was offered, the engine being essentially that from the MG Metro. It was but 2bhp higher in output, but boasted a useful 15 per cent increase in torque.

At the same time as these Rover Coopers were being made at Longbridge, one could take the car to John Cooper's garage at Feering near Worthing and have it converted to S specification. There was an option of both a Cooper S and a Cooper Si, the difference explained by the first having twin SU carburetters and second fuel injection. There was rather more to these conversions than that and much

attention to the cylinder head and exhaust gave an increase over the standard Rover Cooper unit, amounting to a very useful 28 per cent and 22 per cent respectively, whether carburetter or fuel injection set-up. Similar increases in torque were achieved. All manner of other goodies were also available with this Cooper conversion, from even more power, through suspension uprating, to leather and wood interior and so forth. I am sure John Cooper Garages at Ferring would be happy to oblige with more details for those interested!

The result of all this sees that some 400 out of every 1000 Minis which come off the line every day are Coopers. Doubtless, John Cooper would be glad of his £2 a car now! Spurred on by this success in Japan, many European markets were approached. Switzerland had not bought the Mini for ten years but, once the particularly strict Type Approval for that country had been attained, the 1.3i was shown at Geneva in 1992. Apparently, 250 orders were taken before the show

Much of the revival of interest in the Cooper is due to the enthusiasm of private entrants like these with their 970S in the Pirelli Classic Marathon.

Paddy Hopkirk gives a demonstration run at Gaydon prior to the '94 Monte.

officially opened! Similar success has been achieved in the rest of Europe. Not only has this revival made the factory far more amenable to talk to again, just as approachable as they were in the days under George Harriman, according to Cooper himself, but it is greatly ironic that this has all come to pass thanks to the great interest shown in the Mini and Mini Cooper by the Japanese. For this Cooper rebirth has almost certainly meant a reprieve the Mini itself. While we normally associate the Japanese with threatening the very existence of some European car manufacturers simply because of the undeniable excellence of their products, they seem to have been instrumental in prolonging this treasured one of ours. This is perhaps all the more surprising, since the Japanese already made many different varieties of these so-called microcars themselves, all with the most up-to date specification.

Mini Cabriolet

A recent newcomer to the Mini range has been a cabriolet. It is hardly the first such conversion to be seen, but it is the first factory version. Sharing the same fuel-injected engine as the revitalised Cooper, it looks fine with the hood up, but awful with it down. This is because there is nowhere for the hood to go without sacrificing the rear seats, which are retained, so there is a bulky hump behind them. The main disadvantage of open versions of

full four-seater saloon cars is a noticeable loss of torsional stiffness of the body. Mercedes seems to be one of the precious few to offer a de-roofed four-seater with no detectable scuttle shake. It is, amazingly, joined by Rover Group with this Mini.

Apart from the strengthened sills, stronger cross-member under the seats, beefed-up B-pillars and stronger windscreen frame, the main reason for this achievement must be the shortness of the car. Another must be the absence of heavy axle and complex suspension components in the rear, the

mass of which would help try to bend the floorpan when the going is less than smooth. Also, the lack of roof has meant that other Mini bugbear - body resonance - has gone. Therefore, most of the time this new cabriolet is quieter and more refined than the saloon version. Normally, it's the other way around. The body kit does nothing at all for the car's looks - already heavily compromised in hood-down mode. A relatively high price puts it close to BMW territory and this may prove a handicap to match the perambulatorial appearance. That said, in suitable weather it is a fine

Austin Mk 1 Cooper S at Tower Bridge; corner bars are missing from bumper, and chrome is absent from windows.

little car and one that has already had a great deal of praise deservedly heaped upon it. Not bad at all for the 34-year-old design that is the basis of this new machine,

Paddy goes to Monaco

A most welcome postscript in this revival of interest in the Mini Cooper is the recent news that Paddy Hopkirk will be taking part in the 1994 Monte Carlo Rally, a mere 30 years after his historic win. He will drive - of course - a Mini Cooper, with the inspirational registration L33 EJB. This trick could not have been done with any of the other Mini Cooper Monte winners. Sadly, his original co-driver in that '64 event, Henry Liddon, is no longer alive, but Ron Crellin, Hopkirk's co-driver on the '67 and '68 Montes, will sit beside the Irishman. Hopkirk has recently taken part in the odd historic rally from time to time, winning the Pirelli Classic Marathon in 1990, but this one is for real. Apart from being great entertainment for everyone, it is a brilliant piece of publicity for the parent company and, just like the first Mini Cooper, was thought of by someone (Brigden and Coulter) outside the factory. The two modern Mini Coopers (the other crewed by Louise Aitken-Walker and Tina Thorner) are privately entered but with considerable factory support. A third car will be entered by Rover Japan. This whole venture is also excellent and welcome publicity for the rally itself, ironic, perhaps, when one considers that its organisers tried so hard to stop Mini Cooper successes in the past ...

XIII

FUTURE
COOPER

What does the future hold for the Mini and its more powerful Cooper cousin? When judged by today's standards, the original 1960s Cooper suffers from two significant drawbacks, fundamental to the design of the original Mini. The first is in the ride quality, which is greatly hampered by the meagre wheel travel. This constraint on suspension movement is itself a legacy of allowing as little wheelarch intrusion into the car as possible, achieved by tiny wheels and the ingenious use of rubber cones as a space-saving springing medium for the suspension. The result is that the Mini can still boast a ratio of interior space to overall size unmatched by any car made since its introduction, and probably before as well, although this claim may have to be changed when the new Mercedes A-class goes into production in 1997. Still, 38 years to catch up ... Whilst the 'rising rate' behaviour under compression of the rubber contributed to the exceptional handling and roadholding of the Mini, ride comfort was not much praised, even in 1959.

This was ameliorated by the introduction of the interconnected Hydrolastic suspension, brought in on the Cooper models in September 1964. It is sometimes claimed that its introduction greatly weakened the handling when compared to the previous 'dry' suspension models. Certainly, attempts to race and rally the Hydrolastic cars were shortlived - privateer competitors who bought

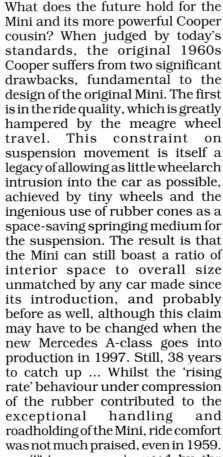

the Hydrolastic models simply returned them to dry suspension before lining up at the start. However, competition use and road use are very different, as all those who have done the former know and of those who haven't, markedly few ever seem to realize. The truth of the matter seems to be that Hydrolastic models offered a useful gain in ride comfort and little detectable difference in handling and roadholding for road use.

With rallying it was a different matter altogether, for the Hydrolastic-equipped cars suffered from too much bottoming - already a serious problem for a Mini with its small ground clearance. The main difficulty encountered when trying to rally a Mini was that the Hydrolastic units were just not tough enough to keep the car off the ground for very long: after a few hectic stages at breakneck speed they began to sag. This was partly cured by using uprated Hydrolastic units for the rally cars.

The second drawback lies in the interior noise levels. Part of the reason for the high decibel readings again stems from the original design aim of excellent interior room for this size of car. The sliding windows - as distinct from the wind-up variety - were a deliberate ploy to give maximum interior space, their trade-off being the excellent door pockets which could be so useful when carrying bottles of milk, or even wine. There's no such thing as a free lunch, as they say, and the

Time has been kind to the Cooper shape - and Pininfarina has been proved wrong.

downside is that the lack of trim panels to mask the window-winding mechanism necessitated by 'proper' windows means that the inside of the Mini can become a veritable sound-box for unpleasant resonant drumming noises. Proper windows on later cars, together with more substantial sound-proofing, helped lessen the noise problem, but the Mini's basic 'squashed together' design of the mechanicals and passenger area will always make for a car that will never be particularly quiet. The wind -up window models are also about 9 inches narrower in hip room - it's that no free lunch syndrome again. Another source of noise is the transfer gear set which takes the drive from the crankshaft down to the gearbox. Also known, less technically, as drop gears, they make that characteristic Mini whine. Distinc-

tive, maybe, discordant, certainly - especially on a long journey. Nowadays, Rover and all other front-wheel-drive designs utilise in-line gearboxes, which obviate the need for these rattling, chattering gear wheels.

The Mini was never styled, as such, which accounts for the fact that it still doesn't look out of date. Because it has never tried to follow fashion in the first place, its looks never dated. Consider some of its contemporaries from 1959 and how very old-fashioned they now seem. We all know what an extraordinary car the Mini was then in terms of dynamics, but there are not many mass-produced family cars which don't look outdated more than 30 years after introduction. It is folklore now that Issigonis was asked by Sergio Farina over lunch, 'When can I do some work on your Mini?'

The retort from the car's designer was a 'styled' car body was like ladies' clothes: 'They'll all be out of fashion in two years' time. My car will still be fashionable when I'm dead.' It must be true that Issigonis was underrated as a designer of car bodies (better not call him a stylist!), since he was absolutely correct. The attempt to modernise the Mini's appearance with the 'Clubman' front end was hardly a design triumph - and these cars now *do* look dated. As with so many things, the original design almost always looks the best.

It is true that many others also have played around with Mini styling, both for a living and just owners having fun. Almost all these attempts are worse, some diabolically so. The recent fashion for skirts looks particularly ungainly. Perhaps the only attempt which actually

managed to improve on the Issigonis design was the Mini-Sprint. However, it was not a practical proposition for the factory to sell cars like this, just as it wasn't viable for it to offer more powerful engines than standard. The reduced headroom in the Mini-Sprint would have lost too many customers, just as providing the car with even more power than the 1275 S produced would have lost sales because of a reduction in tractability and reliabilty.

Viewed by current standards, we therefore have a car which has light weight, good economy, enough room for four adults despite still being one of the smallest cars still in production, wonderful handling and a shape that is loved and recognised by everyone. Sounds promising for a brand-new car, so far, but the drawbacks centre around its suspension and powertrain, neither of which are up to modern levels of comfort and refinement. Would it be feasible for Rover to address these problems and give the Mini an extended lifespan? We know it is possible to put a modern engine in the car, with an in-line gearbox to cure the transmission noise and provide five speeds. (Rumours persist that Rover will give

the Mini Cooper a five-speed underslung 'box before the Mini, but we'll believe that when we see it.) Such a layout would also lower the engine and further improve the handling. If the Rover K-series engine were used, the car would become faster, quieter, smoother and more economical at a stroke.

Dr Alex Moulton has been running a properly-sorted Hydrolastic suspension on his own personal Mini Cooper for years. It gives a ride quality never experienced on any Mini straight out of Longbridge. Such an achievement - a comfortable ride - is therefore attainable, too. After all, the new Metro is a vast improvement on the old one and looks just the same. (It is, of course, essential that our imaginary new Mini is totally unaltered in overall appearance.) There should be a ready market today for such a car, as everyone is thinking smaller, while large cars are becoming harder and harder to sell. Also, the increased affluence of the western world - recession aside - will mean that most people will buy the Mini as a second car, unlike the 1970s when it was selling at its peak. It also means that upmarket versions will be more popular which, in turn,

means good demand for models like the Mini Cooper. If all this sounds exciting, it is probably a trifle naïve because the Mini's body simply costs too much to make and a prohibitively-expensive total redesign of it would be necessary for robotisation of the build process.

How long can it go on, particularly now that Rover Group is owned by BMW? The current car could easily be killed stone dead by changes in emission or safety legislation. If so, the Mini Cooper will still remain in one's memory as the Mini with the pedigree that, in competition, beat countless other cars, every one of which was larger and more powerful. It was developed from a design thought out by a genius, a man who won two F1 championships, and was powered by an engine which won the Formula Junior Championship for single-seaters. It was driven by the very best rally drivers in the world, worked on by the most skilled rally mechanics in the business and raced by some of the fastest saloon car drivers around. If that doesn't make the Mini Cooper a thoroughbred, then Timo Mäkinen was an average driver.

APPENDIX 1

GOING CLUBBING

One of the greatest advantages that the Mini Cooper owner has over owners of many other classic rally-winning legends is that the basic car is still in production, which means that many mechanical parts are still readily available. However, what if the original-style part is no longer obtainable from the factory and nobody seems to know where one can be found? Supposing the owner is stuck during a repair or rebuild due to lack of knowledge, not lack of parts? Life is much easier for the owner if he or she joins a club.

International flavour

Another great advantage of Mini or Mini Cooper ownership is that there are a very great number of clubs: a recent count yielded 250 - rather more than owners of the Goggomobil would have to choose from! The Mini clubs are distributed worldwide: Czechoslovakia,

A banner for one of the French Mini clubs.

Denmark, Finland, Italy, Hungary, Greece, Luxembourg, Malaysia, Mexico, Netherlands, Portugal and New Zealand have one apiece. Norway has two, whilst Ireland, Scotland, Wales, Belgium, France, Japan, Jersey and Spain enjoy three clubs each. Sweden and Austria have four each, Canada six, Switzerland seven, Australia thirteen and the USA - surprising this - has eighteen focal points for Mini activities. England currently has 75. Have I left out Germany? - no, it's last and anything but least. Our Teutonic chums have access to no fewer than 90 clubs! It's true that many of these clubs are small, perhaps having only 20 or 30 members. However, this is also true

A deservedly proud Austrian owner with a fine 1965 Mk 1 Cooper at a club gathering.

It's the Longbridge car park, with a pair of Austrian Innocentis on the Longbridge to Cowley run.

to some degree in the country that made the Mini in the first place - and Germany has more Mini clubs than we do. The reasons for this are unclear; perhaps it is a reaction by German youth against joining very large organisations? Whatever the sociological reason for its disproportionate number of clubs, when compared to other European countries it is very encouraging that such a strong interest in the Mini should exist in the land where, some say, the best cars in the world are made.

Most clubs in the UK publish some kind of newsletter, varying from just a sheet or two of sometimes poorly-reproduced photocopy now and again, to professional-looking glossy magazines every month. The aims of the clubs are several and members will join for different reasons. As mentioned before, help with locating spare parts, spreading of technical knowledge and cheaper spares will be many people's main or sole reason for joining. Indeed, some of the stronger clubs can operate on the strength-by-numbers method and actually persuade suppliers to remanufacture a part that has become unobtainable - at an affordable price, that is. Other members will enrol in order to meet people who share an affection for the same

vehicle as they, or even just to get out and about on the many events the clubs organise. These range from gatherings at suitable ale-houses, hopefully with a decent-sized car park, to driving tests or mini rallies, treasure hunts (once very popular), *concours d'élégance*, or even full-scale race meetings. The Minis that gathered at Silverstone in 1989 for the 30th Anniversary celebrations represented the largest number of Minis ever seen in one place; they're in the Guinness Book of Records to prove it. All club newsletters contain sections for buying and selling whole cars and spare parts - secondhand, of course.

Mini Se7en Club and Mini Se7en Racing Club

One of the first UK Mini clubs established was the Mini Se7en Club, which had a strong element of racing - and therefore Coopers - in its make-up. The club was created in 1961 by some London Mini enthusiasts. Having grown rapidly enough to stage its first race meeting, at Snetterton in Norfolk, England, in 1965, it ran into financial difficulties, mainly thanks to losses connected with race organisation expense. Nevertheless, the club was proving successful enough in membership terms to attract limited support from BMC and, at one time Raymond Baxter, John Cooper and Graham Hill were involved with it. Unfortunately, politics intervened around the time of the Leyland takeover and the club gradually crawled off and

The Mini Cooper Register's prize-winning stand at the 1987 Bromley Pageant, featuring members' club racers in a circuit-paddock setting.

Massed spotlights of three Pirelli Classic Marathon contestants.

Right: Cooper line-up during a visit to Duxford air museum, Cambridgeshire, September 1990.

Below: Hopkirk's 1964 Monte winner, 33EJB.

passed quietly away. There is now the active and well-organised club, the Mini Se7en Racing Club, which operates from Birmingham, England, and is the same thing in (almost) name only.

Mini Cooper Register and Mini Cooper Club

Of the 85-odd Mini clubs in the British Isles, there are only two independent ones catering exclusively for the Mini Cooper and the first to be established was the Mini Cooper Club. For various reasons, there grew up much disaffection amongst its members, some thirty of whom, in 1986, upped

Enjoying a day out at Duxford aerodrome, with a Shackleton and a B52 in the background.

and formed the Mini Cooper Register. The Mini Cooper Club, however, is now "under new management".

The Chairman and Public Relations Officer of the Mini Cooper Register is Philip Splett. He has had many Minis since he first drove one in 1959, the first of which was a 997cc Cooper, acquired two years later. In fact, he still owns several of them, his current Mini and Mini Cooper total being his highest - so far. He is the first to admit that the Mini disease is incurable - if you wanted a remedy, that is. As you'll see from the acknowledgements, Philip was most generous in allowing me to plunder his personal archives for material for the book, and supplied one of his classic Coopers for the driving appraisal.

The Mini Cooper Register is designed to be fully democratic - "a club for its members", says Philip. The current total exceeds 2000. The Register is not operated as a business and takes no profits, as funds raised through membership are all ploughed back into the club. Its monthly newsletter is to a very high standard - which must have a lot to do with the club's membership figure - and the emphasis is on events and meetings, both social and "mildly-competitive". There are registrars appointed for each model of Mini Cooper, that is, not just for

Original and unused production Mk 3 fronts, re-imported from Cyprus.

S-models and the 997 and 998cc cars, but for the Mk 1, 2 and 3 versions, where applicable. A list of honorary members of the Register looks like the index for this book: Lady first - Christabel Carlisle, John Rhodes, Warwick Banks (who does handling and performance conversions on Land-Rover Discoveries these days), Peter Browning, Paddy Hopkirk, John Handley, Ginger Devlin, Bill Price, Julien Vernaeve, Jack Daniels, Sir John Whitmore, Steve Neal and Don Moore.

Occasionally, members are treated to a celebrity guest appearance at a chosen area meeting. People such as John Rhodes, John Cooper and Christabel Carlisle have all put in appearances and, no doubt, answered many questions.

The Register also has helped to organise National Mini Cooper Day which occurs on a yearly basis and looks like becoming a regular feature. The 1993 venue was Beaulieu, in June, when around 700 Mini Coopers took part.

There are various regions for the Mini Cooper Register. For more information, contact Philip Splett at Burtons Farm, Barling Road, Barling, Essex, SS3 0LZ, England. The telephone number is 0702 216062. And while you're at it, ask to try his excellent home-made sausages; Philip is a master butcher.

Mini World Magazine
Of further interest to the Mini Cooper fan will surely be the magazine *Mini World* which first appeared in the summer of 1991 as

A Mk 1 Morris Cooper S is admired at Silverstone during the 1987 Norwich Union Classic Car run.

a quarterly. Demand was strong enough to warrant a switch to a monthly issue before a year had elapsed. The magazine is published by Link House, by the same crew who produce *Cars and Car Conversions*. Let's get one thing straight: it is a first-class publication, perhaps the best one-make mag there is. It has a full-colour, glossy format of around 75 pages with excellent photography, containing articles on technical matters, road and track appraisals, archive photos from the vaults of *Cars & Car Conversions*, historical pieces, news from around the car clubs and so forth. A particular bonus is that John Cooper contributes a couple of pages of reminiscences nearly every month. The magazine has, of course, attracted a host of suppliers of Mini hardware who advertise in its pages - another good reason to buy it. It is very well written, too. If there is a criticism it must be that the section where readers send in pictures of their Minis has got out of hand. The sight of these mostly standard-looking (fancy paint jobs aside) Minis, with no competition (or otherwise) history, usually with owner standing by, is wearing a little thin. Perhaps they could just show one car - the most interesting one - each month?

Mini World organised a London to Brighton run of its own where, no doubt, several quite veteran Minis were at the Crystal Palace starting point. Rather more than the offi-

This Cooper owner clearly means business: suspension is lowered as far as it'll go, headlamps taped and ready for anything!

cially-entered 1200 entrants took part in May 1993, thanks to those who joined in unofficially. In rapidly-improving weather, the total convoy was reckoned to exceed 2000. This about doubled the 1992 figure for the same event, making it a great success. It all goes to illus-trate the immense continuing popularity of these little cars.

Directory of clubs

AUSTRALIA
Mini Car Club of NSW,
Jenny Trayhurn,

A line of assorted 'hot' Minis ready for a session on the circuit at Thruxton. On these occasions only a handful of cars is allowed out at the same time to avoid competition, but some drivers are inevitably carried away by the thrills.

PO Box 1145,
Auburn,
NSW 2144,
Australia.

Mini Owners Club of Western
AUstralia Inc.,
Ruth Onofaro,
5, Southwary Way,
Morley 6062,
Western Australia.

AUSTRIA
Mini Club O.O.,
Gerhard Kaiser,
Strauchgasse 5,
4210 Mittertreffing,
Austria.

BELGIUM
Mini Owners Club of Belgium,
Regis Kalut,
2, rue Fontenelle,
B-1350 Marilles,
Belgium.

BRAZIL
Mini Austin Morris Club De Brazil,
Paulo Reisinger,
Rua Tabupua 726,
04433-Itaim Bibi,
Sao Paulo,
Brazil.

BRITAIN
Mini Owners Club,
Chris Cheal,
15, Birchwood Road,
Bolet Park,
Lichfield,
Staffs.

Mini Cooper Club,
Joyce Holman,
1, Weavers Cottages,
Church Hill,
West Hoathly,
West Sussex RH19 4PW.

Mini Cooper Register,
T.Salter,

20, Batchelor Green,
Lowford,
Nr Southampton,
Hants SO3 8JF.

Mini International Mini Club
Register,
Martin Bell,
151, Waverley Road,
Stoneleigh,
Epsom,
Surrey KT17 2LN.

Mini-Twini,
Helene Blankspoor,
30, Cavendish Road,
Tile Hill,
Coventry CV4 9LW.

CANADA
Kamikazee Kooper Club,
Sandy Smith,
9693 120th Street, Surrey,
British Columbia V3V 4C4,
Canada.

1965 Mk 1 Morris Cooper S, with seven slat grille, in the Silverstone paddock, 1987.

Maritime Mini Owners Network,
Brian Townsend,
R.R. No.1 Albert,
New Brunswick E0A 1AO,
Canada.

CHANNEL ISLANDS
Guernsey Mini Owners Club,
Vanessa Paver,
Les Capucines,
Epinelle Road,
St Sampsons,
Guernsey,
CI.

Jersey Mini Owners Club,
38 Ville de L'eglise,
St Peter,
Jersey,
CI.

DENMARK
Mini Club Denmark,
Soren Carlsen,
Vonsyldsgade 19,
9000 Aalborg,
Denmark.

FRANCE
Club Mini France,
B.P. 96,
94223 Charenton-Cedex,
France.

Mini Club France,
Dominique Bourg,
18, Rue de Louis David,

93170 Bagnolet,
France.

GERMANY
Hannoverscher Mini Club,
Thoralf Harder,
Heisterkamp 18,
30966 Hemmingen,
Germany.

Mini Clique Wesermarsch,
Michael Ruessbuelt,
Geroldstr. 15,
26919 Brake,
Germany.

Mini Club Berlin e.V.,
Lilienthalstr. 14,
10965 Berlin,
Germany.

Mini Club Leverkusen,
Ralf Gerkens,
Im Weidenblech 1a,
51371 Leverkusen,
Germany.

Mini Club Olderburg e.V.,
Henning Brandes,
Ahornstr. 29,
26160 Wehnen,
Germany.

Mini Club Stuttgart,
Gunter Koch,
Olgastr. 137,
70180 Stuttgart,
germany.

Mini Cooper Club Herne,
Reiner Wardenbach,
Dorstener str. 535,
44653 Herne,
Germany.

Mini Cooper Club Offenburg,
Roland Kohler,
Schauenburgstr. 8,
77654 Offenburg,
Germany.

Mini Register von Deutschland,
Robert Webster,
Bloherfelder Str. 40,
DS-26129 Oldenburg,
Germany.

GREECE
Hellenic Mini Club,
Theotokopoulou 32,
Athens GR-111-44,
Greece.

HONG KONG
Hong Kong Mini Fans Club,
Yeung Wan Fai,
81, 3rd Street,
Section H, Fairview Park,
N.T. Hong Kong.

HUNGARY
Mini Club Hungary,
Ferenc Kiraly,
Kisujszallasi UT No.,
59 "1" H-5300 Karcaq,
Hungary.

IRELAND
Irish Mini Owners Club,
Killian O'Carroll,
49, Ardlea Road,
Artane,
Dublin 5,
Ireland.

ITALY
Mini Cooper Club Italia,
Angelo Bortesi,
Via Matteotti 6,
43044 Collechio (Parma),
Italy.

Rear view of Mk 1 1275 Cooper S; wheels and spats are not standard, but otherwise the car is nice enough.

JAPAN
Club Mini of Japan,
Osamu Kobayashi,
c/o Water Land,
2142-1 Oosato,
Kofu,
Yamanashi 400,
Japan.

Club 305,
Masahiko Yamaguchi, 2-25-8,
Setagaya,
Setagaya-ku,
Tokyo 154,
Japan.

LUXEMBOURG
Sweet Mini Club Luxembourg,
Patrick Breuskin,
160, route de Niedercom,
L-4991 Sanem,
G.D. Luxembourg.

MALAYSIA
S.M.O.C. Malaysia,
Raja Kobat,
No. 131 Jalan Lee Woon,
Taman Zooview,
Ulu Kelang 68000,
Ampang-Selgangor,
Malaysia.

MEXICO
Mini Asociados Mexico,
Alejandro Jimenez Landa, Prol.
Mario Talavera No. 220,
Col Estadio,
C.P. 78280,
San Luis Potosi S.L.P.,
Mexico.

NETHERLANDS
Mini Seven Club Nederland,
Ronald van Sonsbeek,
PO Box 234,
3340 AE Hendrik Ido Ambacht,
Netherlands.

NEW ZEALAND
Cooper Car Club of New Zealand,
Tony Maulder,
PO Box 970,
Newmarket,
Auckland,
New Zealand.

Mini Cooper Enthusiasts Club Inc.,
Ralph Taylor,
PO Box 12 189,
Hamilton,
New Zealand.

NORWAY
Sverre Lochen,
Bjornebaerstien 37,
N-1349 Rykkinn,
Norway.

PORTUGAL
Portugal Mini Club,
Axel Champagne,
Apartado 941,
Areias Sao Joao,
8200 Albufeira,
Algarve,
Portugal.

SINGAPORE
Singapore Mini Owners Club,
Victor Chan,
17 Jalan Minggu,
Singapore, 2057,
Republic of Singapore.

SOUTH AFRICA
Mini Cooper Club of South Africa
(inc Mini Owners Club),
Laurie LeRoy,
PO Box 170,
Ferndale 2160,
South Africa.

SPAIN
Club Espanol Del Mini,
Felipe Torres,
C/Espronceda 22,
28003 Madrid,
Spain.

Club Mini Cooper,
C/Viladomat.
176, 3-4,
08015 Barcelona,
Spain.

SWEDEN
Mini Dalarna Sweden,
Kjell Wiklund,
Landa 309,
78393 Stora Skedvi,
Sweden.

SWITZERLAND
Austin Innocenti Morris Mini Cooper
Club Zurich,
Stefan Kunz,
Widmerstr. 44,
8038 Zurich,
Switzerland.

Mini & Mini Cooper Club,
Regula Keller & Thomas Baumann,
alte Bahnhofstrasse 23,
CH-8957,
Spreitenbach,
Switzerland.

USA
California Cooper Club,
Mike Kimball,
18820 Roscoe Blvd,
Northbridge,
CA 91324,
USA.

Capital Mini Register,
Bob Johns,
746 Tiffany Drive,
Gaithersburg,
Maryland 20878,
USA.

Cooper Car Club,
D. Cooper,
14, Biscayne Drive,
Ramsey,
NJ 07446,
USA.

Mini Owners of America - SF,
Chris Pegues,
101, Madora Pl.,
San Ramon,
CA 94583,
USA.

Mini Owners of New Jersey,
Rich & Debbie Franks,
1011 Walnut Street,
Linden,
NJ 07036,
USA.

APPENDIX 2

WORKS CARS
COMPETITION RESULTS

1959

Sept	Viking Rally	Austin Seven	M.Chambers/P.Wilson	YOP663		51st oa
Oct	German Rally Mini Miglia National Rally	Morris Mini Minor	Pat Ozanne/Ann Shepherd			
		Morris Mini Minor	Pat Moss/S.Turner	TJB199		1st oa
Nov	RAC Rally	Morris Mini Minor	Pat Ozanne/N.Gilmour	TMO559	129	Ret
		Morris Mini Minor	K.James/I.Hall	TMO561	126	Ret
		Morris Mini Minor	A.Pitts/A.Marston	TMO560	135	Re
Dec	Portugese Rally	Morris Mini Minor	Nancy Mitchell/Pat Allison	TJB199	57	2nd Ladies, 54th oa
		Austin Seven	P.Riley/A.Ambrose	618AOG		64th oa

1960

Jan	Monte Carlo Rally					
		Austin Seven	P.Riley/R.Jones	618AOG	110	23rd oa
		Austin Seven	T.Wisdom/J.Hay	619AOG	229	55th oa
		Austin Seven	Nancy Mitchell/Pat Allison	617AOG	18	Ret
		Morris Mini Minor	D.Morley/E.Morley	TMO561	263	33rd oa
		Morris Mini Minor	A.Pitts/A.Ambrose	TMO560	284	73rd oa
		Morris Mini Minor	Pat Ozanne/N.Gilmour	TMO559	307	Ret
April	Geneva Rally (Crit. de Divonne-Les Bains & Rallye des Allobrogues)	Austin Seven	Pat Ozanne/Pat Allison	617AOG	47	27th oa, 3rd Ladies, 2nd class
		Austin Seven	D.Morley/E.Morley	618AOG	44	14th oa, 1st class
		Austin Seven	A.Pitts/A.Ambrose	619AOG	45	Ret - accident
	Circuit of Ireland Rally	Morris Mini Minor	D.Hiam/A.Ambrose			Ret

May	Tulip Rally	Morris Mini Minor	T.Christie/N.Paterson	TMO560	161	36th oa, 3rd class
		Morris Mini Minor	P.Ozanne/P.Allison	TMO561	159	72nd oa, 6th class
		Morris Mini Minor	I.Sprinzel/M.Hughes	TJB199	99	43rd oa, 2nd class
	Acropolis Rally	Austin Seven	Pat Ozanne/Pat Allison	617AOG	120	Ret - ball joint
		Austin Seven	M.Sutcliffe/DS.Astle	618AOG	122	31st oa, 5th class
		Austin Seven	J/Milne/W.Bradley	619AOG	124	16th oa, 4th class
June	Alpine Rally	Morris Mini Minor	R.Jones/K.James	TMO559	5	Ret - accident
		Morris Mini Minor	A.Pitts/A.Ambrose	TMO560	1	4th class
		Morris Mini Minor	T.Gold/M.Hughes	TMO561	19	14th GT cat., 1st class
Nov	RAC Rally	Morris Mini Minor	D.Seigle-Morris/V.Elford	TMO559	183	6th oa, 2nd class
		Morris Mini Minor	T.Christie/N.Paterson	TMO560	174	Ret
		Morris Mini Minor	M.Sutcliffe/D.Astle	TMO561	170	8th oa, 4th

1961

Jan	Monte Carlo Rally	Morris Mini Minor	P.Garnier/R.Jones	TMO559	254	Ret - accident
		Morris Mini Minor	T.Christie/N.Paterson	TMO560	227	Ret - illness
		Morris Mini Minor	D.Astle/S.Wooley	TMO561	226	Ret - accident
March	Lyons-Charbonnières Rally	Morris Mini Minor	Pat Moss/Ann Wisdom	TMO560		Ret - engine
May	Tulip Rally	Morris Mini Minor	D.Seigle-Morris/V.Elford	TMO559	135	23rd oa, 3rd class
		Morris Mini Minor	P.Riley/A.Ambrose	TMO561	136	12th oa, 1st class
	Acropolis Rally	Austin Seven	D.Astle/M.Sutcliffe	619AOG	115	Ret
		Austin Seven	D.Morley/Ann Wisdom	363DOC	117	Ret - accident
		Morris Mini Minor	D.Seigle-Morris/V.Elford	TMO560	125	Ret - suspension

1962

Jan	Monte Carlo Rally	Morris Mini Cooper	Pat Moss/Ann Wisdom	737ABL	304	26th oa, 1st Ladies, 7th class
		Austin Seven	R.Jones/P.Morgan	363DOC	97	77th oa, 3rd class
		Morris Mini Cooper	R.Aaltonen/G.Mabbs	11NYB	100	Ret - accident
May	Tulip Rally	Morris Mini Cooper	Pat Moss/Ann Riley	737ABL	104	1st oa, 1st Ladies
		Austin Seven	D.Seigle-Morris/A.Ambrose	363DOC		Ret
June	Alpine Rally	Morris Mini Cooper	R.Aaltonen/G.Palm	407ARX	63	Ret
Aug	1000 Lakes Rally	Morris Mini Cooper	R.Aaltonen/A.Ambrose	407ARX		Ret
Sept	Baden-Baden German Rally	Morris Mini Cooper	Pat Moss/Pauline Mayman	737ABL		1st oa, 1st Ladies &class
Oct	Geneva Rally	Morris Mini Cooper	Pat Moss/Pauline Mayman	737ABL	135	3rd oa, 1st class
Nov	RAC Rally	Morris Mini Cooper	R.Aaltonen/A.Amrbose	977ARX	6	5th oa, 1st class
		Morris Mini Cooper	T.Makinen/J.Steadman	107ARX	00	7th oa, 1st class
		Morris Mini Cooper	L.Morrison/R/Finlay	477BBL	32	13th oa, 3rd class

1963

Jan	Monte Carlo Rally	Morris Mini Cooper	R.Aaltonen/A.Ambrose	977ARX	288	3rd oa, 1st class

		Morris Mini Cooper	P.Hopkirk/J.Scott	407ARX	66	6th oa, 2nd class
		Morris Mini Cooper	Pauline Mayman/Val Domleo	737ABL	58	28th oa, 4th class
		Morris Mini Cooper	L.Morrison/B.Culcheth	477BBL	155	44th oa, 1st class
April	Tulip Rally	Morris Mini Cooper	P.Hopkirk/H.Liddon	17CRX	130	2bd oa, 1st class
		Morris Mini Cooper	Pauline Mayman/Val Domleo	737ABL	129	21st oa, 4th class
May	Trifels Rally	Morris Mini Cooper	Pauline Mayman/ Val Domleo	737ABL		1st Ladies, 1st class
June	Scottish Rally	Morris Mini Cooper	L.Morrison/D.Brown			Ret - accident
	Alpine Rally	Morris Mini Cooper	R.Aaltonen/A.Ambrose	277EBL	63	1st oa, 1st class
		Morris Mini Cooper	Pauline Mayman/Val Domleo	18CRX	73	6th oa, 1st Ladies & class
		Morris Mini Cooper	J.Sprinzel/W.Cave	977ARX	24	Ret - steering
		Morris Mini Cooper	Denise McCluggage/ Rosemary Sears	17CRX	64	Ret - trans
Sept	Tour de France	Morris Mini Cooper S	P.Hopkirk/H.Liddon	33EJB	38	3rd oa, 1st class
		Morris Mini Cooper	R.Aaltonen/A.Ambrose	477BBL	24	44th oa
		Morris Mini Cooper	T.Makinen/L.Morrison	407ARX	17	Ret
		Morris Mini Cooper	Pauline Mayman/ Elisabeth Jones	277EBL	39	Ret
Nov	RAC Rally	Morris Mini Cooper S	P.Hopkirk/H.Liddon	8EMO	21	4th oa, 2nd class
		Morris Mini Cooper	L.Morrison/R.Finlay	407ARX	36	19th oa, 1st class
		Morris Mini Cooper S	Pauline Mayman/V. Domleo	277EBL	38	30th oa

1964

Jan	Monte Carlo Rally	Morris Mini Cooper S	P.Hopkirk/H.Liddon	33EJB	37	1st oa, 1st class
		Morris Mini Cooper	T.Makinen/P.Vanson	570FMO	182	4th oa, 2nd class
		Morris Mini Cooper	R.Aaltonen/A.Ambrose	569FMO	105	7th oa, 3rd class
		Morris Mini Cooper	R.Baxter/E.McMillen	477BBL	39	43rd oa, 2nd class
		Morris Mini Cooper S	Pauline Mayman/ Val Domleo	277EBL	189	Ret - accident
		Morris Mini Cooper 1275	J.Thompson/F.Heys	18CRX	187	Ret - accident
April	Tulip Rally	Morris Minor Cooper S	T.Makinen/A.Ambrose	AJB66B	119	1st oa, 1st class
May	Acropolis Rally	Austin Mini Cooper S 1275	P.Hopkirk/H.Liddon	AJB55B	67	Ret - battery
		Austin Mini Cooper S 1275	R.Aaltonen/A.Ambrose	AJB33B		Ret - steering
June	Alpine Rally	Austin Mini Cooper S 1275	R.Aaltonen/A.Ambrose	AJB55B	70	4th cat, 1st class, Coupé des Alpes
		Morris Mini Cooper S 970	Pauline Mayman/Val Domleo	AJB66B	8	6th cat, 1st Ladies & class
		Morris Mini Cooper S 1275	P.Hopkirk/H.Liddon	AJB44B	18	Ret
		Morris Mini Cooper S 1275	T.Makinen/P.Vanson	BJB77B	19	Ret
Aug	1000 Lakes Rally	Morris Mini Cooper S	T.Makinen/P.Keskitalo	AJB33B		4th oa, 1st class
	Spa-Sofia-Liége Rally	Morris Mini Cooper S	J.Wadsworth/M.Wood	570FMO	68	20th oa
Sept	Tour de France	Morris Mini Cooper S 970	Pauline Mayman/ Val Domleo	AJB66B	20	1st class
		Morris Mini Cooper S	P.Hopkirk/H.Liddon	AJB44B	19	Ret
		Austin Mini Cooper S	R.Aaltonen/A.Ambrose	AJB55B	30	Ret
		Morris Mini Cooper S	T.Makinen/P.Easter	BJB77B	18	Ret - accident
Nov	RAC Rally	Morris Mini Cooper S	P.Hopkirk/H.Liddon	CRX90B	1	Ret

		Austin Mini Cooper S	R.Aaltonen/A.AMbrose	CRX89B	2	Ret
		Morris Mini Cooper S	C.Orrenius/R.Dahlgren	AJB44B	37	Ret
		Austin Mini Cooper S	H.Kallstrom/R.Haakansson	AGU780B	42	Ret

1965

Jan	Monte Carlo Rally	Morris Mini Cooper S	T.Makinen/P.Easter	AJB44B	52	1st oa, 1st class
		Morris Mini Cooper S	P.Hopkirk/H.Liddon	CRX91B	56	26th oa, 1st class
		Morris Mini Cooper S	D.Morley/E.Morley	CRX90B	72	27th oa, 2nd class
		Austin Mini Cooper S	R.Aaltonen/A.Ambrose	CRX88B	283	Ret
		Austin Mini Cooper S	H.Kallstrom/P.Haakansson	AGU780B	176	Ret
		Morris Mini Cooper S	R.Baxter/J.Scott	8EMO	91	Ret
Feb	Swedish Rally	Austin Mini Cooper S	P.Hopkirk/H.Liddon	AJB33B	28	Ret - transmission
		Austin Mini Cooper S	R.Aaltonen/A.Ambrose	DJB93B	22	Ret - transmission
		Morris Mini Cooper S	T.Makinen/P.Easter	DJB92B	31	Ret - transmission
		Austin Mini Cooper S	H.Kallstrom/P.Kaakansson	AGU780B		Ret - transmission
March	Circuit of Ireland	Austin Mini Cooper S	P.Hopkirk/T.Harryman	CRX89B	2	1st oa
April	Tulip Rally	Morris Mini Cooper S	T.Makinen/P.Easter	AJB33B	124	3rs cat, 1st class
May	Luxembourg Slalom	Austin Mini Cooper S	P.Hopkirk	CRX89B	66	7th oa, 1st class
	Acropolis Rally	Austin Mini Cooper S	T.Makinen/P.Easter	DJB93B	60	Ret - engine
June	Scottish Rally	Austin Mini Cooper S	P.Hopkirk/H.Liddon	CRX89B	3	Ret - final drive
	Geneva Rally	Morris Mini Cooper S	R.Aaltonen/A.AMbrose	EBL55C	64	1st oa, 1st class
July	Rallye Vltava Czechoslovakia	Austin Mini Cooper S	R.Aaltonen/A.Ambrose	EJB55C	102	1st oa
		Morris Mini Cooper S	T.Makinen/P.Easter	AJB66B	100	Ret
	Nordrhein-Westfalen Rally	Morris Mini Cooper S	P.Hopkirk/H.Liddon	DJB92B	58	6th oa, 1st class
	Alpine Rally	Austin Mini Cooper S	T.Makinen/P.Easter	AJB33B	70	2nd cat, 1st class
		Morris Mini Cooper S	P.Hopkirk/H.Liddon	EBL56C	60	4th cat, 2nd class
		Morris Mini Cooper S	R.Aaltonen/A.Ambrose	EBL55C	56	14th cat
		Austin Mini Cooper S	Pauline Mayman/ Val Domleo	DJB93B	66	13th cat, 1st Ladies
	Polish Rally	Austin Mini Cooper S	R.Aaltonen/A.Ambrose	CRX89B	55	1st oa, 1st class
Aug	1000 Lakes Rally	Austin Mini Cooper S	T.Makinen/P.Keskitalo	AJB33B	28	1st oa, 1st class
		Austin Mini Cooper S	R.Aaltonen/A.Jaervi	EBL55C	26	2nd oa, 2nd class
		Morris Mini Cooper S	P.Hopkirk/K.Ruutsalo	EBL56C	22	6th oa, Man Team Prize
Oct	Munich-Vienna- Budapest Rally	Austin Mini Cooper S	R.Aaltonen/A.Ambrose	CRX89B	72	1st oa
		Austin Mini Cooper S	A.Fall/R.Crellin	AJB55B	65	2nd class
		Morris Mini Cooper S	G.Halliwell/M.Wood	CRX90B	71	Ret - accident
Nov	RAC Rally	Austin Mini Cooper S	R.Aaltonen/A.Ambrose	DJB93B	5	1st oa
		Morris Mini Cooper S	J.Lusenius/M.Wood	DJB92B	44	6th oa, 1st class
		Morris Mini Cooper S	P.Hopkirk/H.Liddon	EBL56C	8	13th oa, 2nd class
		Austin Mini Cooper S	A.Fall/R.Crellin	CRX89B	36	15th oa, 3rd class
		Morris Mini Cooper S	H.Kallstrom/N.Bjork	EJB55C	37	Ret - exhaust

1966

Jan	Monte Carlo Rally	Morris Mini Cooper S	T.Makinen/P.Easter	GRX555D	2	(1st oa) disq
		Austin Mini Cooper S	R.Aaltonen/A.Ambrose	GRX55D	242	(2nd oa) disq
		Austin Mini Cooper S	P.Hopkirk/H.Liddon	GRX5D	230	(3rd oa) disq
		Morris Mini Cooper S	R.Baxter/J.Scott	GRX195D	87	Disqualified
Feb	Swedish Rally	Morris Mini Cooper S	R.Aaltonen/H.Liddon	GRX310D		Ret - transmission

	San Remo Flowers' Rally	Morris Mini Cooper S	T.Makinen/P.Easter	DJB92B	35	Ret - transmission
		Austin Mini Cooper S	P.Hopkirk/R.Crellin	GRX309D	50	15th oa, 6th class
		Austin Mini Cooper S	A.Fall/H.Liddon	GRX5D		Disqualified - air cleaner
April	Circuit of Ireland	Morris Mini Cooper S	A.Fall/H.Liddon	DJB92B	4	1st oa
		Austin Mini Cooper S	P.Hopkirk/T.Harryman	GRX55D	1	Ret - accident
	Tulip Rally	Morris Mini Cooper S	R.Aaltonen/H.Liddon	GRX310D	89	1st oa
		Austin Mini Cooper S	T.Makinen/P.Easter	GRX5D	100	9th oa, 1st class, Man Team Prize
May	Austrian Alpine Rally	Morris Mini Cooper S	P.Hopkirk/R.Crellin	DJB92B	58	1st oa
		Morris Mini Cooper S	A.Fall/M.Wood	GRX310D	97	Ret - steering
	Acropolis Rally	Morris Mini Cooper S	P.Hopkirk/R.Crellin	GRX311D	67	3rd oa, 1st class
		Morris Mini Cooper S	T.Makinen/P.Easter	HJB656D	82	10th oa, 2nd class
		Austin Mini Cooper S	R.Aaltonen/H.Liddon	JBL172D	77	Ret - engine
June	Scottish Rally	Austin Mini Cooper S	A.Fall/M.Wood	DJB93B	2	1st oa
	Geneva Rally	Morris Mini Cooper S	A.Fall/H.Liddon	EBL56C	75	2nd oa, 2nd class
		Austin Mini Cooper S	P.Hopkirk/T.Harryman	JBL495D	50	Ret, Man Team Prize
	London Rally	Austin Mini Cooper S	P.Hopkirk/R.Crellin	JBL495D	6	Ret
		Austin Mini Cooper S	A.Fall/M.Wood	DJB93B	4	Ret
July	Vtava Rally Czechoslovakia	Austin Mini Cooper S	R.Aaltonen/H.Liddon	JBL494D	75	1st oa
		Morris Mini Cooper S	T.Makinen/P.Easter	JBL493D	77	3rd oa
		Morris Mini Cooper S	S.Zasada/Z.Leszczvk	EBL56C	16	4th oa, 1st class, Man Team Prize
	German Rally	Morris Mini Cooper S	P.Hopkirk/C.Nash	GRX311D	42	Ret - engine
		Austin Mini Cooper S	A.Fall/H.Liddon	JBL172D	49	Ret - engine
Aug	Polish Rally	Austin Mini Cooper S 970cc	A.Fall/A.Krauklis	GRX309D	56	1st ao
		Morris Mini Cooper S	T.Makinen/P.Easter	GRX555D	37	2nd oa, 1st class
		Morris Mini Cooper S	R.Aaltonen/H.Liddon	HJB656D	29	Ret
	Welsh Rally	Austin Mini Cooper S	A.Fall/M.Wood	GRX309D		Ret
	1000 Lakes Rally	Morris Mini Cooper S	T.Makinen/P.Keskitalo	JBL493D	45	1st oa
		Morris Mini Cooper S	R.Aaltonen/V.Numimaa	GRX310D	49	3rd oa, 2nd class
		Austin Mini Cooper S	J.Lusenius/K.Lehto	JBL494D	27	6th oa, 3rd class
Sept	Alpine Rally	Austin Mini Cooper S	R.Aaltonen/H.Liddon	JBL495D	62	3rd oa, 2nd class
		Morris Mini Cooper S	T.Makinen/P.Easter	JMO969D	68	Ret - engine
		Morris Mini Cooper S	P.Hopkirk/R.Crellin	GRX311D	67	Ret - transmission
		Morris Mini Cooper S	A.Fall/M.Wood	GRX195D	66	Ret - driveshaft
Oct	Munich-Vienna-Budapest (Three Cities) Rally	Morris Mini Cooper S	T.Makinen/P.Easter	HJB656D	57	1st oa
		Austin Mini Cooper S	A.Fall/H.Liddon	JBL494D		Ret
Nov	RAC Rally	Austin Mini Cooper S	H.Kallstrom/R.Haakansson	JBL494D	66	2nd oa, 1st class
		Morris Mini Cooper S	R.Aaltonen/H.Liddon	GRX310D	18	4th oa, 2nd class
		Morris Mini Cooper S	A.Fall/M.Wood	GRX195D	21	5th oa, 3rd class
		Morris Mini Cooper S	Marjatta Aaltonen/ Caroline Tyler	EBL56C	117	37th oa
		Morris Mini Cooper S	P.Hopkirk/R.Crellin	JMO969D	10	Ret - driveshaft coupling
		Austin Mini Cooper S	T.Makinen/P.Easter	GRX5D	12	Ret - engine
		Austin Mini Cooper S	S.Lampinen/A.Ambrose	JBL495D	29	Ret - accident
		Austin Mini Cooper S	G.Hill/M.Boyd	GRX309D	5	Ret - diff

1967

Jan	Monte Carlo Rally	Morris Mini Cooper S	R.Aaltonen/H.Liddon	LBL6D	177	1st oa
		Austin Mini Cooper S	P.Hopkirk/R.Crellin	LBL666D	205	6th oa, 5th class
		Austin Mini Cooper S	A.Fall/R.Joss	LBL606D	32	10th oa
		Morris Mini Cooper S	S.Lampinen/M.Wood	HJB656D	178	15th oa
		Morris Mini Cooper S	T.Makinen/P.Easter	LBL66D	144	41st oa

Month	Event	Car	Crew	Reg	No.	Result
Feb	Swedish Rally	Austin Mini Cooper S	R.Aaltonen/H.Liddon	JBL495D	26	3rd oa, 1st class
		Morris Mini Cooper S	T.Makinen/P.Easter	JMO969D	22	Ret - brakes
	Rally of the Flowers (San Remo)	Austin Mini Cooper S	P.Hopkirk/R.Crellin	LBL590E	67	2nd oa, 2nd class
March	East African Safari	Morris Mini Cooper S	R.Aaltonen/H.Liddon	HJB656D	8	Ret - engine
	Circuit of Ireland	Austin Mini Cooper S	P.Hopkirk/T.Harryman	GRX5D	1	1st oa
	Sebring 3-Hr Race	Austin Mini Cooper S	P.Hopkirk/J.Rhodes	GRX309D	48	1st class
April	Tulip Rally	Morris Mini Cooper S	T.Makinen/P.Easter	LRX827E	64	2nd oa, 1st cat
		Morris Mini Cooper S	R.Aaltonen/H.Liddon	LRX829E	65	3rd oa, 2nd cat
		Austin Mini Cooper S	D.Benimra/T.Harryman	GRX5D	73	Ret - clutch. Man Team Prize
May	Acropolis Rally	Austin Mini Cooper S	P.Hopkirk/R.Crellin	LRX830E	89	1st oa
		Austin Mini Cooper S	R.Aaltonen/H.Liddon	LRX828E	92	Ret - accident
		Morris Mini Cooper S	T.Makinen/P.Easter	GRX195D	99	Ret - gearbox
June	Scottish Rally	Morris Mini Cooper S	L.Ytterbring/L.Persson	GRX311D	1	2nd oa
		Austin Mini Cooper S	A.Fall/M.Wood	GRX5D		Ret
	Geneva Rally	Morris Mini Cooper S	A.Fall/M.Wood	LRX829E	79	1st oa
	Criterium de Crans-sur-Sierre	Morris Mini Cooper S	J.Vernaeve/H.Liddon	LRX27E	80	2nd oa, 2nd class
July	London Rally	Austin Mini Cooper S	A.Fall/M.Wood	GRX5D	8	Ret - accident
	Danube Rally	Austin Mini Cooper S	R.Aaltonen/H.Liddon	LRX828E		Ret - no visa
Aug	1000 Lakes Rally	Morris Mini Cooper S	T.Makinen/P.Keskitalo	GRX195D	29	1st oa
	Marathon de La Route	Austin Mini Cooper S 970cc	A.Fall/J.Vernaeve/A.Hedges	GRX5D	39	2nd oa, 1st class
		Austin Mini Cooper S 970cc	A.Poole/R.Enever/C.Baker	LRX830E	40	Ret - accident
Sept	Alpine Rally	Morris Mini Cooper S	P.Hopkirk/R.Crellin	LRX827E	107	1st oa
		Austin Mini Cooper S	R.Aaltonen/H.Liddon	JBL172D	106	Ret - gearbox
		Morris Mini Cooper S	T.Makinen/P.Easter	GRX311D	103	Ret - engine
		Morris Mini Cooper S	A.Fall/M.Wood	GRX310D	40	Ret - accident
Nov	Tour of Corsica	Austin Mini Cooper S	P.Hopkirk/R.Crellin	GRX5D	79	Ret - fan belt
		Austin Mini Cooper S	R.Aaltonen/H.Liddon	JBL172D	73	Ret - fan belt
	RAC Rally: cancelled	Morris Mini Cooper S	T.Makinen/P.Easter	GRX311D	24	
	Foot & Mouth disease	Mini Cooper S	T.Fall/M.Wood		27	
		Mini Cooper S	P.Hopkirk/R.Crellin		26	
		Mini Cooper S	L.Ytterbring/L.Persson		80	

1968

Month	Event	Car	Crew	Reg	No.	Result
Jan	Monte Carlo Rally	Morris Mini Cooper S	R.Aaltonen/H.Liddon	ORX7F	18	3rd oa, 1st cat
		Austin Mini Cooper S	A.Fall/M.Wood	ORX707F	185	4th oa, 2nd cat
		Austin Mini Cooper S	P.Hopkirk/R.Crellin	ORX777F	87	5th oa, 3rd cat
		Morris Mini Cooper S	T.Makinen/P.Easter	ORX77F	7	55th oa
Feb	Flowers Rally	Morris Mini Cooper S	R.Aaltonen/H.Liddon	ORX77F	40	Ret
		Morris Mini Cooper S	A.Fall/M.Wood	ORX777F	44	Ret
April	Tulip Rally	Austin Mini Cooper S	L.Vernaeve/M.Wood	ORX707F	74	3rd oa, 1st cat
		Morris Mini Cooper S	T.Makinen/P.Easter	LBL66D	73	41st oa
	Circuit of Ireland	Morris Mini Cooper S	P.Hopkirk/T.Harryman	JMO969D	1	Ret - diff
		Austin Mini Cooper S	L.Ytterbring/L.Persson	OBL46F	3	Ret - accident
	Canadian Shell 4000 Rally	Austin Mini Cooper S	P.Hopkirk/M.Kerry	GRX5D	119	Disqualified
May	Acropolis Rally	Morris Mini Cooper S	R.Aaltonen/H.Liddon	RBL450F	46	5th oa, 1st class
		Morris Mini Cooper S	T.Makinen/P.Easter	GRX310D	49	Ret - head gasket
June	Scottish Rally	Morris Mini Cooper S	L.Ytterbring/L.Persson	JMO969D	3	2nd oa, 1st class
Oct	TAP Rally	Austin Mini Cooper S	P.Hopkirk/A.Nash	LBL606D	71	2nd oa, 2nd class

Dec	ITV Rallycross Croft	Mini Cooper S	J.Rhodes			3rd oa
		Mini Cooper S	J.Handley			6th oa

1969

Jan	BBC Rallycross Lydden Hill	Mini Cooper S	J.Rhodes			Ret - diff
Feb	BBC Rallycross Lydden Hill	Mini Cooper S	G.Mabbs			Ret - accident
	ITV Rallycross Croft	Mini Cooper S PI	J.Rhodes			2nd oa + FTD
		Mini Cooper S PI	J.Handley			5th oa
March	ITV Rallycross Croft	Mini Cooper S PI	J.Handley			4th oa
April	ITV Rallycross Croft Final	Mini Cooper S PI	J.Rhodes			4th oa, 2nd Championship
	High Egborough Rallycross	Mini Cooper S PI	J.Handley			1st in Heat
		Mini Cooper S PI	G.Mabbs			1st in Heat
March	Brands Hatch Saloon Car Race	Mini Cooper S	J.Rhodes	OBL45F		Ret - accident
		Austin Mini Cooper S	J.Handley	OBL46F		Ret - accident
	Silverstone Daily Express Meeting	Morris Mini Cooper S	J.Handley	LRX827E	15	10th oa, 4th class
		Morris Mini Cooper S	J.Rhodes	GRX310D	14	11th oa, 5th class
April	Snetterton Guards Trophy Meeting	Morris Mini Cooper S	J.Rhodes	GRX310D		12th oa, 4th class
	Thruxton Easter Monday Meeting	Morris Mini Cooper S	J.Handley	LRX827E		9th oa, 4th class
		Morris Mini Cooper S	J.Rhodes			22nd oa
	Circuit of Ireland	Morris Mini Cooper S	P.Hopkirk/A.Nash	GRX311D	2	2nd oa, 2nd class
May	Silverstone Martini Race Meeting	Austin Mini Cooper S	J.Rhodes	LBL666D	17	6th oa, 2nd class
		Morris Mini Cooper S	J.Handley	LRX827E	16	7th oa, 3rd class
	Crystal Palace Annerley Trophy	Austin Mini Cooper S	J.Rhodes	LBL666D	134	4th oa, 4th class
		Morris Mini Cooper S	J.Handley	LRX827E	135	3rd oa, 3rd class
June	Hockenheim Race Meeting	Morris Mini Cooper S	J.Rhodes	URX560G		6th oa, 3rd class
		Morris Mini Cooper S	J.Handley	URX550G		5th class
	Brands Hatch 6Hr Race	Morris Mini Cooper S	J.Handley/R.Enever	RBL450F		4th oa. 2nd class
		Morris Mini Cooper S	J.Rhodes/P.Hopkirk	GRX310D		7th oa, 3rd class
	Mallory Park Guards International	Austin Mini Cooper S	J.Rhodes	LBL666D	118	8th oa, 4th class
		Morris Mini Cooper S	J.Handley	LRX827E		Ret - engine
July	Nürburgring 6Hr Race	Morris Mini Cooper S	J.Handley/R.Enever	RBL450F	74	Ret - rear suspension
		Morris Mini Cooper S	J.Rhodes/G.Mabbs	GRX310D	73	Ret - rear suspension
	Silverstone British GP Meeting	Austin Mini Cooper S	J.Rhodes	LBL666D	16	8th oa, 4th class
		Morris Mini Cooper S	J.Handley	LRX827E	15	10th oa, 6th class
	Spa 24Hr Race	Morris Mini Cooper S	J.Handley/R.Enever	RBL450F	78	Ret - engine
		Morris Mini Cooper S	J.Rhodes/G.Mabbs	RJB327F	79	Ret - engine
Aug	Thruxton Race Meeting	Morris Mini Cooper S	G.Mabbs	RJB327F		BBC Camera Car
	Oulton Park Race Meeting	Austin Mini Cooper S	J.Rhodes	LBL666D		12th oa, 4th class
		Morris Mini Cooper S	J.Handley	RJB327F		15th oa
Sept	Tour de France	Austin Mini Cooper S	P.Hopkirk/A.Nash	OBL45F	57	14th oa, 1st class
		Morris Mini Cooper S	J.Handley/P.Easter	URX560G	56	Ret - accident
		Morris Mini Cooper S	B.Clucheth/J.Syer	URX550G	12	5th Trg car, 2nd class
	Brands Hatch Guards Trophy	Austin Mini Cooper S	J.Rhodes	LBL666D	244	10th oa, 4th class
		Morris Mini Cooper S	J.Handley	LRX827E	245	Ret

Oct	Salzburgring Saloon Car Race	Austin Mini Cooper S Morris Mini Cooper S	J.Rhodes J.Handley	LBL666D LRX827E	30 31	1st oa 2nd oa

1970

April	London/Mexico World Cup Rally	Mini Clubman 1275	J.Handley/P.Easter	XJB308H	59	Ret - engine
June	Scottish Rally	Mini Clubman 1275 GT	P.Hopkirk/A.Nash	XJB308H	14	2nd oa, 1st class
Sept	Marathopn de La Route	Mini Clubman 1275 GT	J.Handley/A.Poole J.Vernaeve	SOH878H	20	Ret - head gasket
Oct	Southern Cross	Mini Clubman 1275 GT Morris Mini Cooper D	A.Cowan/R.Forsyth B.Clucheth/ R.Bonhomme	YMO881H RJB327F	12	Ret - accident Ret - OTL
Nov	Rally of the Hills	Morris Mini Cooper S	B.Clucheth/ R.Bonhomme	RJB327F		4th oa

MONTE CARLO RALLY RECORD
(Top 3 Mini Coopers by year)

1960	23rd	33rd	55th
1961	-	-	-
1962	26th	77th	-
1963	3rd	6th	28th
1964	1st	4th	7th
1965	1st	26th	27th
1966	1st	2nd	3rd
1967	1st	6th	10th
1968	3rd	4th	5th

RALLY WINS BY DRIVER

AALTONEN	9
MAKINEN	6
HOPKIRK	6
FALL	4
PAT MOSS	2

TOP THREE PLACINGS AS PERCENTAGE OF RALLIES ENTERED

DRIVER	RALLIES	1st	2nd	3rd
AALTONEN	16	63%	6%	31%
HOPKIRK	16	44%	44%	12%
MAKINEN	11	55%	36%	9%
MOSS	10	30%	40%	30%
FALL	7	71%	29%	0%

COOPER RALLY WINS

REG NO	RALLY	DRIVER
737 ABL	1962 TULIP GERMAN	MOSS MOSS
277 ABL	1963 ALPINE	AALTONEN
33 EJB	1964 MONTE	HOPKIRK
AJB 33B	1965 1000 LAKES	MAKINEN
AJB 44B	1965 MONTE	MAKINEN
AJB 66B	1964 TULIP	MAKINEN
CRX 89B	1965 CCT OF IRELAND POLISH THREE CITIES	HOPKIRK AALTONEN AALTONEN
DJB 92B	1966 CCT OF IRELAND AUSTRIAN ALPINE	FALL HOPKIRK
DJB 93B	1965 RAC 1966 SCOTTISH	AALTONEN FALL
EBL 55C	1965 GENEVA	AALTONEN
EJB 55C	1965 CZECH	AALTONEN
GRX 5D	1967 CCT OF IRELAND	HOPKIRK
GRX 195D	1967 1000 LAKES	MAKINEN
GRX 309D	1966 POLISH	FALL
GRX 310D	1966 TULIP	AALTONEN
HJB 656D	1966 THREE CITIES	MAKINEN
JBL 494D	1966 CZECH	AALTONEN
JBL 493D LBL 6D	1966 1000 LAKES 1966 MONTE	MAKINEN AALTONEN
LRX 827E	1967 ALPINE	HOPKIRK
LRX 829E	1967 GENEVA (CRITERIUM)	FALL
LRX 830E	1967 ACROPOLIS	HOPKIRK

APPENDIX 3

SPECIALIST
ADDRESSES

British Mini Company *(Interior trim)*
Brambles, Catsash Road, Christchurch, Newport, Gwent NP6 1JJ, England.
Tel: 0633 423976

John Cooper Garages *(Sales, conversions, accessories)*
Ferring Street, Ferring, Worthing, West Sussex BN12 5JP, England.
Tel: 0903 504455

Janspeed Engineering Ltd *(Preparation and tuning)*
Castle Road, Salisbury, Wiltshire SP1 3SQ, England.
Tel: 0722 321833

Midland Mini Centre *(New and used spares, accessories)*
317 Highfield Road, Hall Green, Birmingham B28 0BX, England.
Tel: 021 777 1961

John Kelly, **Mini Machine** *(Restorations, panels, new and used parts, mechanical rebuilds)*
Units 1 & 2, North Road Industrial Estate, Whessoe Road, Darlington, County Durham DL3 0QR, England.
Tel: 0325 381300

Keith Dodd, **Mini Spares** *(Restorations, new and used spares, engine rebuilds)*
29-31, Friern Barnet Road, London N11 1NE, England.
Tel: 081 368 6292

Mini Sport *(New and used parts)*
Thompson Street, Padiham, Lancashire BB12 7AP, England.
Tel: 0282 778731

Mini and Metro Spares Centre *(New and used components, restorations, electrics)*
105, Brinksway, Stockport, Cheshire SK3 0BZ, England.
Tel: 061-480 8808

Roger Tello, **Mighty Minis** *(Restorations, competition preparation)*
Aykroyd Drive, London E3 4AP, England
Tel: 081-981 2055

Newton Commercial *(Interior trim)*
Eastlands Industrial Estate, Leiston, Suffolk IP16 4LL, England.
Tel: 0728 832880

APPENDIX 4

SPOT THE FAKE

Superficially, it's pretty easy to fake a Cooper by mixing standard Mini components with genuine or Cooper lookalike parts. The details in this appendix - kindly supplied by the Mini Cooper Register - should help you to verify whether or not a particular car is genuine.

CYLINDER HEAD IDENTIFICATION CHART	
Casting No.	**Engine application/comments**
2A 628	850 Mini, 998 Mini, 948cc 'Frogeye' Sprite (Mk 1)
2A 629	948 Morris Minor, Austin A35 and A40 (22A 629 head had no water temperature boss)
12A 1456	Fitted to later 850s and 998s
12G 185	997 Cooper
12G 202	Austin/Morris 1100s, Mk 1 Midget, Mk 2 Sprite
12G 206	Early rare headcasting fitted to early MG 1100, 998 Cooper, Mk 2 Midget and Mk 3 Sprite
12G 295	Most common head found on the 998 Cooper. Also the MG 1100, Mk 2 Midget and Mk 3 Sprite
12G 940 (9 stud)	Small valve head found on Austin/Morris 1300, 1275 Sprite/Midget, Mini 1275 GT. Also 1300 Marina and Allegro
12A 185 (Yellow) AEG 16 (Brown/Blue)	Big valve heads used on early 1071 Cooper S engines. Used on later1071 and 970/1275 Cooper S. **WARNING!** Prone to cracking between inlet and exhaust valves.
12G 940 (11 stud)	Big valve head found on MG 1300, 1300 GT and Mk 3 Cooper Ss. Look for 12G 1805 stamped adjacent to thermostat housing
12G 940 (Sculptured)	9 stud head found on Metro 1300cc range

	Inlet	Exhaust
Ord 1300	33.2mm	29mm
MG Metro	35.6mm	29mm
Metro Turbo	35.6mm	29mm (exhaust sodium filled)

Courtesy of the Mini Cooper Register © 1992

GEARBOX CASING IDENTIFICATION NUMBERS

The gearbox casing number is stamped on the front of the gearbox adjacent to the oil filter bowl. WARNING! Correct gearbox identity can only be confirmed by inspection of the gears themselves.

Casing No.	Application
22A 363	Early 850 Mini
22A1128	Non S B type 3 synchro box
22G 68	A & B type 850, 998, 1100, 997 and 998 Cooper
22G 333	970 and 1275 S B type gears
22G 190	970 and 1071 S A & B type gears
22G1128	4 synchro box

DISTRIBUTOR IDENTIFICATION CHART

997cc Cooper HC	Lucas 25 D4 40774
997cc Cooper LC	Lucas 25 D4 40873
998cc Cooper HC	Lucas 25 D4 40955 or 41032
998cc Cooper HC	Lucas 25 D4 41958 or 41031
970cc & 1071cc S	Lucas 23 D4 40819
1275cc S (Mk 1 & 2)	Lucas 23 D4 40819 or 41033
1275cc S (Mk 3)	Lucas 23 D4 41033

The automatic advance on 997 and 998 Coopers was both centrifugal and vacuum, whilst on Cooper S models it was centrifugal only. HC/LC - High/Low Compression.

TRANSMISSION UNITS IMPORTANT PRODUCTION CHANGE POINTS

Description	Change point
Coil spring clutch replaced by diaphragm clutch	997 N/A (all coil spring type) 998 9FA-SA-H3780 to 4999 9FD-SA-H101 on 9FA-SA-L101 on 9FD-SA-L101 on 1071 9F-SA-H33260 on 970 9F-SA-X29001 on 1275 9F-SA-Y31001 on
Cone type transmission replaced by baulking ring type with 'A' type gears	997 9F-SA-H10667 to 26376 (excluding 19201 to 20410) 9F-SA-L10448 to 28575
'A' type gears replaced by 'B' type gears	997 9F-SA-L28576 to 28950 998 9FD-SA-H1961 (plus H1916 to H1924) 9FD-SA-L645 on 1071 9F-SA-H19201 to 20410 9F-SA-H26501 on 970 9F-SA-X29041 on 1275 9F-SA-Y31001 on
Rubber drive couplings replaced by solid inboard driveshaft universal joints (1275 Cooper S only)	1275 9F-SA-Y41234 on
Introduction of 4-speed all synchromesh gearbox	998 9FD-XE-H101 on 9FD-XE-L101 on 1275 9F-XE-Y51501 on

Notes
1) The letters 'H' and 'L' preceding an engine number denote High and Low compression respectively.
2) Engines built out of sequence are shown in brackets.
3) The above change points have been sourced from the official BMC parts lists. With the exception of the introduction of 4-speed synchromesh, they are only approximate. It is quite possible that engines exist with features out of sequence with the official change points.

SU CARBURETTOR TAG IDENTIFICATION CHART

Although all of the A-series engines shared the same 1 1/4 inch SU carburettor, the jet needle specifications were usually different. This is denoted by the small, pear-shaped alloy tag attached to the top of the float chambers. Stamped on it are the letters 'AUD', followed by a number. It is this number which identifies the vehicle model the carburettor was jetted to fit.

Model	I.D. Tag
997 Cooper	AUD 15
998 Cooper	AUD 104
1071 Cooper S	AUD 99
970 Cooper S	AUD 151
1275 Cooper S	AUD 146
1275 Cooper S	AUD 440 (1970/71)

Identification tags belonging to other models -

1300 GT (1275cc)	AUD 344
Riley Kestrel (1275)	AUD 318 or AUD 344
948cc MG Midget	AUC 990
MG 1100	AUD 69
1098 MG Midget	AUD 73
1098 MG MIdget Mk 2	AUD 136
1275 MG Midget Mk 3	AUD 136
MG 1300 Mk 2	AUD 344
Austin 1300 GT	AUD 454 or AUD 431
AH Sprite	AUD 327

Note
Tags are identical for both 'Austin' and 'Morris' variants.
TAG CHART COMPILED BY RICHARD MANSFIELD

GLASS CODES

A common item often overlooked by prospective purchasers when inspecting a Mini Cooper is the glass. In addition to the manufacturer's name, all car window glass will also bear a date code indicating both the year and month or quarter during which the glass was made. Armed with this knowledge it should be possible to corroborate the year of manufacture of the vehicle. Where the two differ significantly, the prospective buyer should be wary.

The two most common makes of glass used in pre-1972 Minis and Mini Coopers are Indestructo and Triplex.

Indestructo

This manufacturer was taken over by Triplex in 1968 and closed down. The name is usually etched in an arch shape with two letters under the bottom of each leg. The letters of interest are the two underneath the letter 'I' of the company's name (B & R in the illustration). The letters below the 'O' should be ignored for dating purposes (T& S in the illustration

Of the two letters marked beneath the 'I', the one on the extreme left is used to indicate the quarter of the year of manufacture using the code word BRIT.

B - First quarter   R = Second quarter
I = Third quarter   T = Fourth quarter

The year is indicated by the second letter below the 'I', using the code word Indestructo -

1=7	N=8	D=9	E=0	S=1
T=2	R=3	U=4	C=5	O=6

(The second 'T' was ignored, except for the first six months of 1966 when T=6 and O was ignored.)

The example illustrated (BR) shows the First Quarter of 1953 or 1963 (clearly, only 1963 applies in the case of a Mini).

Triplex

The date code of this company in shown by dots above or below words in the company motif.

The year is shown by a dot under one of the letters of the words 'Laminated' (where this applies to a windscreen) or 'Toughened' (this being the most common). A dot under the first letter of either word represents a year ending in a '1'; e.g. 1961/1971. A dot

under the second letter would represent 1962/1972, and so on.

Although only a single dot is used the format showing which letter represents each year is as follows -

```
LAMINATED   TOUGHENED
1234567890  1234567890
```

Prior to January 1969, only the quarter was shown using a dot above the letters 'T', 'R', 'E' and 'X' of the word Triplex: T-1st, R=2nd; E=3rd and X=4th.

```
          ·
TRIPLEX
TOUGHENED  = 3rd qtr 1964
```

After January 1969 the month is shown by one, two or three dots above the letters 'T', 'R', 'E' and 'X' of the word Triplex, as follows:

January	T R I P L E X	July	T R I P L E X
February	T R I P L E X	August	T R I P L E X
March	T R I P L E X	September	T R I P L E X
April	T R I P L E X	October	T R I P L E X
May	T R I P L E X	November	T R I P L E X
June	T R I P L E X	December	T R I P L E X

Example: May 1970 =

```
  ··
T R I P L E X   T O U G H E N E D
                           ·
```

APPENDIX 5

ORIGINAL ROAD TEST DATA

The leading British motoring magazine Autocar *tested the new Austin 7 Cooper in October 1961. Its description of road testing what was a very exciting mew model from a major manufacturer is rather deadpan. Autocar's team was impressed by the new Mini's performance and in particular the engine's tractability. They mention that father and son team, Charles and John Cooper, used Formula Junior technology to increase the 997cc unit's output to 55bhp (standard Mini 37bhp).*
Autocar thought the gear ratios well chosen and the gearchange accurate; if a little stiff.
The Lockheed disc/drum brake system came in for strong praise - disc brakes being a novelty still as far as affordable mass-production cars were concerned in the early 1960s.
The Cooper buyer was told that the optional heater was very desirable to avoid the problems of windscreen misting in such a small car.

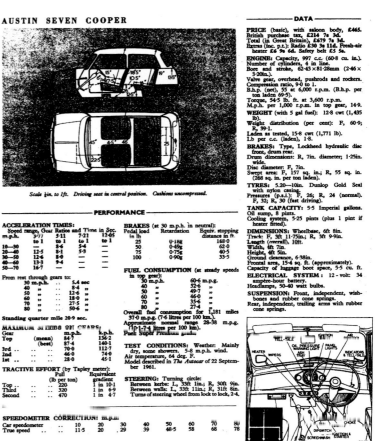

APPENDIX 6

PAINT AND TRIM

MK 1 COOPER & COOPER S BODY COLOURS & TRIM			
Body exterior & BMC paint code	**Seats**	**Liners**	**Carpet mats**
Surf Blue/ (BU 35)	Silver Brocade Grey/ Powder Blue	Silver Brocade Grey	Powder Blue
Old English White roof (WT3)	Gold Brocade Grey/ Powder Blue	Gold Brocade Grey	Powder Blue
Smoke Grey/ (BU15)	Dove Grey/ Dark Grey	Dove Grey	Grey
Old English White roof	Dove Grey/ Dark Grey	Dove Grey	Cumulus Grey
Almond Green (GN37) Old English	Dove Grey/ Porcelain Green	Dove Grey	Grey
White roof (WT3)	Dove Grey/ Porcelain	Dove Grey	Cumulus Grey
Tweed Grey (GR4) Old English White roof (WT3)	Dove Grey Dark Grey	Dove Grey Dove Grey	Cumulus Grey
Tartan Red (RD9) Black roof (BK1)	Gold Brocade Grey/ Tartan Red	Gold Brocade Grey	Tartan Red
Old English White (WT3) Black roof (BK1)	Gold Brocade Grey/ Tartan Red	Gold Brocade Grey	Tartan Red

Fiesta Yellow/ (YL11) Old English White roof (WT3)	Silver Brocade Grey/ Powder Blue	Silver Brocade Grey	Powder Blue
	Gold Brocade Grey/ Powder Blue	Gold Brocade Grey	Powder Blue
Island Blue/ (BU8) Old English White roof (WT3)	Gold Brocade Grey/ Cumulus Grey	Gold Brocade Grey	Cumulus Grey

Notes:
1) Smoke Grey was never a colour option on the 1275S
2) Some cars left the factory with monotone body colours. Black and Police White were also available but only as special orders
3) As you can see, all brocade is not gold. Some of the very early cars had either silver or gold brocade.

MK 2 COOPER & COOPER S BODY COLOURS & TRIM

Body Exterior & BMC paint code	Seats	Liners	Carpet mats
Almond Green (GN37) Snowberry White roof (WT4)	Black	Black	Black
El Paso Beige (BG17) Snowberry White roof (WT4)	Black	Black	Black
Sandy Beige (BG15) Snowberry White roof (WT4)	Black	Black	Black
Island Blue (BU8) Snowberry White roof (WT4)	Black	Black	Black
Tartan Red (RD9) (No.2) Black roof (BK1)	Black	Black	Black
Snowberry White (WT4) Black roof (BK1)	Black	Black	Black
Black Mono (BK1)	Black	Black	Black

RSP ROVER COOPER BODY COLOURS & TRIM

Body Exterior & BMC paint code	Seats	Liners	Carpet mats
Flame Red (COF) White roof (NMN)	Half leather/ Black 'Lightnng'	Black/ 'Lightning'	Red
British Racing Green (HNA) White roof (NMN)	Half leather/ Black 'Lightning'	Black/ 'Lightning'	Red
Black (PMF) White roof (NMN)	Half leather/ Black 'Lightning'	Black	Red

Note:
1) RSP Coopers have door mirrors and wheelarch extensions colour coded to the body

MK 3 COOPER S BODY COLOURS & TRIM

Body exterior & BMC paint code	Seats	Liners	Carpet mats
Antelope (BLVC7)	Black	Black	Black

Body exterior (BMC paint code)			
	Icon Red	Icon Red	Icon Red
Aqua (BLVC60)	Black	Black	Black
	Navy	Navy	Navy
Blue Royale (BU38)	Galleon	Galleon	Galleon
	Blue	Blue	Blue
Bronze Yellow (BLVC1)	Black	Black	Black
	Navy	Navy	Navy
Flame Red (BLVC61)	Autumn Leaf	Autumn Leaf	Autumn Leaf
	Black	Black	Black
	Navy	Navy	Navy
	Geranium	Geranium	Geranium
Glacier White (BLVC59)	Black	Black	Black
	Navy	Navy	Navy
	Icon Red/ Geranium	Icon Red/ Geranium	Icon Red/ Geranium
Teal Blue (BLVC18)	Limeflower	Limeflower	Olive
	Navy	Navy	Navy
Blaze (BLVC16)	Navy	Navy	Navy
Bedouin (BLVC4)	Autumn Leaf	Autumn Leaf	Brown

Notes:

1) The Mk 3 Cooper S was offered only in monotone colour schemes. Black was not quoted as a standard colour but may have been available to special order. Police White may have been available for Police orders.

2) Navy trim did not become available until approximately July 1970, at which time Teal Blue, Blaze and Bedouis were added to the colour range. Black trim was deleted in early 1971, along with the Antelope body colour.

3) Blue Royale was listed as a body colour very early on in Mk 3 Cooper S production. However. since no cars of that colour appear on the register, it is thought doubtful it was ever used.

ROVER COOPER 1.3i BODY COLOURS & TRIM

Body exterior & BMC paint code	Seats	Liners	Carpet mats
Flame Red (COF) White roof (NMN)	Half leather/ Black 'Lightning'	Black/ 'Lightning'	Red
British Racing Green (HNA) White roof (NMN)	Half leather/ Black 'Lightning'	Black/ 'Lightning'	Red
Black/(PMF) White roof (NMN)	Half leather/ Black 'Lightning'	Black/ 'Lightning'	Red
White Diamond (NMN) Black roof (PMF)	Half lether/ Black 'Lightning'	Black/ 'Lightning'	Red
Storm Grey (LOZ) Black roof (PMF)	Half leather/ Black 'Lightning'	Black/ 'Lightning'	Red
Quicksilver (MNF) Black roof (PMF)	Half leather/ Black 'Lightning'	Black 'Lightning'	Red

MAINSTREAM ROVER COOPER BODY COLOURS & TRIM

Body exterior & BMC paint code	Seats	Liners	Carpet mats
Flame Red (COF) White roof (NMN)	'Racing Crayons' fabric	Plain Black	Black
British Racing Green (HNA) White roof (NMN)	'Racing Crayons' fabric	Plain Black	Black

Black (PMF) White roof (NMN)	'Racing Crayons' fabric	Plain Black	Black
White Diamond (NMN) Black roof (PMF)	'Racing Crayons' fabric	Plain Black	Black
Storm Grey (LOZ) Black roof (PMF)	'Racing Crayons' fabric	Plain Black	Black
Quicksilver (MNF) Black roof (PMF)	'Racing Crayons' fabric	Plain Black	Black

Note:
1) *Mainstream and 1.3i Rover Coopers have door mirrors colour coded to match the roof and unpainted wheelarch extensions*

INNOCENTI 1300 COOPER BODY COLOURS & TRIM

Exterior body colour	Seats	Liners	Carpet mats
Rosso 72/Nero (Red/Black)	Black	Black	Grey or Black
Castoro/Bianco (Brown/White)	Beige	Beige	Beige
Blu Scuro/Bianco (Dark Blue/White)	Beige	Beige	Beige
Rosso 74*/Nero (Red/Black)	Black	Black	Grey or Black
Bianco Avorio/Nero (White/Black)	Black	Black	Grey or Black
Verde Chiaro*/Nero (Green/Black)	Black	Black	Grey or Black
Bluette/Bianco Light Blue/White	Black	Black	Grey or Black
Prugna/Nero (Plum/Black)	Black	Black	Grey or Black
Aragosta*/Nero (Orange/Black)	Black	Black	Grey or Black
Pesca/Nero (Peach/Black)	Black	Black	Grey or Black
Sabbia*/Nero (Sand/Black)	Black	Black	Grey or Black

* *colours introduced during production*

APPENDIX 7

SPECIFICATIONS & EVOLUTION. PRODUCTION & PERFORMANCE DATA

Power unit

Every Mini uses a version of the BMC A-Series engine, which has four cylinders, in-line, and is mounted transversely in the car, with the gearbox underslung. The engine uses a cast iron cylinder head and a cast iron block which, on the earlier engines, carried two tappet chest covers on the side of the block.   All heads contain two valves per cylinder, in-line, which are operated by pushrods and rockers from the camshaft mounted in the side of the block on the rearward facing side..

Construction

The body is constructed of pressed sheet steel panels built as a box unit with front and rear subframes for the suspension.

Basic data is as follows with variations noted under individual model headings:

Overall length	10ft 0.25in
Width	4ft 7.5in
Height	4ft 5in
Wheelbase	6ft 8in
Front track	3ft 11.75in
Rear track	3ft 9..875in
Tyres & wheels	10in x 3.5in
Front suspension	transverse wishbones with Moulton rubber cone and tie rod
Rear suspension	trailing arm and Moulton rubber cone
Steering	rack and pinion

Austin Seven & Morris Mini-Minor (later called Austin & Morris Mini, then just Mini)

Introduced	August 1959
Ceased production	1980
Engine	Type 8MB
Capacity	848cc
Bore	62.94mm
Stroke	68.26mm
Compression ratio	8.3:1
Max power	34bhp at 5500rpm, later 37bhp (33 DIN) at 5250rpm
Max torque	44lb/ft at 2900rpm, later at 2500rpm
Gear ratios	1st, 13.658:1; 2nd, 8.177:1; 3rd, 5.316:1; 4th, 3.765:1
Final drive	3.765:1
Brakes	7in drums front and rear

Austin Mini Cooper, Morris Mini Cooper 997

Introduced	October 1961
Ceased production	December 1963
Engine	Type 9F
Capacity	997cc
Bore	62.43mm
Stroke	81.28mm
Compression ratio	9:1 (8.3:1 optional)
Valve sizes	inlet 29.4mm; exhaust 25.4mm; lift 7.29mm
Max power	55bhp at 6000rpm
Max torque	54lb/ft at 3600rpm
Carburation	twin SU HS2, 31.75mm choke diameter. Two wire air cleaners
Gear ratios	Std: 12.95, 7.213, 5.11, 3.765:1; Option: 11.01, 6.598, 4.674, 3.765:1
Final drive	3.765:1 (3.44 option)
Brakes	front: 7in discs. rear: 7in drums x 1.25in wide

Austin Mini Cooper, Morris Mini Cooper 998

Introduced	January 1964
Ceased production	November 1969
Engine	Type 9FA
Capacity	998cc
Bore	64..588mm
Stroke	76.20mm
Compression ratio	9:1 (7.8:1 optional)
Valve sizes	inlet 30.86mm; exhaust 25.4mm; left 7.29mm
Max power	55bhp at 5800rpm
Max torque	57lb/ft at 3000rpm
Carburation	twin SU HS2, 31.75mm choke diameter. Two wire air cleaners
Gear ratios	Std: 12.95, 7.213, 5.11, 3.765:1. Option: 11.01, 6.598, 4.674, 3.44:1
Final drive	3.765:1 (3.44 option)
Brakes	front: 7in discs. rear: 7in drums x 1.25in wide

Austin Mini Cooper 998: Evolution

March 1963	Brakes improved from chassis L/A257 313830 (rhd) and C/A257L212740 (lhd)
January 1964	998cc Cooper introduced
February 1964	Windscreen wiper arc reduced to avoid fouling screen surround
March 1964	Dunlop SP41 radials fitted
July 1964	Rear brakes get lower anti-lock pressure settings
September 1964	Hydrolastic suspension fitted. From engine 9FD SAH1701, new gearchange forks with larger contact area fitted. Diaphragm spring clutch fitted from enginee 9FS SAH3780
October 1964	Improved driveshaft couplings
November 1964	Driver's seat gets three position setting
January 1965	Better radiator fitted - 16 grilles per inch
May 1965	Primary gears get scroll-type oil seall from engines 9FD SAH6448 and 9FD SAL935
January 1966	Leading edge of exterior handles gets safety boss
October 1967	Plastic fan fitted. Mk2 bodyshell introduced with larger rear window and rear lamps and Super de-luxe trim

September 1968	All-synchro gearbox introduced

Mini Cooper S 1071

Introduced	March 1963
Discontinued	August 1964
Capacity	1071cc
Bore	70.60mm
Stroke	68.26mm
Compression ratio	9:1
Valve sizes	inlet: 35.71mm; exhaust 30.96mm; lift 7.29mm
Max power	70bhp at 6000rpm
Max torque	62lb/ft at 4500rpm
Carburation	twin SU hS2, 31.75mm choke diameter. Two wire air cleaners
Gear ratios	Std: 12.05, 7.213, 5.11, 3.765:1. Option: 11.01, 6.598, 4.674, 3.44:1
Final drive	3.765:1 (3.44 option)
Brakes	front: 7.5in discs. rear: 7in drums x 1.25in wide
Front track	4ft 0.58in
Rear track	3ft 11.3in
Wheels	10 x 4.5in

Mini Cooper S 970

Introduced	September 1964
Discontinued	January 1965
Capacity	970cc
Bore	70.60mm
Stroke	61.91mm
Compression ratio	9.75:1
Valve sizes	inlet 35.71mm; exhaust 30.96mm; lift 7.29mm
Max power	65bhp at 6500rpm
Max torque	55lb/ft at 3500rpm
Carburation	twin SU HS2, 31.75mm choke diameter. Two wire air cleaners
Gear ratios	Std: 12.05, 7.213, 5.11, 3.765:1 Option: 11.01, 6.598, 4.674, 3.44:1
Final drive	3.765:1 (3.44 option)
Brakes	front: 7.5in discs. rear: 7in drums x 1.25in wide
Front track	4ft 0.58in
Rear track	3ft 11.3in
Wheels	10 x 4.5in

Mini Cooper S 1275

Introduced	September 1964
Discontinued	July 1971
Capacity	1275cc
Bore	70.60mm
Stroke	81.33mm
Compression ratio	9.5:1
Valve sizes	inlet 35.71mm; exhaust 30.96mm; lift 7.29mm
Max power	76bhp at 5800rpm
Max torque	79lb/ft at 3000rpm
Carburation	twin SU HS2, 31.75mm choke diameter. Two wire air cleaners
Gear ratios	Std: 12.05, 7.213, 5.11, 3.765:1. Option: 11.01, 6.598, 4.674, 3.44:1
Final drive	3.765:1 (3.44 option)
Brakes	front: 7.5in discs. rear: 7in drums x 1.25in wide
Front track	4ft 0.58in
Rear track	3ft 11.3in

Mini Cooper S: Evolution

February 1994	Windscreen wiper arc reduced to avoid fouling windscreen surround
July 1964	Rear brakes get lower anti-lock pressure setting
September 1964	Hydrolastic suspension fitted Diaphragm spring clutch fitted from engines 9F SAX29001 (970cc), 9F SAH33260 (1071cc) and 9F SAY 31001 (1275cc) Positive crankcase ventilation from engines 9FD SAX29004 (970cc) and 9FD SAY31406 (1275cc)
November 1964	Driver's seat gets three position setting
January 1965	970S car discontinued. Only 1275cc version of S-type remains in production
January 1966	Twin petrol tanks fitted as standard. Oil cooler fitted as standard
April/May 1966	Higher rate Hydrolastic units, new steel and rubber lower wishbone bush, plus rear hub bearings get roller bearing. Also inboard end of driveshaft gets solid universal joint. Suspension mountings strengthened from chassis C/A 257 851199 (Austin) and K/A 254 851028 (Morris)
October 1967	Mk2 bodyshell introduced with larger rear window and Super de-Luxe trim. Gradual fit of all-synchro gearbox started
March 1970	Mk3 bodyshell introduced with wind-up windows and Clubman trim, seats and doors (including concealed hinges). Ignition shield from N20 D528A

MINI COOPER PRODUCTION

A total of 99,281 Mini Coopers were built between 1961 and 1969.

	Morris	Austin
1961	781	863
1962	6633	7283
1963	5008	5338*
1964	4683	4546
1965	4002	4267
1966	8493	5037
1967	8727	4375
1968	9911	4756
1969	9702	4276
Total	**57,940**	**41,341**

Austin Rover statistics do not allow a precise split between Mk1 and Mk2 Coopers (the switch came in 1967), nor between 997 and 998cc versions. Estimated production of the original 997cc Cooper (1961-63) is 25,000 cars.

Included here are CKD (knocked-down kit) production in Eire, Belgium, Portugal, South Africa and Australia. This may account for the larger proportion of Morris versions; Australia took a large number of CKD cars, the majority of which were badged Morris.

*The 1963 Austin figure includes the Austin Cooper S which was not separated from ther standard Coopers in this first year of production. Approximate 1963 volume of Austin Cooper S is 820 cars.

PERFORMANCE FIGURES

	Mini Cooper 997	998	Mini Cooper S 1071S	970S	1275S	1275GT	Cooper Conversion 998cc	Mayfair
Power	55bhp	55bhp	70bhp	65bhp	76bhp	59bhp	64bhp	41bhp
Max speed	85mph	90mph	95mph	92mph	97mph	90mph	88mph	78mph
Acceleration								
0-30mph	4.8sec	4.5sec	4.0sec	Full	3.6sec	3.9sec	3.9sec	5.7sec
0-40mph	7.7sec	6.5sec	6.9sec	test	5.6sec	6.0sec	6.1sec	8.9sec
0-50mph	11.8sec	9.6sec	9.0sec	figures	7.7sec	9.3sec	8.9sec	13.7sec
0-60mph	17.2sec	14.8sec	12.9sec	not	10.9sec	13.3sec	13.2sec	22.0sec
0-70mph	26.3sec	21.4sec	17.1sec	available	14.4sec	19.sec	19.4sec	40.8sec
0-80mph	47.3sec	33.6sec	23.2sec		20.9sec	29.4sec	31.2sec	-
0-90mph	-	-	40.1sec		37.5sec		-	-
Standing quarter mile	21.1sec	20.0sec	18.9sec		18.2sec	19.0sec	18.8sec	21.8sec
Top gear acceleration								
10-30mph	10.7sec	-	11.6sec		7.8sec	-	14.4sec	20.6sec
20-40mph	11.8sec	9.9sec	10.4sec		7.6sec	8.6sec	14.4sec	20.6sec
30-50mph	12.7sec	10.2sec	11.0sec		7.3sec	8.5sec	14.6sec	21.5sec
40-60mph	13.3sec	11.1sec	10.8sec		7.7sec	9.8sec	15.6sec	28.5sec
50-70mph	16.5sec	14.3sec	12.1sec		9.2sec	12.2sec	19.5sec	-
60-80mph	30.6sec	19.9sec	16.0sec		11.5sec	16.0sec	26.9sec	-
70-90mph	-	-	26.4sec		15.6sec	-	-	-
Speed in gears								
1st gear	28mph	28mph	37mph		31mph	31mph	32mph	29mph
2nd gear	46mph	46mph	62mph		52mph	50mph	53mph	49mph
3rd gear	63mph	65mph	84mph		75mph	77mph	81mph	75mph
Fuel consumption								
Overall	34.6mpg	31.5mpg	26.8mpg		29.9mpg	30.5mpg	29.6mpg	38.0mpg
Tyres	5.2x10in Dunlop Gold Seal	5.2x10in Dunlop SP41	5.5x10in Dunlop SP41		5.5x10in Dunlop SP41	4.5x10in Dunlop SP68	4.5x12in Pirelli CN54	4.5x12in Pirelli CN54
Kerb weight	1400lb	1411lb	1425lb		1440lb	1555lb	-	1498lb

MINI COOPER S PRODUCTION

A total of 45,629 Mini CooperSs were made between 1963 and 1971.

	Morris	Austin	Mk3
1963	770	**	
1964	2659	3020	
1965	2591	2359	
1966	2338	1673	
1967	2489	1407	
1968	2527	1174	
1969	2126	985	
1970			9436
1971			10,075
Total	**15,500**	**10,618**	**19,511**

As with Mini Cooper production figures, it is not possible to make a precise split between Mk1 and Mk Cooper S models - the switch occurred in 1967. The Mk3 S models were badged only as Mini Cooper and not Austin or Morris. The numbers of the three engine capacity variants of the Mini Cooper S can only be estimated. The most reliable source gives the number of 1071cc S models built between 1963 and 1964 as 4005, while the 970cc 'homologation special' production was 972. That leaves a balance of 21,141 1275cc S models, of which approximately 14,000 were Mk1 and the rest Mk2s built between 1967 and 1969.

From 1990 to date a total of 41,835 Rover Coopers have been built, of which 21,407 had carburettors.

**As noted in the previous table, the Austin figures for 1963 included the S with the standard Mini Coopers. The total figure for Austin Cooper S is therefore some 820 cars greater than shown above. As in the Mini Cooper table, CKD models assembled overseas are included here, hence the greater proportion of Morrises.

INDEX

Dear Reader,
We hope you enjoyed this
Veloce Publishing production. If
you have ideas for books on
the Mini or other models,
please write and tell us.
Meantime, Happy Motoring!